For

JOHN E JONES
(1920-2005)

who loved theatre

Comedy is simply a funny way of being serious.

Peter Ustinov

John Wright

WHY IS THAT SO FUNNY?

A Practical Exploration of Physical Comedy

Foreword by Toby Jones

NICK HERN BOOKS

London

www.nickhernbooks.co.uk

A Nick Hern Book

Why Is That So Funny?
first published in Great Britain in 2006
by Nick Hern Books Limited
The Glasshouse, 49a Goldhawk Road, London W12 8QP

Cover designed by Ned Hoste, 2H
Cover photograph of Hayley Carmichael by Jon Barnes
Author photograph by Robert Golden

Typeset by Country Setting, Kingsdown, Kent CT14 8ES
Printed in the UK by CPI Books (UK) Ltd

A CIP catalogue record for this book
is available from the British Library

ISBN   978 1 85459 782 3

MIX
Paper from
responsible sources
FSC® C013604

Contents

Foreword

At some point in the last forty years, theatre directors started bringing balls into the rehearsal room. Actors know the day has begun when the stage manager rolls a football or tennis ball into the centre of the hall. Conversations around the tea urn peter out. Gradually, the cast drifts dutifully to the centre of the room where the director waits, smiling. Something more desultory than a game begins, as the ball is lobbed from hand to hand. There is nervous laughter and head-shaking, as jackets are removed and the ball is caught or dropped. Names may be shouted. Then, after a little while, it's all over. The ball is given back to the stage manager, tables are pulled out, everyone sighs, more shakes of the head and the proper rehearsal begins. The actors sit down and disappear behind their scripts.

In John Wright's rehearsal rooms there are no such disappearances. The ball is not given back, because the play has already begun. Games and improvisation are the way in, not just a vigorous way of saying 'Good morning'.

For John, games are how we make dramatic action real. To discover the play is to discover the games at work in the play, the games that generated the play in the first place. Not an optional extra, an ice-breaker or a nod to 'directorial process', games force us to be present in the rehearsal room here and now. In the theatre this is fundamental. The circumstances of the play, the 'there and then' of the story, are in constant play with the 'here and now' of the actors' shifting relationship with the audience. And this can't be discovered by reading books or discussing plays, you have to get up.

'Just get up. It's as simple as that...'

It's 1989 and I've just been introduced to John Wright for the first time. It's the summer before I go to study at the Lecoq School in Paris.

A mutual acquaintance has told me that John knows a lot about masks; that he, too, trained with Lecoq. So I've asked him what I should expect.

' . . . keep getting up.'

He's nodding and chuckling now. Eyebrows raised. What does this mean? He obviously knows something, but he's not going to tell me. I probably look bemused. He smiles, slaps his knees.

'That's all you need to remember. Get up.'

' . . . er, right. Thanks.'

That was the advice. Good advice, the best he could have given me. It was only by getting up and following the scant but precise instructions of an improvisation that I could begin to learn. Learning how to make theatre is not about 'understanding advice', it is a journey through failure as much as success. Getting up when you've just fallen down.

This book is a map of some of the many places John has succeeded and failed on his journeys as a director and teacher. There are many stories of unexpected revelation. Strange and hilarious theatre founded on accidents of misdirection, incomprehension and sheer persistence. You can hear the excited, curious and passionate teacher perched on the edge of his seat giggling, exhorting and provoking the actors to play. Is the game still working? John, glancing at the audience alongside him, gauging not just the action on stage but the action in the audience too. What is happening there? Are we bored? How can we improve this game?

The games described in this book are often simple. Simple games are sometimes the hardest to play, the hardest to keep interesting, but they are starting points, to be developed, adjusted and mis-played, until they work as new 'plays'. Here, as at Lecoq, the inspiration is partly the *Commedia dell'Arte*: not the prettified 'masked theatre' we see in paintings, but the earlier, eminently pragmatic form of popular theatre, adapting and adjusting itself to the marketplace.

Somehow, to describe the *Commedia* as a specific genre is to underestimate the legendary resourcefulness of its performers – theatrical athletes negotiating ever-changing landscapes, languages and laws. This vision of a highly flexible, dissident, vagabond theatre is inspirational because of what it must have required of the actors. Actors needed to improvise, yes, but also to write, dance, declaim, sing, vault, mime, parody, to adapt to survive. *Commedia dell'Arte* was not, after all, the comedy of art, it was comedy of skill and there are physical skills to be learned.

John has devised exercises to explore 'the stops, turns, interruptions and sudden surprises' of physical comedy. This is technical work, for which he has developed a concrete language with which to teach. Nothing is mystified. By breaking down and articulating how physical comedy operates technically – the rhythms, the tensions, the trips, the drops, the takes – we can begin to see how different kinds of comedy work.

Only by distinguishing the physical properties of pastiche, caricature, burlesque and buffoon can we begin to appreciate the different colours of a particular comic spectrum such as parody. More than that, we can begin to revive our experience of theatrical style as a whole. Here, John understands style practically in terms of different levels of physical and emotional engagement with a character or story. By playing with these levels we can begin to integrate other colours – the tragic, the melodramatic, the soap operatic – and notice how these styles might combine and collide within a single story. John is always pushing beyond the orthodox, reaching for other possibilities – the pratfall that makes us weep; the clowns who start to poison each other…

'Why is that funny?' John asks, looking along the row of actors who sit there, mouths open, delighted or perhaps aghast at what they might have just seen. John rocks with laughter, feet jigging up and down, cajoling the clown who has just been murdered:

'Get up! Find a new game! Just keep on getting up!'

TOBY JONES

Preface

On receiving his lifetime achievement award at the 2002 British Comedy Awards, Michael Palin said that comedy was a great leveller. He explained that his facility for making people laugh had been a key element in enabling him to find something in common with those he had met on his travels to the most far-flung corners of the world. He finished his speech with the conclusion that he was so confident in the unifying power of comedy that, instead of dropping bombs on Iraq, we should drop comedians instead. This idea was received with great enthusiasm – but then he was preaching to the converted. Had he been making that speech at a theatre function it is unlikely that these sentiments would have been received with such unanimous and uncritical acclaim. John Peter, the drama critic for the Sunday Times, criticised Mark Rylance for finding comedy in his performance of Shakespeare's *Richard II* at the Globe Theatre on London's South Bank (May 2003). He wrote:

> **66** He treats some of Richard's great speeches as oddball comedy. The timing of pauses and the nerdish self-deprecating chuckles during 'my large kingdom from a little grave – a little, little grave – an obscure grave' reduce tragic self-pity to smug stand-up comedy. **99**

Clearly, Mark Rylance hadn't read the rules properly, but I don't suppose Shakespeare had either. The idea that 'comedy' and 'tragedy' are mutually exclusive and that 'comedy' will inevitably result in a 'reduction' of 'tragedy' goes back to Aristotle. Comedy has always been the poor relation in theatre. Oh, it might put bums on seats occasionally, but alongside tragedy (whatever we mean by that today), comedy is regarded as the lesser of the two genres. The tighter we cling to the idea that comedy and tragedy are as compatible as hot fat and water, the more distorted our view of life becomes. In life, the comic and the tragic are interdependent. We see this on film and we see it on television. Our best sitcoms freely interweave the two. *Steptoe and Son* is as moving as it is funny, and *One Foot in the Grave* killed off its comic hero, Victor Meldrew, at the end of the series. The writers weren't inhibited because they were supposed to be doing comedy. We've seen it on the big screen and we've seen it on prime-time television and not only in 'smug stand-up comedy'. Over the years we've seen people laughing at funerals, laughing in the face of pain. We've seen people laugh at misfortune, injustice, violence and death. We've even seen people laugh during sex. Laughter is more a survival strategy than an idle diversion because real life is a far more complex and disorderly affair than ancient literary theory would have us believe.

But comparisons with life will only take us so far. Life isn't like art. Art is a reflection of life, and sometimes that reflection is deliberately distorted. We sell ourselves short if we confuse theatrical credibility with verisimilitude. Art is a carefully selected view of life, and different generations of artists make different choices according to contemporary values. For instance, today the notion of kingship is an anachronism. Most of us don't believe in God any more and *Harry Potter* is outselling the Bible. Big texts in the theatre – a Christopher Fry play or a Webster, for example – no longer hold big audiences, at least not for as long as they used to. The visual image has never been so powerful, and genre boundaries are being deliberately broken down. We can't agree what art is and we don't know what is beautiful any more. Popular culture has never been so diverse, and the old rule books have all been thrown away. There's only one rule in theatre: Don't be boring!

Elitism in theatre runs much deeper than John Peter's opinions on tragedy. This elitism goes right back to the basic premise behind our approach to actor training, and how we deal with emotions. It's this elitism that divorces comedy from life, and laughter from other forms of emotional expression.

In most of our drama schools far more attention is paid to making students cry than is ever paid to making them laugh. This is partly due to the legacy of Stanislavski, and the majority of our acting teachers base their approach on some aspect of his teaching. There probably isn't a drama student in the country who hasn't encountered ideas like the 'magic if', inner monologue, motivation, or emotion memory. I once worked with a self-styled Stanislavskian who, in the best traditions of the great man, would place a chair at the end of the studio with a box of tissues nearby. Then, one at a time, each person was asked to talk to the group about some traumatic incident in their lives. They had to stay there talking until they had made themselves cry. A student came to me in floods of tears after one of these sessions saying that she'd been told she couldn't make contact with her emotions. On another occasion, a student confessed that everyone had complimented her for her description of the death of her mother when in reality her mother was alive and well and living in France. What infuriated me about this approach wasn't the exercise itself – it's actually quite a good one – it was the spurious value placed on so-called 'truth'. Who cares if you slept with your grandmother? It's none of my business. And it's beyond my professional expertise to be able to handle this information. I'm not a therapist and neither was my colleague. If the worst thing that has ever happened in your life is the death of your hamster, it's difficult to score high in the personal-experience stakes.

Being able to cry at will is a useful skill, and tears can be induced in a variety of ways, but this exercise was only the tip of the iceberg. That same colleague told me that comedy was an emotional cop-out and that it was simply a get-out clause to avoid our 'big' feelings. He divided the world into comic actors, on the one hand, whom he referred to as 'comedians', and 'actors', on the other, who presumably were very serious, could cry at the drop of a hat, were perfectly in touch with their emotions and didn't do comedy. This is the real elitism in theatre: the belief that comedy is incapable of ever being profound and, by implication, is always superficial and essentially trivial.

Let's be under no illusions here, comedy can wreck anything. It can debunk, it can trivialise and 'reduce' anything you like down to some puerile idiot doing nothing in particular just for a laugh. But, like it or loathe it, there's skill in this destruction – sometimes great skill. The fact that comedy is capable of being such a wrecker is all the more reason for exploring how it works. Live theatre is a tightrope act. We all admire the skill and the grace and the daring of somebody up there on the high wire. But 'no one can be that good', we think to ourselves, 'no one can be that clever.' Let's face it – rock-solid virtuosity is boring. Deep down, the only thing that really keeps us watching is the thought that the acrobat up there might fall off at any minute. Then at least we'd see something a bit more human. It would destroy everything, of course it would, it could be life threatening, of course it could, but at least it would be a bit more like us. The thought is delicious. We watch in anticipation for the first telltale wobble. Live theatre is at its most compelling when things are just slightly off-balance. These wobbles aren't jokes, they're not clever and they're not witty. They're funny because they're scary, and they're scary because they're slightly out of control. We all keep watching that person up there because they're only just all right. Too much security, too much control, too much purity, or too much aestheticism is ultimately very boring.

The masks of comedy and tragedy are misleading. Having worked with masks for years, I can assure you that a big smiley face doesn't take long to become deeply irritating, and if you put that mask in slightly different circumstances it will soon appear to be barking mad. But if you put a party hat on the frowning face of tragedy it will immediately become amusing, and if you can then persuade that mask to dance, it will become very funny indeed. Comedy and tragedy are unhelpful distinctions. Rather than being opposite sides of a coin, they're just equal parts of the whole. The fact that we see theatre as a predominantly literary medium – and psychological realism remains our dominant form of theatrical representation – does nothing for our rediscovery of theatre as a live event. To appreciate that, we need to refer back to those pre-literary skills of performative acting and presentational drama from the age-old popular forms of *Commedia dell'Arte* and clowning, when the contract between 'you up there' playing to 'us down here' was much clearer – you had to be compelling or you had to get off. I'm not talking about historical authenticity here and I'm not taking about genre either, but rather, that oral tradition amongst actors concerning what's going to be funny.

It's understandable that John Peter wrote that review at the Globe – as a full-size recreation of an Elizabethan playhouse, it is the most confrontational performance space in the country. At the Globe we can't sit back and nestle into our familiar notion that theatre is an illusion. The audience configuration of this space demands physical levels of engagement that are very alien to us today. The notions of acting as play and theatre as game, and the role of laughter in the event as a whole, are genuine imperatives when you've been standing in the cold for a couple of hours. You can't be passive at the Globe. Here, listening to the text is as active as playing tennis. We're not sitting in a darkened room with only our imaginations for company. We're continually aware of everyone around us all the time. This space is volatile – anything can happen in it. The sacred and the profane sit side by side and we want to see them both because, deep down, we all know that the one provokes the other.

This book is a notebook on physical comedy. It's a reference and a brief record of the key ideas, games and exercises that have shaped my work in provoking comedy over the years.

I'm a director, deviser and teacher of theatre. I'm not an academic. But that doesn't mean that I'm not interested in theory. On the contrary, I'm preoccupied with it; only, in my case, theory is continually tempered by practice. All the games and exercises in this book have been included because they work. They are derived from years of working with different actors and struggling with them to make theatre and to keep the audience laughing. I'm quite eclectic in my approach and I'll take anything from anywhere.

I'm not trying to propose a method here – I don't have one. I rarely approach two different projects in the same way. I use games to make things happen in the rehearsal room. If I don't like what's happening, I change the game so I'm continually inventing or devising new ways to make things happen as the work develops. For me this work is never fixed, it's continually evolving. By the time you read this book I'll most likely be trying something else, but my precepts will probably remain the same. My intention here is to give you a vocabulary of starting points, processes and provocations that can be used immediately and that will inform your own practice. You may not agree with everything I say, in which case at least I've provoked you to do something else and to find another way, and we'll all be the richer for it. There isn't a 'right way' or a 'wrong way'; there are only differences. Differences are interesting. Differences are creative.

JOHN WRIGHT

WHY IS THAT SO FUNNY?

From the moment I picked up your book until I laid it down, I was convulsed with laughter. Some day I intend reading it.

Groucho Marx

Introduction
About Laughter

One of the first jobs I had as a director was to stage 'the blasted heath scene' from *King Lear* as an exercise at a north London drama school. The student I found to play Lear was a loveable lunatic with a huge sense of humour. He was a bear of a man – Hungarian, I think – and had very little English, but what he lacked in language he made up for in passion. His terror of the elements was of biblical proportions – as indeed were the elements themselves. The wind and the rain were created by Henry, who played Lear's Fool. Henry was a small Japanese actor who would throw himself across the room and attack a thundersheet and then throw buckets of water over himself and the King. This would send Lear into blind terror one minute but, as he tried to control the text with his wayward English, he became a gentle and genial host the next. During 'Blow, winds, and crack your cheeks', he talked to the wind and rain as if they were his friends that he was inviting round to tea. We all has a great time, except the principal of the school and his immediate acolytes, who all loathed it. They described our interpretation as disrespectful to the text and accused me of reducing tragedy to farce and of behaving irresponsibly. I was stunned. I had never met such prurience. Once they'd all gone we sat there in dispirited silence, looking at the wreckage of the rehearsal room.

Henry, who'd excelled himself on the thunder sheet, told us a disturbing little story that has stuck in my mind ever since. In halting English he said, 'This is story of first performance ever. Before rules.' (I have since learnt that it was first recorded in an ancient book *The Kojiki*, known as *The Record of Ancient Matters*, written about 7 1 2 AD in Japan.)

This is my version of Henry's story, with no conscious additions on my part:

66 *The great Sun Goddess is in a petulant rage after an argument with her brother. She hides herself in the depths of a dark cave to sulk, and the world is plunged into the deepest darkness. All the other gods start to gather round the dim glow at the mouth of her cave and try to persuade her to come out again.*

A young goddess is particularly angered and frustrated by the darkness and, on seeing an old wooden bathtub near the mouth of the cave, turns it upside down to make a small platform and starts to stamp on its base. The other gods look round to see what all the noise is. Her stamping turns into a small child having a tantrum. She laughs, and they laugh, and they all want more. More and more gods gather round to watch her scream and stamp and fret and punch the ground. She laughs, and they laugh, and they all want more. She stamps again and again and her stamping turns into a silly little dance. She laughs and they laugh, and they all want more.

Her dance becomes more graceful and more delicate with pretty little jumps. She laughs and they laugh, and they all want more. Her dance becomes slower and her smile becomes coy and playful, and the more she dances, the more she laughs, and they laugh and they all want more. She begins to touch her body and the gods begin to roar, and she laughs, and they laugh, and they all want more. She unfastens her kimono and lets the silk slip from her shoulder, and she laughs, and they laugh, and they all want more. Her kimono drops to the ground and she shakes her naked body, she struts and stamps and dances and jumps. And she laughs, and they laugh, and they all want more. She begins to stroke her body and her nipples become erect, and she laughs, and they laugh, and they all want more. She stamps, she kicks, she slaps and punches her body all over and she grabs her nipples and rips them out and holds them up for all to see, with the blood running down her arms, and she laughs, and the gods roar and roar and roar, and in the depths of the cave, the sulking Sun Goddess hears the roar and, fearful that she is missing something, comes charging out, and the world is once again filled with light. **99**

Before rules, apparently there was no such thing as genre. One element bled into the other. The parodic and the comic, the aesthetic, the erotic, the dramatic and eventually the tragic were all part of one great whole. Before rules, there was no conscious acting, and no conscious art. This young goddess got up on her upturned bathtub for a bit of fun. Simplistic, you might think. I'm not so sure. Today, God is no longer in 'His heaven', and we are what we are, but none of us knows quite what that is. Genre is breaking down and the margins between reality and illusion are continually being eroded. Back then, in the bright blue ether, this 'first performance ever' was inspired by the desire to keep the audience's attention and to keep them amused. Back then, in the year minus zero, when none of these questions existed, the gods were having a laugh. What started as a bit of fun resulted in being something else entirely, but their starting point was laughter, and laughter runs through this story like 'Blackpool' runs through rock.

I prefer to talk about laughter rather than comedy because laughter is less conceptual and more specific. You do something in a certain way and either we all laugh or we don't, as the case might be. It is a simple contract and it is non-negotiable. We know exactly where we stand with laughter. Laughter has universal coinage. Through laughter, we establish a reciprocal relationship with the audience; you're not doing comedy if nobody laughs.

We tend to define laughs by their context. For example, we might say 'That's a cruel laugh', or 'That's an ironic laugh', or 'That's a dirty laugh.' But if we look at laughter from the point of view of how lifelike you might be, or how out of control you might look, or how outlandish your behaviour might be, or simply how surprising your action might seem, then we can start to narrow things down to four different kinds of laugh elicited in an audience, indicating four different aspects of comedy:

- The Recognised Laugh
- The Visceral Laugh
- The Bizarre Laugh
- The Surprise Laugh

Each type of laugh defines a different level or quality of audience response, and each type is a catalyst that enables us to identify different levels of emotional engagement and rational understanding of the work. The four aspects of comedy operate either independently, each with its own specialised dramatic function, or in conjunction with each other as a part of an entire comic sequence.

Why Do We Laugh?

In 2003, the BBC Radio 4 Reith Lectures were given by the eminent neurologist Dr Vilayanur S. Ramachandran. In his first lecture he asked the question 'Why do we laugh?' and went on to say that laughter is a specific and universal trait for us humans:

> 66 *Every society, every civilisation, every culture, has some form of laughter – except the Germans.* 99

He explained that a Martian ethnologist would be perplexed to see large groups of people 'suddenly stop, look round, throw their heads about and make a funny staccato, rhythmic hyena-like sound.' Apparently our species of Homo sapiens has a laughter mechanism 'hardwired' into our brains. But 'why did the brain evolve like this?' he asked, 'and how did it evolve through natural selection?'

He outlined what he described as 'the common denominator of all jokes and all humour, despite their diversity':

> 66 *You take a person along the garden path of expectation and you suddenly introduce an unexpected twist that makes us reinterpret all the previous facts.* 99

He emphasised that the vital comic element in this reinterpretation is that our conclusions must be inconsequential or trivial if we are going to laugh. He went on to cite the classic banana-skin routine:

> 66 *A portly gentleman striding purposefully along, only to slip on a banana skin and be sent sprawling on the floor.* 99

If the gentleman had cut his head open in the fall and was left lying there in a pool of blood then, he argues, we'd all be on the phone for an ambulance. It would be a potentially serious accident that would arouse our feelings of empathy. In this instance there would be no twist in the story and our original interpretation would have been borne out. The ending would be anything but trivial and we would have no cause to laugh. According to Dr Ramachandran:

> 66 *Laughter evolved as Nature's way of signalling the all-clear.* 99

In other words, if the portly gentleman were to get up again with no apparent harm being done, then we would probably laugh in order to reassure each other that he is OK, and to share the fact that now he looks more stupid than he did before. For a more atavistic example, imagine the following:

A small group of our Stone Age ancestors are hunting in the forest, armed to the teeth with stone axes and pointed sticks. Suddenly they're stopped in their tracks by what sounds like a wild beast caught in a thorn bush. Instantly, they surround the spot and are just about to attack when the foliage parts to reveal the tousled head of one of their children, wild with rage.

The sound of laughter would dispel the hunters' aggression and re-assure everyone, including the child, that everything was OK after all.

Our desire to assure each other that there is no cause for alarm accounts for the refrain in the Japanese myth: 'She laughed, and they laughed, and they all wanted more.' We share big laughs in a way that's spontaneous and empathetic. We'll seek eye contact with complete strangers standing next to us. We might even hold on to each other, as if for support. Laughter is infectious and spreads quickly in an eager crowd. In the circumstances of the myth, where there were no prece-dents for young goddesses leaping up and cavorting about on upturned bathtubs, I should imagine that they all needed continual reassurance and continual 'OK signals', and I'm not surprised that they wanted more.

This young goddess was playing her audience. She was following her impulses and entertaining the crowd. She started off playing with pleasure but, as the story went on, her laughter became increasingly ironic and eventually grotesque. We don't know whether she's laughing out of pleasure or not. The incessant refrain after each unit of the story only emphasises this ambiguity and highlights the role of the audience. Are they goading her on or simply joining in her game?

The Recognised Laugh

I don't suppose you laughed out loud when you read the Japanese myth, but the event started as a joke. The goddess's stamping was reminiscent of a child having a tantrum. The audience laughed because they recognised the parody. Now their laughter had a context. They not only recognised the accuracy of the tantrum but they also recognised the pertinence of the parody of the behaviour of the Sun Goddess sulking in her cave. From then on, the propensity towards laughter is sustained throughout the entire incident because everyone knew exactly what she was doing, so they all laughed. The 'OK signals' were sent back and forth and, with that much assurance, she felt a wild freedom up there on her bathtub, and her need for assurance became addictive. Her desire to keep the attention of the audience was palpable. She had to keep them watching or their attention would drift off to the cave. This was the motor behind everything she did. At the beginning I should think she was really enjoying herself. I can imagine the parody being very funny in that context, as is the silly little dance that it leads into. She probably enjoyed the striptease, but only a mad person would have enjoyed playing anything that happened after the kimono came off. At this point, darker feelings started to show behind the laughter. The audience started to match her audacity with their own. They were more interested in the shock value of what was happening in front of them than anything else. It reminds me of an American television series, *Jackass*, where a team of people are filmed doing painful and potentially dangerous feats like attempting to ski down steps, or having baby alligators bite their nipples. (There seems to be a common theme emerging here.) People laugh at these things, and the team members laugh at each other, but it's more bravado than comedy that we're looking at here, where the most disgusting antics get the biggest laughs.

It's as if our young goddess was laughing in spite of herself towards the end, but those final roars of the crowd, as the blood ran down her arms, remain ambiguous. Are they roaring out of approval or outrage or disappointment? We shall never know. This is the point behind the myth. Ambiguity is at the heart of our theatrical response. What's chalk to me is cheese to you. The fact that we're still wrestling with this awkward question is evidence of its theatrical potency. It's all gone that step too far for everybody involved. The crowd can't stop watching, and some of them even seem to like it. This is the point where events overtake the game and make laughter impossible.

But the 'act' started from an idea that was childlike in its simplicity. She was poking fun at the Sun Goddess in the cave. She was doing 'a take off', and everyone had a clear reference point. In the beginning, the laughter was recognisable.

It is a common misconception amongst students that they should try to be original. We've all been taught to be wary of stereotype and cliché and, as a result, we've learnt to mistrust the ordinary and the mundane.

Keith Johnstone in his book, *Impro*, makes a similar point. 'What's for tea?' somebody says in an improvisation. 'Fried mermaid,' comes the reply. Of course everyone laughs. That's what I'd call a bizarre laugh, which is more challenging to sustain. Keith Johnstone goes on to explain that 'sardines on toast' would probably have been a much more useful reply because we would all know exactly where we were and the action could develop in a more recognisable way – which is what I'd call a recognised laugh. This isn't funny in itself, although it could well get a laugh because it is so ordinary.

When running a series of workshops at a festival in Norway, I was once in the embarrassing position of being required to do an impersonation of a typical Norwegian to a large audience. In the absence of anything else to do, I sat down, leant forward, and looked intense, which was exactly the way I saw the audience looking at me. They recognised what I was doing, and they laughed. They laughed at the normality of the situation. Originality might be funny in the short term, but after any length of time, it's simply baffling. Typicality is much more useful. Which is why the vast majority of our comedy is based on recognition. We laugh because we can see ourselves in that situation. We laugh because we understand and because we can share that understanding. Recognition is at the heart of the way we represent our humanity on stage. But it must be remembered that in art, all our representations of life, no matter how real they might appear to be, are the product of carefully made choices. Verisimilitude might be at the heart of recognition but it isn't the key to theatrical truth. We want something more.

Today, with reality TV and sitcoms like *The Royle Family*, *The Office*, *Curb Your Enthusiasm* and the work of Steve Coogan, we've taken recognition comedy just about as far as we can go. In the case of *The Office* and *The Royle Family,* immense care has been taken in the writing and the acting to appear completely spontaneous and avoid the slightest trace of 'theatricality'. Dramatic moments are deliberately missed. Nothing is allowed to appear to happen deliberately. There are no neat endings, and obvious climactic moments are avoided or made to happen in the wrong place. The playwright Terry Johnson said that he felt that *Big Brother* was generating more interesting drama than the majority of the scripts submitted to the Royal Court Theatre. He might be right, but the laughter of recognition is only one colour in a much more varied palette. It is the bruising ironies that are most fascinating. 'How real,' we think, 'how lifelike', 'how appalling these people are' and 'how hypocritical' or 'how incompetent'. Recognition has become what we expect, and we've grown to rely on it because in the end, it is the easiest way of establishing the world of the story.

Even in the Japanese myth, for example, the gods might be in their heavens before the beginning of time, but we see them living in an everyday kind of world. They're so naive. They might be gods, but they still have rows and go into sulks. They still have baths and they're still all frightened of the dark. It's a sort of celestial kindergarten. As is to be expected, the myth works primarily at the level of recognition. The audience recognise the tantrum, they recognise that the goddess is just being silly, that she's being very graceful, or sensual, or erotic, and her constant laughter of recognition tells them that everything is all right – it's only a game.

The Mistaken Fart

I directed a play called *Meeting Myself Coming Back* by Kerry Hood at Soho Theatre in London (2002). It was almost exclusively written with recognition in mind, but what fascinated me about the writing was the way Kerry managed to clash different types of recognition.

> *In one scene, Catherine, a mute, traumatised young woman with 'non-stop aching hips' (played by Joanna Holden), was lying in a hospital bed, terrified by the prospect of a lonely death. Just as a nurse started to move her legs to make her more comfortable, the friction between her naked buttocks and the rubber sheet she was lying on made a sound like a ripping fart. It was an unmistakable comic moment.*

Catherine's situation was so appalling that we were all in danger of keeling over with emotional exhaustion, but as soon as the nurse thought she had farted, all the agonies of the hospital bed were sent flying out of the window. Instantly, this pathetic victim became one of us. That mistaken fart tapped into our humanity, and the old cliché of redemption through suffering was instantly promoted to redemption through laughter.

Even looking as she does, Catherine still has her dignity, she still gets embarrassed, but in spite of everything that's happened to her, she has the courage to laugh about it. That mistaken fart makes her heroic, and for the first time we start to admire her. From victim to hero in a single fart. Once the nurse had gone away and Catherine was alone again, our feelings for her helplessness in that hospital bed were made even more poignant. All our empathy came flooding back, and it was even stronger than before.

We're too precious about empathy in the theatre. It's far more robust than we think. It's perfectly possible to be dripping with pity, then to laugh at a crude joke and finally to return to an image of even greater despair than we had before. It's what we do in life, so as an audience, we welcome this emotional agility. We're energised by the contrasts, and when we experience them, we're more active, more engaged and the entire event is more credible. Laughter may momentarily drag our feelings of empathy away from the protagonist, but for the audience, laughter is a huge empathetic boost. A shared laugh is a shared feeling. Instantly, we're all 'in each other's shoes'; we've all gone to the same place and now we have a common understanding.

Empathising with each other is just as important as empathising with you on stage. Of course it's important to empathise with you on stage, but we don't have to do it all the time. In a vibrant piece of theatre our empathy goes to and fro. Comedy throws the dynamic to us in the auditorium, whereas moments of drama draw it into 'you up there'. The more we are drawn in, the quieter we become. We enter one of those sustained moments of stillness that give rise to all those questions of what we might be thinking individually. These moments are as compelling as they are ambiguous. We only go as still as that when something appalling or momentous has happened, so you must have touched a nerve. Moments like that are theatrical gold, but you can't demand them, you can't take them for granted. If you give it away – that you're going for the big stillness – from the very beginning, we'll all fall asleep because you'll be so boring. To keep us on our toes you have to keep that ball flying to and fro, and you can't do that without comedy. Don't forget that we go to the theatre primarily for fun. I enjoy language and poetry and ideas, I enjoy laughing as much as I enjoy being appalled by something, and I'll certainly enjoy something momentous – but I like it all on the same plate!

The Visceral Laugh

Things start to look slightly strange in that Japanese myth when 'she stamps, she kicks, she slaps herself and punches herself all over'. There's desperation here. It's the first clue we get that things might be getting out of control, or that the audience might be goading her that one step too far. She might still be laughing, but things are definitely getting out of hand. Her 'OK signal' is ambiguous; we can't decide if this is an attempt at comedy or self-mutilation, and we're confronted with an ascending spiral of violence. The stamping clearly isn't enough to get a response from the audience, so she tries kicking. That isn't enough, so she tries scratching and punching herself. The crowd still want more, but she's incapable of thought and she's become a victim of her own gut reactions. She has become grotesque: what she's doing is more alarming than funny. This is precisely the level of play that has given rise to some of our richest, climactic moments of physical comedy. Disturbing violence and raucous laughter are a hair's breadth apart, and our ability to laugh depends entirely on whether we believe the 'OK signal' or not.

This is the journey towards a visceral level of play:

1. I see that you appear to be terrified. I am convinced of this because I recognise the symptoms of terror and because the dramatic context tells me that terror is an appropriate response to the circumstances of the drama.

2. You develop the physical rhythm of terror to a point that you look as if your body is out of control. I see this as a sort of dance of terror.

3. I recognise that your dance is pertinent to the drama, so I believe it. But I also recognise that this is preposterous behaviour, so I feel free to laugh at you. This is what I call the visceral laugh.

The Italian *Commedia dell'Arte* is our clearest reference for visceral comedy. Time after time in *Commedia* we see those three steps of action as a scene is pushed towards a visceral climax. Often the action goes beyond the visceral and into the bizarre. For example, if your final action of terror involves you running up the walls then banging your head on the table, you might try to eat the table and dig your teeth into it. This action has nothing in particular to do with terror but because of the context, I read what you're doing as an image of terror. Basically, at this stage you can do what you like and I'll see it as a logical development of what has gone before. You can see examples of this sort of comic action in any episode of *Fawlty Towers* when John Cleese panics or loses his temper. *Commedia* is the prototype of farce.

The action in cartoon films follows a similar pattern: a sneeze can blow a character across the room, through the window and into a tree where he could spin round and round a branch and end up staggering dizzily about the road in a disorientated dance until he's squashed by a passing car. *Commedia* is the theatrical version of a cartoon.

The Banana Debate

Visceral humour emerges when life overtakes us. In other words, when the events around us appear to be moving faster than what's going on in our heads. An accident, like a trip, a fall, or a near miss, can provoke visceral humour. Hits, acts of aggression or violence are all capable of inspiring a visceral response. We laugh at the way you move and at what you do and what you look like. This work has more to do with agility and sudden changes of rhythm than wit or clever ideas. We're back to 'the banana-skin incident' that Ramachandran mentioned. It's worth noting that the French philosopher Henri Bergson (1859-1941) based his ideas on comedy on a similar incident.

Writing in the 1890s, Bergson maintained that sustaining a rhythm in inappropriate circumstances makes us laugh:

66 *A man, running along the street, stumbles and falls. The passers-by burst out laughing . . . They laugh because he's sitting down involuntarily . . . Perhaps there was a stone on the road. He should have altered his pace and avoided the obstacle. Instead of that, through lack of elasticity, through absent-mindedness, and a kind of physical obstinacy as a result, in fact, of rigidity or of momentum, the muscles continued to perform the movement when the circumstances of the case called for something else. This is the reason for the man's fall and also for the people's laughter.* 99

He then went on to formulate his law of physical comedy:

66 *The attitudes, gestures and movements of the human body are laughable in exact proportion as that body reminds us of a mere machine.* 99

Machines were the brave new world of the nineteenth century just as consciousness is the brave new world of the twenty-first century. Words like 'mechanical' and 'rigidity of momentum' fail to warm the heart today, but Bergson's law of physical comedy intrigued me.

In 1992, I tried out the famous banana-skin routine on a group of Performance Arts Students at Middlesex University. I asked them to walk like a person whose movements are so habitual that they have become mechanical. Without breaking this rhythm of their walk, they were to slip on a banana skin. It was surprisingly difficult to do at first – to slip without breaking the rhythm. But working outside, on grass, enabled most of them to become very credible and very funny. Not breaking the rhythm of the walk gave the fall a huge momentum. Some of them flew into the air in wild pratfalls. At the end of the day, I came to the conclusion that basically it didn't matter what they did in the air because our laughter was triggered by the credibility of that slip.

In other words, if your impulse to go flying through the air is phoney, then the laugh will be irretrievable. In full flight you'll do what comes naturally and any attempts to influence this part of the movement are going to be a waste of time. We've just got to believe in that trip. If it looks even slightly premeditated, even slightly hesitant or set up, then nobody is going to laugh. If we believe in the fall, then we enjoy seeing you out of control. Your actions are mechanical in the sense that they are automatic and not in the sense that they are machine-like. We'll all fall in a different way. We're all different. It's pointless trying to copy somebody else's movement. It's too personal and too idiosyncratic. It's the impulse to move that's the vital component of physical comedy and not the movement itself. This is the essence of the visceral laugh. If the impulse is strong enough, your movements will be instinctive. You won't know what you look like and you don't need to know.

I came to the conclusion that Bergson's law was more a conceptual interpretation of physical comedy than an empirical one. We're in the same area of instinctive movement here as the 'fright-flight syndrome' that psychologists talk about. For example, if you're almost hit by a recklessly driven car and you discover that you've jumped back on to the pavement without realising it at the time, this is described as an automatic 'fright-flight' response. It isn't the being hit that's funny so much as how you avoid being hit. It's not the falling off the tightrope that makes us laugh so much as what you do to try to stay on.

Memme's Mad Chase

The most effective visceral action sequence that I've been associated with was in a play called *On the Verge of Exploding* (Told by an Idiot, 1993). The situation was this:

> *Memme, a young peasant girl* (played by Hayley Carmichael), *had fallen in love with a young chicken thief* (Paul Hunter). *They used to meet secretly in the bathroom of the girl's house. Unfortunately for both of them, Memme's mother* (Sarah Brignall) *was an inveterate man-hater and was likely to kill any man she met.*
>
> *On this particular evening, Memme ran upstairs to the bathroom in eager expectation of a night of love, only to find her mother stubbornly in occupation of the lavatory bucket. Terrified of the consequences, Memme ran out of the house in an attempt to catch her boyfriend along the way. She missed him and ran about looking for him in an increasing state of panic. She called, she searched, she threw herself across the space. She ran headlong into the audience and climbed up the theatre walls, only to see from a distance that her boyfriend had already climbed into the garden and was doing a striptease right under her mother's nose. So she had to scramble all the way back, taking even more risks than before, and arrived just in time for her mother to absent-mindedly empty the contents of the lavatory bucket over her boyfriend's head.*

That run and that hapless scramble became an aria of despair. The extremes of Memme's situation inspired her to take enormous physical risks. She was beside herself. The striptease, though very funny to us, was a provocation to Memme to make yet another turn of the emotional screw in her nightmare journey back down to the garden. The mad mother sitting on the bucket was the grenade about to go off, the striptease was the equivalent of the boyfriend playing with the pin.

This sequence was hysterical and exhausting to watch. Every element in it was designed to keep the stakes rising for Memme's mad chase. The more the situation worsened, the funnier and the more painful Memme's predicament became. The desperation of her run, the risks she took in the space, were all visceral expressions of the dramatic situation. None of these actions was funny in itself – far from it – they could have been the actions of a lunatic.

The visceral laugh comes from extremis. Madness, as well as magic, the supernatural, and intoxication, can all be harnessed dramatic devices that enable us to go beyond the limits of realism and into our dreams and nightmares. These are worlds where anything can happen just for the sake of it. Here, things don't have to make sense. The story tells us that Memme is scared to death, so anything she does is likely to be seen as an extreme expression of that fear. Whilst laughing at her boyfriend's striptease, we would glimpse her hanging off the wall, her body contorted and apparently screaming too loud to make a sound, as in Munch's painting. We'd see her slapping the wall or sprawled on the floor, unable to move, trying desperately to drag herself up for another pathetic dash.

This is visceral comedy. It's passionate and not necessarily funny out of context. After the event, it is often difficult to pinpoint exactly what it was that we were all laughing about, yet it all made perfect sense at the time. The crucial element is the level of emotional intensity. We empathised with Memme whilst laughing at the absurd eroticism of her lovesick boyfriend, as layer after layer of filthy rags were elegantly tossed in the air with the panache of a seasoned stripper, right under the nose of the brooding figure of Memme's mad mother sitting on her bucket. The scene was played as a drama. No one was trying to be funny. We deliberately ran the farce and the drama head to head. The resulting mix of feeling was so strong that the audience was laughing more out of hysteria than anything else.

Just like the young goddess in the Japanese myth, Memme's dilemma is all too horrible to contemplate. In both stories, this visceral comedy is about building emotional intensity to unbearable levels and taking the action beyond the representation of real life to something more surreal and absurd. In Memme's case, the sequence ended as well as it could: the boyfriend's ardour was cooled with the contents of the bucket and the mad mother watched in disbelief as her 'little girl' drove the naked body of a man out of her garden. It's one thing to sustain an intense feeling for a period of time and another thing entirely to be able to develop that feeling higher and higher on a Richter scale of emotional expression. Visceral sequences like this are knee-trembling journeys that are capable of taking us through the limitations of logic and reason and on through the absurd, and on again to the surreal, and eventually on to levels of madness and poetry.

The final incident in the Japanese myth follows a similar pattern to Memme's chase. In this case, the grenade with the loose pin is the crowd the goddess is trying to please. Having made them laugh and amused them and aroused them with her striptease, now, with her erotic dance over, what is there left for her to do if she isn't to do some sort of a sex act on stage? That's the 'hot spot' of the scene. That's what most of the crowd wants to see in their heart of hearts. The pin is slipping out so all her stamping, kicking, punching, and slapping herself up to that final image represent the same visceral development, but unlike with Memme, the action in this story takes us to the highest level of all: the bizarre.

The Bizarre Laugh

Take a look at these corny one liners. The first is from Jimmy Tarbuck and the second is from Spike Milligan:

    "   *Put the kettle on, it suits you.*   **"**

" *That man is screaming out in anguish. Fortunately I speak it fluently.* **"**

In each case the 'set-up' of the joke is pure recognition. The familiarity of the context lulls us into a false security, but the punchlines of both these jokes are bizarre. Here we have that trivial and inconsequential element of comedy that Dr Ramachandran was referring to as being the most crucial part of his 'lowest common denominator of humour'. This is the nonsense that flips conventional logic onto its back and makes us think again. These images of somebody wearing a kettle on their head or somebody having a conversation in 'anguish' are compellingly stupid.

If *Commedia dell'Arte* is a fruitful reference for the visceral, then the clown is an equally fruitful reference for the bizarre. I'm not interested in the big shoes or baggy trousers of the circus clown so much as clowning as a level of play – an imaginative key into the bizarre – and for some people, this key is immensely liberating. This is a place where you aren't required to be clever or witty or obviously skilful. Here, you're simply invited to generate meaning from the inconsequential and the trivial – from the lowest common denominator of comedy.

A normal person can stand on the beach, look out to sea and scan the horizon, but a clown is unlikely to know what the horizon is. The clown lives in a world of bafflement where one thing leads to another. It's a state of perpetual free association where we no longer have to ask the question 'why?' The bizarre laugh is the exact opposite to the recognised laugh. To get to a point where we all know exactly where we are and what we're doing requires detailed analyses and constant questioning. It's impossible to make anything that we can describe as being typical without this. The bizarre laugh, however, comes out of nowhere. It defies conventional logic. The bizarre laugh comes from a place of immense honesty, simplicity and naivety.

There was a famous debate in the fifties between Jacques Lecoq (1921-1999) and Dario Fo about whether clowns could ever be political. Dario Fo reckoned that they could, but Lecoq was adamant that the clown is incapable of being political or subversive because he or she is incapable of seeing that far ahead. He maintained that they'd always be more taken by the uniform than what that uniform might represent.

We can all touch this part of our imagination in the right circumstances, but few of us are prepared to stay there for any length of time. Angela de Castro, an extraordinarily accomplished clown with a huge international reputation, was invited to an interview with Sir Peter Hall. He had heard of her and was interested in working with her on Beckett's *Waiting for Godot*. 'What part would you like to play?' he asked her, 'Pozzo, Vladimir, Estragon, Lucky?' 'The Tree,' she replied emphatically, 'that is the only part in the play that relates to everybody.' Inevitably, that was the end of the interview and the end of her association with Sir Peter Hall. Her suggestion was too bizarre for words. True clowns aren't actors and they don't fit comfortably into theatrical conventions, which is why we have much to learn from clowning in the theatre today. Clowns don't respect the text and they're not interested in role or character. True clowns are motivated by their contact with the audience. Only a clown would have thought that 'The Tree' was a part and only a clown would have valued the playing of it.

The bizarre is an ancient form of comedy; today, it's endemic in our popular culture. *The Goon Show* put it on the map in the fifties and sixties, but *Monty Python's Flying Circus* made it respectable in the seventies by presenting us with a constant stream of surreal images and nonsensical situations: delinquent grannies roaming the streets of small seaside towns, recklessly mugging passing youths and terrorising the neighbourhood, or a man going into a pet shop to complain that he'd been sold a dead parrot.

We don't need explanations with the bizarre. It is funny in its own right. Even these isolated images are amusing but they really come into their own in a dramatic context. John Cleese as Basil Fawlty in *Fawlty Towers* thrashing his broken-down car with the branch of a tree is an excellent example of a bizarre image. It works because it makes a satisfying conclusion to all the previous disasters that had befallen him already that day. The thrashing scene comes at a point in the story when we think that things can't get any worse. Logically, they can't. The only place to go is into the bizarre. We've all dreamt about thrashing the car when it won't start, and to this extent, the action is completely recognisable, but few of us have actually done it. Basil Fawlty actually does it. In the context of a narrative, bizarre imagery accrues meaning. At its best, a bizarre image will encapsulate a scene perfectly and leave uncomfortable questions dangling in the air.

This is precisely what happens in our Japanese myth. The final image of our young goddess standing there stark naked, smiling at us, and holding her nipples in the air, dripping in blood, is grotesque. Do we laugh or don't we laugh? Is it funny or just plain revolting?

When the Laughter Stops

Imagine staging a version of this myth where there was no blood when the goddess tears her nipples out. Imagine instead that she peels her nipples off like so much dead skin and then looks at the audience as if to say, 'Look, they came off in my hands!' It's certainly bizarre, and it might even be funny, but it would bowdlerise the story completely. As soon as we see that the nipples are false, the action would lose all its resonance. This once disturbing event would be reduced to a tawdry bit of smut. All those difficult questions like, 'Why did she go that far?' 'Why did she do it?' 'Why ruin something so beautiful?' and 'Why make us all feel so bad about it?' would go unanswered. Art's job is to ask the questions, it isn't required to answer them. That's for us to do, and in this case it's the final image that poses all the questions. This image isn't remotely comic: it's bizarre and it's grotesque. At this point in the story, the gods didn't laugh, they roared. By now their 'OK signals' had turned nasty. Having assured each other that everything that had happened so far was only play, by now their games had become carnal. The audience had become a crowd and the crowd had become a mob and they were baying for blood. It was more like a boxing match than a stage show.

Something significant happens on stage with the letting of blood. But we've got to believe it. If we don't believe that actual physical harm has been done then it's little better than the false nipple joke. The letting of blood is only funny if you have no respect for human life. To see someone seriously hurt and bleeding is the ultimate act of recognition and it is irrevocable. It implies that something has been done that can't be undone and that things will never be the same again.

In the film *A Fish Called Wanda* (1988), Michael Palin played a gentle animal lover with a heavy stutter. He was given the task of murdering an eccentric old lady. The method he chose to kill her consisted of dropping a large concrete block on her from a great height as she came out of her house. As fate would have it, she came out of her house to walk her two poodles and, instead of flattening the old lady, it flattened the dogs instead.

When this incident was filmed, it contained a short sequence where blood was seen to ooze from under the concrete block. This was cut from the final edit because it was felt that it would have compromised the comedy. They wanted to keep us laughing so they didn't show us any blood. The sequence finished with our hapless dog murderer inconsolable in his remorse, hiding up a tree, weeping copiously as he watched two tiny coffins lowered into the ground. Another bizarre image.

Laughter and violence go well together, laughter and blood don't, and that's why they make such wonderfully resonant clashes. This is prime territory for the bizarre. Of course you can bleed and laugh at the same time. You could be at death's door and we'll laugh with even more enthusiasm provided we believe that you're really going to die in the first place. Some time ago Channel 4 broadcast *The Boy Whose Skin Fell Off*, a documentary about the last few weeks in the life of Jonny Kennedy, who was born with the genetic skin condition, dystrophic epidermolysis bullosa. This causes his skin to fall off under the slightest pressure, leading to scars and sores and, ultimately, skin cancer. We watched agonising scenes as his mother peeled bloodstained dressings off his back, and we joined him on a trip to the undertakers to be fitted for his coffin. The only thing that made the film remotely watchable was Jonny's inimitable sense of humour. He was warm, engaging, ironic and self-deprecating – if that was possible in his condition. We laughed, not because he was witty, but because he was brave, unsentimental and realistic. He met his end with grace and empathy, and the effect was life-enhancing.

In the late sixties, Peter Brook devised a play called *US*. It was about the Vietnam War. At a crucial dramatic moment, one of his actors burnt a live butterfly on stage. It provoked a national outcry. The press attacked him. Even butterflies have rights – never mind the people dying in Vietnam. They wanted to know if it was an actual butterfly that was killed or if it was a trick. Brook promised to tell them, but if they printed it, he would certainly burn a live butterfly on every subsequent occasion. He had to make the moment credible and this was his attempt at making the act irrevocable and making us respect the letting of blood. He was prepared to go to any length to avoid that fake nipple moment.

If you never pause to respect the blood, if we don't buy that you are dying in agony, then the laughter will lose its edge. Had Jonny Kennedy been played by an actor, we'd have felt cheated and the comedy would have been grotesque. There would have been no recognition. The stakes wouldn't have been high enough to engage our humanity. But the moment we believe that death is imminent then you can play the comedy and the drama head to head with equal commitment. Then our laughter will take on all the varying tones of the drama. Sometimes that laughter will be raucous and sometimes it will be more muted, as in the crucifixion scene at the end of *The Life of Brian* (1979). Sometimes the action will be ridiculous and sometimes it will be almost too painful to watch, but our capacity to laugh is just as strong as our capacity to em-pathise. The knowledge that the tension could be broken at any moment keeps us watching at times when many of us would rather look away. We're perfectly capable of laughing and crying at the same time. Once we believe that blood has been spilt, we bring the appropriate gravitas to the scene. We know what to do.

The Surprise Laugh

This is the most basic of all the laughs to be looked at, and it's the one to be the most forgotten. This laugh goes back to that infant game of 'peek-a-boo'; to the infant delight of the jack-in-the-box. It's the little surprise, the little trick that catches us unaware. The table that's up-ended to make a door that somebody opens and walks through, the quick-change artist who walks behind a flat in one costume, and appears almost instantly in something entirely different. Good theatre thrives on moments like these. They're evidence of our invention and our imaginative interpretation. Some of the most effective surprise laughs work on a scenic level. I remember watching a presentation when, at a crucial moment, we heard a violent noise at the back of the auditorium and everybody turned round to see what was going on. When we turned back again, the scene had been changed. We laughed because we'd been caught out by a simple and effective little trick. Scenic sur-prises are a reminder that you're one step ahead of us and that theatre is a live event happening in the 'here and now'.

The Japanese myth was a fictitious account of an incident of theatre. There is nothing illusory about what happened on that upturned bathtub. The gods were never invited to suspend their disbelief. For them, everything was actually happening in front of them. Everything that the young god-dess did was a surprise. No one had ever seen anything like it before. She probably surprised herself, which is why she felt free to share her laughter with her audience all the way through. That little refrain, 'she laughs, and they laugh, and they all want more' kept everybody firmly in the 'here and now'. Laughter always does that. Even the most bizarre image has the effect of emphasising the 'here and now'. Laughter is always real. Pretend laughter is excruciating because laughter and credi-bility are one and the same thing.

Surprises come in many forms. Memme running up the stairs to the bathroom only to find her mother sitting on the pot is the little dramatic surprise that turned the story. Our empathy for the predicament of both the goddess and Memme sucks us in, and our laughter at their predicaments knocks us back again. Every stage in our journey towards believing in them and their predicament is marked by laughter. We laugh when we recognise what they're doing, when we see them getting out of control, when events are pushed beyond reason and when they take us by surprise. Sometimes we laugh at all four elements at the same time, sometimes individually and sometimes in sequence. In each case, our laughter is shared with each other, and we all want to see how far we can go.

When the Sun Goddess came charging out of her cave on hearing that final roar from the crowd, this was a huge surprise. We had completely forgotten about her. Her entrance wiped out that final horrific image and shocked us into catharsis. In other words, everything that we'd experienced whilst she was sulking in the cave had all been worthwhile because it brought her out again and restored light to the world. It is the element of surprise that brings the story to a satisfying conclusion.

Part One

The Gentle Art
of Playfulness

Humanity has advanced, when it has advanced,
not because it has been sober, responsible and cautious,
but because it has been playful, rebellious and immature.

Tom Robbins

Play

If you look up the word 'play' in the Shorter Oxford English Dictionary you'll find that the various definitions take up some seven inches of column space. It's a complex little word. When I use the word 'play' in the context of acting, I use it in the sense you might say, 'Moonlight plays on a pool of water.' It implies something absorbing, beautiful and pleasurable to watch. But at the same time, it's something frivolous, pointless and meaningless. It's these last three adjectives that give us all the trouble. We live in a rational and a literary culture that doesn't value the frivolous, the pointless and the meaningless. These things go against everything we've ever been taught. After all, how can frivolity and meaninglessness ever be a responsible way to proceed? But if the work is playful it becomes pleasurable, and when you're enjoying yourself you get bolder and take more risks. Choices proliferate. Problems become more manageable because our perspectives change once the work becomes a pleasure.

So far I've used the word 'pleasure' when talking about play, but that isn't the most appropriate word in this context. In English we have a better word and one unique to English: 'fun.' This isn't the namby-pamby, nursery word that it first appears to be. If you thought that 'play' was a complex word, then 'fun' is a semantic hornet's nest. On one level, it means a naive physical exuberance that you might experience having a snowball fight or riding the dodgems, but to do something 'for the fun of it' also implies a joke. To 'poke fun' or to 'make fun' is to ridicule, cajole or to mock. To say that someone is 'a very funny man' is generally taken as a great accolade, but to say that someone's 'a bit funny' implies a social deviance that's more 'funny peculiar', than 'funny ha-ha'. If we say a line like 'something funny happened on the way to the forum' we mean that something remarkable happened. To do something 'for the fun of it' is a robust choice, and less earnest than 'to have pleasure' in doing something. To do something 'in fun' implies a distancing. We're admitting that what we're doing isn't real. We're declaring the game but we're also enjoying the activity. To 'have fun' with something invites invention and gives us even more licence to do what we will. Fun gives us our objectivity and our engagement at the same time. The sensation of playing is empowering and it's liberating. You'll find innumerable techniques and devices for making physical comedy in this book, but they'll all be dead in the water if you don't have fun with them.

Several years ago I was rehearsing a group of students for a lecture demonstration at the National Student Drama Festival, hosted by one of our most respected universities. A lecturer approached me: 'Could I sit in for a bit? – I've heard so much about you, and I'd love to see what you get up to at first hand.' He arrived late and still opening his mail. I indicated where he should sit and carried on. 'Games,' he said after about half an hour or so. 'Excellent icebreakers. I'd no idea that your warm-up would last so long. Tell you what. Why don't I do a bit of work in the office and you send down for me when the work really starts?'

In Dickens' *Great Expectations*, Pip was commanded to play by mad Miss Havisham, and he found that he couldn't. The circumstances just weren't right: he was helplessly self-conscious and didn't know where to start. Play is unconscious in our own childhood, but in adulthood, Miss Havisham is always in the room somewhere, so we have to conscientiously establish the appropriate circumstances that enable us to feel free to do what we like, or we'll end up feeling awkward and self-conscious like Pip. Play is a discipline for me, with its own ground rules and its own procedures. Let's not kid ourselves; theatre-making can be tough and making comedy even harder. The spectre of Miss Havisham will rise up in the form of lack of time, lack of money, intractable material or interpersonal conflicts. You might be tearing your hair out in the office with interminable discussions but in the rehearsal room, play always generates more material than discussion.

Back at my rehearsal, we were convulsed with laughter over a horse-racing scene we'd just made. It turned out that the piano stool had made an astonishing racehorse and had just won by four lengths against the office chair and the top of an old sewing machine that had been forced to retire from the race after refusing the first jump. It was the antics of this delinquent little pony that were causing all the hilarity.

'Now – why is that so funny?' came a voice from the back of the room as our laughter died down. Our visitor had returned. 'I haven't a clue,' said one of my students. 'Whatever it was, it just flew out the window.' More laughter. 'No – it's back. It's sitting over there.' Our Miss Havisham was resolute and unperturbed. 'To what extent can illustration ever be profound?' Illustration is the bane of psychological realists everywhere. Some students gathered round our visitor while I started to clear up. Words like 'mimicry' and 'mimesis' were banded about. 'We were only playing, Sir,' I heard somebody say with heavy sarcasm.

Psychologists have long maintained that there is a vital link between children's play and their emotional and social development. They cite the case of Jeanie, a child who was strapped in a cot for thirteen years by her tyrannical father. She emerged from her ordeal terrified of the world around her with no social skills and with severely impaired movement. Hardly surprising, you might think, because today the significance of children's play is undisputed, but there are still strong misconceptions about the role of play in conventional approaches to acting.

'You weren't being a racehorse: you were illustrating the movement of a racehorse,' our Miss Havisham remarked. The discussion was becoming intense.

About forty years ago, the great movement teacher Jacques Lecoq developed the idea of *mime de fond* by which he meant fundamental, basic or essential mime. Lecoq maintained that children instinctively indulge in mimetic play in order to experience the world around them. He observed how children mime cars, planes, the movement of animals and concepts like size and distance in order to experience these things so that they understand them. He concluded that mimetic play is at the core of our understanding of the world. To theatre practitioners, the word 'mime' is about as acceptable as paedophilia, but mimetic play is as close to the heart of theatrical invention as it ever was.

The game of using a piano stool as a horse was funny because we knew that on the one hand it was only a piano stool but on the other it was an Arab thoroughbred. This wasn't achieved by illustrating the movement of the horse but by recreating that movement. We weren't laughing at the illusion of a horse so much as at the ridiculous and imaginative journey that took us there. That horse was credible because we all knew it was only a piano stool. It was an audacious game. To a child, play like this is exploratory. To an actor, it's metaphorical. The piano stool becomes a metaphorical horse, and the game of turning a piano stool into a horse is eminently theatrical.

Play occupies a liminal world between the actual and the imaginary where anything can become something else and metaphors breed like rabbits. Comedy thrives in this atmosphere, and if you're riding a piano stool as if it were a racehorse, laughter is a reassurance because it tells you that we're seeing what you're seeing so it must be OK. This same laughter gives us permission to carry on doing silly things with a piano stool when our more rational selves are inhibited and alarmed by our persistent stupidity. Our visitor was more interested in big ideas than silly games. He wanted things to be like life because then he knew where he was. He wanted substance, insight and meaning. He wanted a beautifully conceived and expertly written play rather than the sight of us playing. He wanted to see us up and running, when we were still working out how to stand up. We laughed at the piano stool becoming a racehorse because the idea was as recognisable as it was bizarre and as shocking as it was credible. In favouring the game of the piano stool becoming a horse over other options like creating a mimetic illusion of a horse or devising some other more realistic representation of a horse, we were capitalising on our natural capacity for making associations. Theatrical play is associative action.

Neuroscientists tell us that the brain is like a computer with a multitude of programmes all open at the same time, allowing us to flip from sense memory to observation to ridiculous fantasy or to rational conclusions at great speed, and in a highly personal and totally subjective manner. We leap from one association to another like a series of random stepping-stones that are just as likely to take us down the stream as across it.

Whilst working on a children's play at the Polka Theatre in Wimbledon, I was wrestling with the idea of how to stage the psychotic dream of a young child who was having a nightmare about collecting the first breath of a baby. I was thinking about how to stage this as I passed the supermarket Tesco, and I suddenly asked myself: 'Do they have Tesco in Ireland?' I was remembering my production of *Hamlet* that had toured to Ireland years ago. At one performance to an audience of a thousand schoolchildren in Cork, a child had shone a laser torch in the eyes of one of the actors and stopped the show. Two burly ushers lifted him bodily from his seat and I noticed he was holding a Tesco bag, so . . . 'We could use a laser torch for the baby's first breath,' I thought to myself. Associations. We have the facility to associate anything with anything: words, actions, images, movements, memories, tastes, sounds, smells or textures.

In Virginia Woolf's famous essay 'Modern Fiction', published in 1919, she writes:

❝ *The mind receives a myriad of impressions — trivial, fantastic, evanescent, or engraved with the sharpness of steel. From all sides they come, an incessant shower of innumerable atoms . . . life is a luminous halo, a semi-transparent envelope surrounding us from the beginning of consciousness to the end.* **❞**

This rather florid pronouncement became the manifesto of the style of writing that became know as 'the stream of consciousness', a sort of literary free-association game in which we're invited to follow the eccentric path of those random stepping stones along the stream and up the side of the mountain on a complex and subjective journey. The problem is, of course, that our multi-tasking computer with all its programmes open all the time bombards us with apparently random associations, but language is linear and causal. We string words together in an attempt to make sense of things, and we have a natural propensity for finding meaning in narrative.

It's quite satisfying to play a simple word-association game where I might say the word 'ball', and you say 'dog' and I say 'tree', and you say 'piss', and I say 'grass', you say 'cricket', I say 'bowl' and you say 'out'. These are apparently random associations made more entertaining by being put into a chain of logic. It's easier to produce a vestigial narrative like that one than it is to play a word game where all associations are forbidden. This is much more difficult to do. Something like: 'bed', 'corrugated iron', 'dunce's cap', 'potato' and 'motorcar' is an unrelated list of words. There's no causality here and no logic. The incongruity of these words is baffling but the more we think about them, the more we can't help but try to put them into some sort of story. Our rational mind is confounded but the clashes between the words are intriguing. Take any two words at random like 'dunce's cap' and 'potato', for example. I have a picture of a potato wearing a dunce's cap. There's a game I once played with Roddy Maude-Roxby, a former member of Keith Johnstone's theatre company in the sixties and seventies. He would say 'lobster', for example, and I had to complete the image by saying something to make the initial proposal more incongruous. So I might say 'a lobster on crutches', or he might say 'brick', and I'd say something like 'a brick singing an aria'. These bizarre clashes are comic purely because they're juxtapositions, and juxtapositions make strong theatrical imagery. We might be amused by their audacity, but they'll only acquire any lasting interest for us if we put them into a context where we can find meaning.

I'll warn you now – the vast majority of the games I use are banal. We're dealing with physical interaction here, not lofty concepts. Put any of these games in a dramatic context and they'll generate meaning, but when we look at the games in isolation then they're just silly games. They have to be simple so that we can apply them instinctively to a dramatic situation without thinking about it. We're playing with the substance of acting here rather than the drama itself, and it's a substance that's more about reaction than thought.

Developing the Movement

A group of people stand in a circle. One person makes a simple movement like clenching and releasing their fist, for example. Everybody else copies that movement and the next person develops it. For example, if I'm clenching my fist I might bend my elbow, then everybody else copies that. Then the next person clenches the fist, bends the elbow and then finds the development of extending the arm out. Then the next person round clenches the fist, bends the elbow, extends the arm out and finds the development of lifting the arm straight up above their head. That's the game. You can start with any part of the body.

This is a game of action association: you're required to watch, copy and find the development. That's all. When the game is played well it flows smoothly around the circle, but the slightest hesitation indicates thought. Don't think about what you're going to do; find the action in the doing. This is the skill. You'll probably find that people will want to make movements that are too complicated at first. You can't play the game with complex movement so start small and keep it simple. Have nothing in your head and be content just to copy the others. When it's your turn to find the development, do the easiest, the most comfortable and the most obvious thing that occurs to you.

The Thinking Behind Playful Acting

The conventional approach when rehearsing a scene is to ask: 'What's your objective?' In other words, what do you want at this moment in the action? For example, you might want to throw yourself into an armchair in sheer exasperation over what somebody has just done. We'll read that choice as 'your character' doing it but, to you, it's just a choice that you've made in pursuit of your objective. Alternately, you might want to show your exasperation with somebody by walking slowly out of the room; again, it's a choice in pursuit of your objective. Playing your objective is a valuable device to enable you to interpret the text, and open up the various interactions in a scene. But, if I ask you to find the game of throwing yourself into that armchair, or to find the game of showing your contempt for somebody by the way you leave the room, then I'm inviting you to be much more daring with the action. Now you'll be playing the action just for the fun of it. Suddenly you'll give yourself more options, and you'll be able to make wilder choices. By asking you to find the game rather than to play your motivation for doing something, I'm inviting you to take the action beyond the psychological nexus of the scene, and I'm encouraging you to play the action for its own sake. Of course, if you do this all the time you'll wreck the scene and obscure the drama, but if you rely exclusively on playing your objectives you'll be in danger of becoming too small, and too literal in your playing of the text. If you haven't got a text in the first place, and you're devising the scene from scratch, then relying exclusively on playing your objectives will obstruct the development of the scene. The interaction will become too fixed. Playing an objective is more a device for enabling you to accurately repeat the choices made in rehearsal rather than a method of finding new choices and fresh ideas.

If I ask you to find the game of doing something, I'm inviting you to play, and to do something for the fun of it. I'm encouraging you to be mischievous and provocative and to stir things up a bit.

Devising a play is a bit like building your own house: in my experience, people who've built their own homes have a different attitude to making alterations and changing things round a bit than those of us who've never touched a trowel, let alone built a wall, or put a roof on. Habits picked up over years of making plays from nothing encourage me to see a text as a blueprint rather than a facsimile of the final thing. I'm not happy just to view the accommodation and imagine its potential, I want to knock it about a bit, look at the foundations and worry about the wiring. Of course you can't do this unless you have ownership, but theatre-making is the most collaborative of all the arts. In a really good production, the entire creative team has ownership. If you want to play anything credibly, you must own it in its entirety. If you don't feel that it's yours, you'll soon start to feel phoney and lose confidence or just get bored with it. You can't fake play. You're either really enjoying yourself in a game that's delicate, unpredictable, and compelling to play, or you're not. Whether you're in a high drama or the wildest physical comedy imaginable, if it doesn't feel alive and absorbing to you while you're playing it – how do you think its going to look to us?

Finding the Game

I remember working with a group of acting students on *Two* by Jim Cartwright. The play, set in a pub, is made up of a series of interactions pushed to a level of social realism that becomes so bleak that it's poetic. I was working on a conversation between a man and his wife. She had just been to the loo, and consequently had been out of his control for a few brief minutes. If this was a picture of them on a happy night out, God knows what it must be like at home, when he's had a bad day at the office. The actors had been working on the scene for some time with their acting teacher, so they'd carefully broken the text down into units of thought, they'd constructed a background for their characters, and they'd planned their objectives perfectly. 'The wife' approached 'the husband' with the care of a bomb-disposal expert. He barely looked at her. He was still, and spoke very quietly, and stared into his pint. He wanted to know what she'd been doing in there. Was it 'a number one' or 'a number two'? He actually wanted to know!

'You play a good atmosphere,' I said when they'd finished. They were diffident and unimpressed by my praise. 'We're bored with it,' they said. 'We've been working on it for a week and it's got too technical, and everybody says it's too small.'

I asked them to play the action of the scene and to say the text in their heads, just to make us all aware of exactly what actions they played in the scene:

He sat at the table and stared into his pint. She came through the door and walked towards him, haltingly, and went to her seat next to him. He continued to look at his pint.

He was locked in his world, and she in hers. I didn't want to radically change what they'd done, because I felt much of it was very effective, but I thought there could have been more interaction between them, but it would have to be very subtle.

'Play the scene again, but with the text this time; find the game of allowing her to come to her seat,' I suggested. 'Keep it subtle, and don't talk about it beforehand.'

She came through the door, looked at him, and stood some feet away. She waited uneasily, watching him intently. Like before, he didn't move, and stared into his pint, but this time he was holding his breath. With as much control as he could muster, he breathed out. She walked to her seat, and sat down.

'Now, find the game of letting every question he asks you stop you thinking. And you [the husband] find the game of holding your breath, but still don't look at her.' Every question he asked her made her fumblingly inarticulate, and his smiles and soft-spoken manner made the scene more chilling than before.

The games had made them play off each other more because they brought actuality into the scene. She was genuinely kept waiting. On the inside she probably felt more awkward than terrified. On the outside we saw her discomfort, and as the context became clear, we started to read this discomfort as terror. He was always in control, which is exactly how the scene is written. He could keep her waiting as long as he liked, and he could use this game to provoke her to greater levels of discomfort in every new performance. In this way, the scene was truly theirs. The game of him holding his breath was excellent. Like the waiting, it was an actual restriction. From the outside it looked as if he were trembling in an attempt at controlling a violent temper. On the inside he was trembling because he was trying to breathe out smoothly, and the effort was making him slightly red in the face. She, on the other hand, looked almost relieved as she sat down, as if she had avoided the worst of that interaction. By making each question a different provocation, he was forced to play the text with more pauses than before, and all his attempts at looking affectionate and kind only emphasised the thin gloss he was putting on his almost uncontrollable rage. Her game of 'not being able to think' took her beyond fear, to the point of incredulity. She was terrified and helpless, and we empathised with her completely.

I find the idea that acting must be 'truthful' deeply irritating. The more credible we are in the theatre, the bigger the lies we're trying to tell. Theatre is one big benign lie and the act of telling that lie is a game, so why not admit it? Childhood experiences in the playground have taught us all that games can be nice or nasty. The only difference is that in theatre we've got more scope for deciding how nice or nasty those games are going to be. Games amplify action. They can turn an objective into a contest and make that objective into something that has to be played for. If you try to find the game in everything you do, then we'll want to take you out and disembowel you in the town square, but if you're more selective then you'll play to better effect, and we'll love you for it and admire your daring and your invention but you'll know it's only a game. Even if you're required to play something truly appalling like a rape scene, for example, and if you find the game of being the aggressor and the game of being the victim, then you can enter the nightmare of that situation with impunity. Find the game and you'll empower everyone involved to push that situation as far as you like, safe in the knowledge that you're only playing to have an effect. We'll be the ones left to handle the emotions of the situation, and you'll be free to play the game with greater accuracy and more engagement.

Rapes are such grotesque violations of human dignity that they're difficult to contemplate, let alone to play convincingly on stage. But if you break the events of a rape scene down to a series of games, you'll probably get something like the following: the game of shocking somebody and the game of struggle, chase, and restraint and finally, the game of hinting the worst.

In the mid-nineties I made a play called *She'll be Coming Round the Mountain* for Backstairs Influence Theatre Company. It was a heartbreaking comic drama about the struggles of a father trying to look after his little girl in a devastated, bombed-out world of anarchy and despair. The set consisted of a landscape of literally hundreds of old shoes. They were difficult to walk on without stumbling and falling over.

In the story, a young girl, no more than a child really, struck up an acquaintance with a young soldier. She'd often chat to him but he never said anything. Perhaps he didn't speak the same language, perhaps he was embarrassed, or perhaps he hated her — who knows? One day she met him in the usual place and he was drunk. He made a fumbling pass at her, which developed into a brief chase, and then he caught her, and raped her. It was quick, brutal, and in full view of the audience.

In working on the scene I remember trying to work in very broad strokes. The rape started with the game of the chase, which in reality was the game of trying to run on the rough piles of shoes, which was very difficult and cumbersome to do. The harder the girl tried to run, the more desperate she looked. The harder the soldier tried to run over the shoes the more drunk he looked. They were both stumbling about and soon they fell over. To find the rape I remember asking them to make up a shocking image. After several attempts they came up with the young girl struggling to get up on her hands and knees after having fallen over yet again, and the soldier suddenly reaching under her skirt and pulling her knickers down. She fell, face down, in the shoes and, in the audience, our eyes were instantly distracted by the young soldier struggling to unbutton his trousers with one hand whilst trying to keep her pinned to the ground with the other. Then he fell on top of her and they both struggled, and the play moved on to another scene.

That's about as explicit as I care to go. Those two images gave us all the hints we need to understand and empathise with the action. Some people after the show were convinced that the action was even more explicit but that was all we did and I have no memories of ever discussing the rape, the brutality or the powerful feeling involved. We were all too preoccupied with the games. 'Run faster and it looks worse,' someone might say. 'Try running over here, it's more difficult.' We were all very proud of the image of him pulling her knickers down. We enjoyed its shock value and the image of him struggling to undo his flies hinted at the worst possible outcome.

By focusing on the quality of the games we were able to explore the horrors of the situation with much more confidence than if we had tried to write the action of the rape in a sequential order. The more we came up with another way of playing a game, the more we were exploring the scene and generating new choices and fresh ideas. What were simple games to us were powerful moments of dramatic intensity to the audience. They would have been appalled to know that we were playing games with a subject like child rape and, had they caught even a glimpse of a game in what we were doing, they would have been deeply offended, I'm sure. As it was, the games were hidden deep in the dramatic situation.

In finding the game, you're giving yourself permission to 'get on with it' and to stop thinking. This isn't an invitation to debunk everything, and allow yourself to be trapped in a world of perpetual parody. It's a reminder to keep following those little associations and tiny developments. The best games aren't big ideas – at least they don't start that way. The best games come from tiny moments of silliness, and once you find the game, you'll start to play.

The great thing about working with a text is that the writer will have built in, or at least suggested, most of the games for you already. Your job is to recognise what you're being invited to play, and you're most likely to do this once you've developed the habit of playing in the first place. Whatever material you're working with, games amplify action and bring it alive. Here are two games to help cultivate these habits.

Finding the Game

If a small group of people stand in a circle, and I ask them to 'find the game', they'll need to find something very small, like somebody raising their eyebrows, for example, or just grinning inanely at each other. Once the game has been identified, everyone else copies it, finds variations of it and tries to entertain each other with it.

The big lesson here is that you don't have to be inventive. You've just got to be reactive to everybody else. As soon as you find a game, your job is to let the action develop naturally. Variations will evolve with little effort on your part, and it won't matter if your copy of the original movement is a bit sloppy because it's bound to give someone else another idea. I can get an entire group to play with this game.

If I were to ask two people to find the game between them, then the play will become slightly more linear and less mercurial because there will be fewer imaginations pulling the action in so many different directions.

The skill in 'finding the game' becomes clearer as soon as you try to play it in front of an audience. Our interest lies not so much in the action itself, but in recognising when that action is starting to flop. As soon as the action fails to amuse, we need to move on, and find something else. Everything's going to die eventually, but you can always go back to something that you liked in the first place. The rules are:

1. Find the game.

2. Entertain each other with it.

3. Recognise when the game is over.

4. Find another game.

Finding the game is a crude application of Virginia Woolf's stream of consciousness. It develops our appetite for finding associations, and for taking the action beyond those clearly defined dramatic circumstances of 'Who are you?' 'Where are you?' 'What are you doing and when?' You won't necessarily wreck the scene, because if the dramatic situation is strong enough, these circumstances will be self-evident anyway. By looking beyond them, your work has the potential to become more poetic and more theatrical.

In *On the Verge of Exploding* (Told by an Idiot, 1993), Sarah Brignall, playing Memme's mad mother, would stroll about the set playing a piano accordion. She found the game of drifting off to sleep. She'd do it in the most inconvenient moments. We discovered that she could play the accordion in such a way that it would make no musical sound, but the air coming in and out of the bellows reminded us of breathing. It looked as if she was asleep whilst still playing. She became a sleeping presence, and a not-so-silent witness, to Memme's secret love affair. So finding the game is the same as having an idea, you might think? No, it isn't. Games lead us to ideas. They put us in the vicinity of ideas. They make ideas possible.

Most actors tend to find a game and persist on playing it. They want to make bigger reactions, and they play to develop the situation and to make it worse than ever. In a workshop investigating the relationship between clown and acting, I asked Toby Jones and Selina Cadel to explore the situation of a wife trying to tell her clearly inadequate husband that the marriage was over. We staged the scene in the kitchen area at the rehearsal venue so we had a fully operational kitchen to work with. Toby found the game of washing-up. It was clearly a game. He wasn't really washing-up so much as moving the dishes about in the water and looking busy. Selina, his wife, stood in the doorway, 'I want to have a serious conversation with you,' she said.

'Well, it's not particularly convenient at the moment,' he replied, whilst ostentatiously rattling the dishes in the sink.

Having found the game and found it effective, he sustained it to the end of the scene and his pointless washing-up developed into a poignant metaphor for his hapless relationship.

Had a clown played the same situation as opposed to an actor it's unlikely that the game would have been so insisted on. Clowns tend to play the moment as opposed to the scene. Their games tend to be shorter and more immediate and there tends to be more of them. Clowns don't play for situations so much as reactions.

The 'And . . . And' Game

Working in twos, one person makes a simple action like patting an empty chair. The other person says 'and' which is a command to develop that action. As in developing the movement, the idea is to do the first thing that comes into your head. So I might pat an empty chair next to me, my partner says 'and' so I start to stroke the chair, my partner says 'and' so I kiss the chair, my partner says 'and' so I roll onto the floor and embrace the chair, my partner says 'and' and the chair is bouncing up and down on top of me – 'and' the chair pulls itself off me and stands apart – 'and' I approach the chair – 'and' the chair turns away.

Finding the game demonstrates the inconsequential freedom of free association, whilst the 'And . . . And' Game demonstrates how the rule, the restriction, and the provocation drive these associations forward. Like water in a hosepipe, the most anarchic freedom is channelled into a focused and tightly controlled output. This focus is created by 'the rules' of the game. Rules impose restrictions, and restrictions provoke reactions. All these games were designed to restrict your choices and to put you in a position to make you react. They take you to a place where there is no acting, and where everything's for real. The discipline is to find the game that makes the reaction real – that's all. Any scene, be it comic, deeply disturbing, or just plain weird, can be seen as a series of little games all strung together like beads, to produce a continuous cycle of actions and reactions.

If you find the game of trying to whistle, you'll see that, by restricting yourself to the task, you make yourself genuinely vulnerable to being taken by surprise. If somebody then plays the game of shocking you, and manages to touch you on the neck, making you jump out of your skin, the reaction is amplified. As far as you're concerned, it's actually happened. You've felt it, and we've just seen it, so there's no question of us having to suspend our disbelief. We were witnesses to the fact. This is the mechanism of play in a dramatic context. You invent a game and impose your own rules and play that game as effectively as you can. These are the forces that make play dynamic. If a game is any good it will always, on the one hand, invite you to do what you want whilst, on the other, make you obey precise rules. These rules give the impression that you're getting it right. You're not, of course, because there is no 'right'. All the rules do is to channel your associations in a particular direction. When random ideas meet clearly defined parameters time and time again, as in the 'And . . . And' Game, we tend to make narrative.

The more we develop the action, the more we find ourselves moving from random associative action towards narrative. Most comic sequences can be seen as simple narratives. The insistent 'And' is a provocation to develop the action. All your partner is saying is 'And what happens next?' The 'Ands' force you to make connections, and the simplest connections make a story:

> *A man walks along the street 'and' he lights a cigarette, 'and' he turns round to shelter the flame from the wind, 'and' he walks into a wall.*

It's a simple three-beat story – and we have an insatiable appetite for stories. Stories are much more exciting to play, more interesting to watch, and easier to sustain than random associations.

The Experiential Gap

At the Market Theatre in Johannesburg I met actors who'd been trained by Barney Simons. They explained how Barney would articulate most elements of a drama in the form of a story. He would talk about 'the story of the play' and 'the story of the story of the play' or 'your story in the play' and 'your story of that story'. In other words, what were the forces that spawned the story in the first place? He used questions like these to enable his actors to find a point of political ownership of the emerging drama. In the Johannesburg of the early nineties, just to be there was a political act in itself. But if you pursue this line of questioning in a less extreme political climate, you'll end up back in the world of consciousness, which is the most subjective place you could ever be in. What was most meaningful in that experience to you personally? Answer that and you'll be playing with what scientists and philosophers call 'qualia', meaning all the things that make up the experiential gap. In other words, all those subjective experiences like how we feel when we touch cotton wool, or eat candyfloss, or how we describe the taste of a mango, look at a naked flame, or see a pile of rubble. Qualia dominate our perception of the world around us.

Language is subject to exactly the same experiential gap as anything else. Our personal understanding of the simplest and most ordinary word is determined by our individual experiences of that word, rather than by its literary definition. A linguistics specialist once explained to me that words are like pebbles on the bottom of a stream. Over time they become covered in a moss, which obscures their original form. For example, if you had a deeply loving relationship with your mother, and I had had a violent and eventually estranged relationship with mine, my personal understanding of the word 'mother' will be radically different from yours. It's just another experiential gap. Personal references and associations have no objective scientific meaning. Scientists don't write in the first person: to say 'I feel that . . . ' is hardly an example of objective analytical thought. The taste of a mango might mean something wonderful to me, and something quite noxious to you.

Qualia refer to the specific nature of personal experiences that are so difficult to describe with any accuracy – except in art. Painting, poetry, literature and theatre all freely trade in qualia. The more freely we play, the more individual and unique that play becomes. In the objective rigour of scientific thought, qualia are a pain in the arse because they make it impossible for us to be objective, but qualia are the stock in trade of art in all its forms. Peter Brook once said that effective theatre strives to 'make the invisible visible'. In other words, the task of theatre is to find action that creates such vibrant resonance in our imaginations that it enables us to reach a mutual understanding. When an audience roars with laughter you can be sure that they've reached such an understanding. It's a bridge over that experiential gap.

The National Student Drama Festival is an annual event that brings together student theatre companies from all over the UK, and is the ideal place to glimpse the theatrical zeitgeist in our colleges and universities; not in terms of quality so much as form, content and attitude to theatre-making. If the past few years are anything to go by, it would appear that qualia form a dominant theme in the prevailing approach to performance and theatre studies in higher education.

Every time I've attended the festival somebody has told me, in defence of some enthusiastic but flawed attempt at theatre-making: 'Oh, it can mean whatever you want it to mean.' And in that single short sentence they abdicate all responsibility for the creation of meaning. Ironically, at the same festival, I'm just as likely to hear some bewildered individual ask: 'But what did you mean by . . . ?' and they'll refer to some tiny detail in a theatrical metaphor. This is just as disturbing because this line of questioning implies that theatrical meaning is necessarily literal, when in reality, theatrical meaning is very rarely literal, since that would be two-dimensional and boring.

The 'make of it what you want to' approach is absolutely right. Of course, we'll always make of it what we want to because our perceptions of the world are built up through our experiences, and the relentless activity of countless neurons zooming about the cerebrum tell us precisely what everything means, second by second. But art deals with qualia better than science ever will; art thrives on association and ambiguity. A piece of prose, or even a photograph, is capable of the same subjective meaning as a piece of dance or music. But comedy deals with qualia in a very different way: qualia are blasted out of the sky every time the audience laugh. Few of us will even raise a smile in the spirit of: 'Oh, it can mean whatever you want it to mean.' We laugh because we all reach the same conclusion at the same time. We can only laugh together when we find a common understanding. At that moment, empathy is more important than anything else. Comedy is constantly trying to bridge that experiential gap, or at least letting us signal across it to each other – in the dark.

An eruption of laughter is one of those moments when the penny drops, and we all reach the same conclusion, at the same time. It's significant that those who are most likely to tell me that something can mean whatever I want it to mean, don't do comedy. Their work is invariably cold and deadly serious. Once in a while, a choreographer like Rosemary Butcher or Pina Bausch, or a director like Tadeusz Kantor or Peter Brook, or some anonymous student group who've never made anything for the theatre in their lives before, will do something that will make my eyes fill with tears, and I won't, for the life of me, know why. This is the indomitable power of qualia. But while people more in love with concepts than practice have po-faced discussions about 'spatial landscape' and 'interacting resonances' (whatever they are), then 'nothing will come of nothing'. Such activities only breed more qualia, and as qualia thrive like microbes anyway, they're the last things we ought to be trying to propagate.

Play in its most open and unstructured form is an indulgence of qualia; it's an invitation to run along your own stepping stones and follow your own stream of consciousness just for the fun of it. The great theatre director Jacques Copeau knew all about play, and started one of the most seminal theatre schools in Western Europe: Théâtre du Vieux-Colombier. He only ran the school for three short years, but in that time he turned our approach to acting upside down. Copeau was the first practitioner to investigate acting as play; he was the first to examine the relationship between clowning and acting, the first to investigate the use of masks in acting, and the role of spontaneity in creative practices.

Copeau maintained that there were two types of play: conscious play and unconscious play. If I were to doodle on a pad whilst talking to you on the phone, I'd be idly following the associations in my drawing, and I'd be playing unconsciously. If I were riding a piano stool as if it were a racehorse, and articulating the fear and the excitement of the race, then I would be playing consciously. If my game were any good, I'd probably make you laugh and gasp in equal measure. Laughter, as I've said before, is an 'OK signal', but in this instance it's also an indication of a shared understanding: my game might capture the essence of a horse, but we all know it's only a piano stool. At its best, play enables us to make the invisible visible. The funniest actors in my experience are the most playful actors. They're the ones who'll take the most risks and be the most uncompromisingly honest on stage. These are the actors who'll most willingly embrace the shocking, the visceral, and the bizarre, as readily as they will the recognisable.

Declaring the Game, and Hiding the Game

On stage, all play is conscious play but even here we have choices. The primary choice, once you've found what game you're playing, is whether you declare the game to the audience, or whether you hide the game from the audience completely.

Kids declare the game all the time. I remember as a child playing endless games of being shot and dying horribly. A small group of us would try to outdo each other with impressive deaths, based on what we'd seen in the latest cowboy film. A friend of mine could make his death last from one side of the street to the other. I remember being very impressed. Clowns also declare the game all the time. Watch Angela de Castro make an entrance, and she'll probably walk on a step or two, look round, and then look at the audience, as much as to say, 'So far – so good.' Then she might see a chair, and then she'll look at us again, as if to say, 'Look at that,' then she'll probably walk over to the chair, and sit down, and look at us again as if to say, 'Perfect.' Every little action is declared as a game. If she thought that somebody had missed something, or if somebody were to laugh, she'd probably stop and play the game again.

Once the game is declared, the audience will know you're playing and everything will look as if it's actually happening. They'll be no illusion, and all your actions will be valued for what they are rather than for what they imply. When you declare the game, you play it so as to have an effect on the audience. I can imagine every Stanislavskian in the world would find that statement toe-curling because it flies in the face of the established creed on the subject of acting. But if I ask you to find the game of sitting in a chair, or the game of changing your clothes, or the game of handing in your resignation to your boss, or the game of murdering somebody, and if I ask you to keep it boring, then the game will be hidden. Your action will still be slightly larger than life, and you'll feel just as free to find alternative ways of doing any of these actions, but because I've asked you to be boring rather than entertaining, the economy of your game will invite more subtext. In being boring, you'll give me less information, so I'll be compelled to make up that information for myself. To you, this will still be a game, and the great thing about finding the game of an action rather than just playing the action is that you don't need a particular reason to do it, other than the invitation to play. But if you're going to hide the game effectively, you'll have to find more stillness, which will help you to become even more boring.

The idea that playing to be boring will make your work appear more psychologically interesting comes from Keith Johnstone. It's an excellent device because it demystifies psychological action. Sometimes I say, 'Do less,' or 'Do nothing'; but if I say, 'Be more boring,' you'll have a clearer idea of what I'm talking about. It's an audacious thing to ask you to do – a deliberate flouting of all the rules. To hide the game credibly you'll have to edit out all your little mannerisms, and all your little illustrations of what you think you ought to feel. Suddenly the pressure of having to do something will be lifted from you and you'll find it easier just to walk on stage, to sit, watch the others, and wait for something to happen. We're all terrified of being boring, so it's a great release to be given permission to be just that. The more boring you are, the more you hide the game, and the closer your games will be to what happens in life whilst never falling into the trap of mimicking life. To invite you to be boring isn't the same as you having to restrict yourself to the question: 'What do I do in this situation?' If it's a game, you're playing it for effect, so how hard you play that game depends on the effect you want to make.

The more you hide the game, the more we're likely to believe that you're this particular person in this particular situation, and the dramatic illusion will be stronger. The more you declare the game, the more distanced we'll feel from you as a character, and the closer we'll feel to you as a person. If we see that what you're doing is a game, we'll see you playing a game rather than you playing somebody else. Our interest will lie more in what happens in the game rather than what happens in the dramatic situation. Your action will look deliberately comic, clown-like, or parodic, or, quite simply, theatrical.

Some years ago I directed a production of *Hamlet*. I cast Hamlet as young as I could. He was playful to the point of bitterness with Polonius, Claudius and his mother, Gertrude. The audience laughed at his outrageous behaviour as he rampaged through the royal household. We were shocked and disturbed as circumstances darkened around him as the drama progressed. At the very end of the play, after the duel, when Gertrude has taken the poison, Laertes is dead, and brutal revenge has been taken on Claudius – even in his last dying moments in Horatio's arms, Hamlet mimicked the death agonies of everyone who'd just died as if to mock death and make Horatio laugh. In mocking their deaths, it looked as if he was mocking his own. It was as if he didn't care. We laughed because it was such a relief, after the carnage we'd just seen – and we also laughed because, on another level, the final scene of *Hamlet* is dangerously over the top for a young theatre audience in a small provincial arts centre. But in declaring the game, Hamlet kept us in the 'here and now'. They were all just actors playing dead – it might be horrible but really no more than a few gurgling noises and dramatic twitching. Once the audience were laughing, Matthew Steer, who was playing Hamlet, suddenly stopped playing, looked at Horatio, tried to make a final joke, then died. Having laughed with Hamlet and having shared his trials and his pathetic little victories, now his death was a loss to us, and his bitterness not misplaced. Hamlet's sport of sending everybody up declared the game in a powerful dramatic situation. It pushed our capacity for empathy to its limits and put us all on a theatrical knife-edge.

Complicity

Complicity refers to the act of being an accomplice. We might say 'both parties were complicit in the robbery', meaning that they were both accomplices in the crime. For example, if one person makes a movement and another person copies that movement, in a sort of mirror image, we have the start of a game of complicity. We can develop this game in three ways: I can copy you, or you could copy me, or we could both share the copying as we like, without stopping the action. If we do that, then we'll inevitably reach the stage where you might think that I'm leading and I might be convinced that you're leading. At that point, the action will become less predictable and more playful. This is complicity.

Complicity is the art behind everything; once you know what you're looking for, you'll see it everywhere: in sport, in the military, or in any team of people who have to work together in a way that demands structure and spontaneity. In theatre, complicity is a creative force in its own right.

The Group With No Leader Game

A small group of people move about the space as one, stopping and starting as they like. They see an object. As one, they all approach that object and take hold of it, as far as possible, in the same place. The group then proceed to play with that object in any way they like, going naturally from one idea to another.

This is perhaps the most intense feeling of complicity that you're likely to experience, and it's as simple as that. The most important thing is that we don't see a leader. The group must always move as one. If you were to end up stopping dead in your tracks, waiting for divine intervention, then I'd have to intervene and get you to move from one thing to the next a little quicker.

I love this game because it gives you the safest feeling of being out of control that you're ever likely to experience. For example, the group might look towards a chair. Then the group walk towards the chair. As an individual in the group, you might think you're going to pick the chair up but then all the hands get hold of the jacket on the back of the chair and pick that up instead. No single individual decided that. This is a game where the group 'take over', and to play it effectively everyone has to be prepared to delegate their individual responsibility to the group and let the group get on with it. You don't have to be clever, and you don't have to be original. In fact, you can be quite anonymous in the crowd, and still have a significant influence on what happens. It's an enervating and inspiring feeling, and it's enormously liberating not to be responsible for how something's likely to turn out.

The Ultimate Takeover

The Balinese have a word for this phenomenon. They call it 'taxus' – a trance-like state of mind that enables you to go beyond what you think you can do – where you can transcend your potential. We'd probably call it inspiration or 'getting off' on something. To the Balinese, 'taxus' is the key to all artistic endeavours, be they cooking, carving, painting, dancing, making music, or playing a grotesque little half-mask on a street corner.

66 *I was sitting on a wall, feeling bored. I'd been in the temple for about an hour, and nothing much was happening. I was just about to leave, when an elderly gentleman sitting next to me said:*

'In Bali, we have rubber time.'

'I believe you,' I said, 'When will it start?'

'When everyone is here.'

'When will that be?' I asked.

'Oh, early,' he said, and burst out laughing at my expression of incredulity. It turned out that he was a retired teacher of English.

'Have you looked round the temple?'

'No,' I said, and continuing our conversation, he led me through a narrow gateway, and into a small courtyard dominated by several large stone plinths. I

was expecting to see the customary statues of Shiva and Ganesh, as in Hindu temples in India, but there were none.

'Where are the statues of the gods?' I asked. 'I suppose it's too humid for you to keep them out here in the open all the time.'

'We don't need statues in Bali because gods always come when they smell food.'

I searched his face for irony, but there wasn't any.

'So they're a bit like house pets,' I said, chancing my arm — I didn't want to cause any offence, but he smiled patiently as if he were talking to an inquisitive child.

'They only eat special food.'

'What's that?' I said, guardedly.

'They only eat rasa.'

'What's that?' I asked, and he beamed with delight.

'At the beginning of time, the gods broke the top off the tallest mountain they could find — just as if it was the top of an egg — then they hollowed it out to make a huge bowl, then they put every living thing that they could find into the bowl: every bird, animal, reptile, leaf, flower and insect. Then they ripped up giant tree trunks, and used them to pound all these living things together to make soup. They called this soup 'rasa'. Today, when the gamelan plays, and the dancing is beautiful, the gods smell rasa, and they sit there, and when the dancing is very, very good, they eat. The gods are always hungry.'

'And they'll come tonight?'

'Of course — as soon as they smell it and you will smell it too. The memory of that smell will bring you back to the temple again.' And his smile was the same.

(Personal Journal, Ubud, 1985) 99

In Bali, artistic activity of any kind is seen as making food for the gods, and to the Balinese, all creative acts, no matter how profane, are seen as sacred. They seek 'taxus' to make their work inspiring. When they do that, so they say, they make 'rasa' — a sort of celestial soup. The gods have insatiable appetites. In our culture, money and fame are the nearest we get to the sacred. The profane and the comic never get a look in. Comedy is never sacred. There's an enduring universal belief in the

West, one of those deep-seated concepts that the evolutionary biologist Richard Dawkins would call a 'meme' as opposed to a 'gene': namely, the idea that comedy is more associated with devils than gods. Fun, laughter and impish delight invariably emerge from the darker side of human experience. Goodness is invariably solemn and serious. But we all understand the idea of 'taxus' and we can achieve it, at least our version of it, through complicity. We all want to get off on what we do, and we all want to transcend our potential even if our gods are so much more prosaic.

Here are a few more games to develop complicity.

The Starting and Stopping Game

If I ask the entire group to walk round and to stop, and then to start again, all at the same time, and with no commands from me, and no 'cues' from anybody else, so that there are no leaders in the group, then you'll have complicity.

Here are some variations on the game:

If I ask the group to go as if to stop, and then to change their minds, this will introduce a dynamic uncertainty into the game.

Now people are likely to make mistakes, and to be caught out, which of course is even more entertaining. The slightly ragged nature of big-group complicity games like these keeps everything in the 'here and now'. You'll all desperately be trying to maintain concord, but little conflicts will emerge all the time. 'Are we stopping?' you'll think, looking round. 'Yes, yes, I think we are . . . No, not yet, oh just a minute!' The game of trying to keep things together whilst deliberately messing things up creates a feeling of volatility that brings the smallest incident to life. The key to playing this sort of game is to convince yourself that everybody else knows better than you. Put your attention on everybody else. You've got to keep reacting rather than acting.

If you play the same game, but with the group running and then stopping all at the same time, and with no cues from anybody else, it will be much more demanding to do.

Though this version is more demanding, it's perfectly possible with a little practice. Now the tension when you're about to run will really build up. And when you do run, the energy released will be explosive, which makes the task of stopping much more difficult. Everyone talks about 'awareness' and 'openness' but these things remain abstract concepts unless you can really experience them for yourself. Complicity embraces 'openness' and 'awareness' and turns these things into tangible skills and pleasurable sensations that you'll want to repeat over and over.

The One Person Stops at a Time Game

Everybody runs around except for one person who stands perfectly still. As soon as that person starts to run, then somebody else must stop. The idea is that there's always one person – but only one person – still at any time, and the game is to be that person.

This game focuses the attention of the group down to one point. It becomes most interesting to watch when something goes wrong and two people stop at the same time. Then they have to negotiate wordlessly, and without stopping the momentum of the game. This takes us to the same point of uncertainty, as in the previous game, only now it's between fewer people, so it's easier to see what's happening. To keep the game going, you've got to learn to give way. If two people give way, one of you will have to stop immediately before somebody else does.

The One Person Moves at a Time Game

This is a reversal of the previous game, in that everyone is still and only one person moves at a time. As soon as they stop, somebody else must take the focus immediately. The game is to take the focus as soon as it is given.

This game is more about teasing than negotiating. I'm always astonished when I play this game with a new group how so many people think that they have to perform. 'Just tease each other,' I find myself saying. 'Try to catch the others out. The game is more interesting than your fancy movement.' In any new group I'll invariably see naff dancing and funny walks in the mistaken belief that you have to be extraordinary to be interesting. There are strategies, little tricks and surprises that keep this game alive, and they'll pop into your head once you start playing. The idea is to find the surprises in the game, rather than on anything that you try and impose on the game. The group will pick up that you're about to stop and everybody will be ready to jump in, and if you change your mind, they'll pick that up too. Your job is to be very clear with your intentions. Funny walks are just funny walks but thoughts are eloquent. We can read your thoughts in your movement but funny movement is just baffling and ultimately boring to watch. Clear games – played rigorously with genuine surprises – are fascinating.

Free Dance

I went to Bali in the eighties and again in the nineties to work with a mask-maker and dancer (they don't have a word for actor) called Alit. I'd gone there to study how masks are used in Bali, and I spent most of my time observing some of the most sophisticated levels of complicity I have ever seen. I saw complicity in relation to the materials they were using, in their relationship with the masks, the music, each other and the audience. I say audience but this isn't strictly true. I spent most of my time watching religious ceremonies. To me, they were predominantly theatrical but to the Balinese they were profoundly religious. For the most part I was a member of a 'congregation' who believed in, and who expected to see magic. As a devout secularist, magic has a limited appeal, but skill and sensitivity impress me deeply.

I couldn't work out if the dancers were following the music or the musicians were following the dancers. I asked Alit and he didn't know. At least, he couldn't answer with any certainty. Yet some dances were highly choreographed, visual comedies with characters and stories and wild knockabout sequences. Others were subtle dramas danced with immaculate precision. I watched rehearsals and I observed dance teachers working with children, and it became apparent that traditional motifs were carefully learnt and meticulously practised, but a skilled group of dancers might change them a little or at least combine the elements in a slightly different way. But I don't think that this was ever discussed beforehand.

The situation became clearer for me when, a few weeks into my stay, I suggested that one or two of the dancers might do one of my 'dances'. My interpreter wasn't around that day so I had to rely on a small boy, who was only too pleased to practise his English, to explain. 'What is your dance?' they wanted to know. 'Tell them it's called free dance,' I replied, thinking on my feet. 'You make it up as you go along.' They were intrigued and amused. They were indulging me and I felt flattered.

To get the ball rolling, I set up the Group With No Leader Game, but my interpreter kept dissolving into paroxysms of giggling. We had just started when the drummer from the gamelan appeared. The explanation and the giggling started all over again. 'Free dance,' he said. 'Yes,' I replied. The drummer started to play, and the dancers stood in a small group looking slightly awkward. 'He follows you,' I said, 'and you follow him, and he follows you, and you follow him, and he follows him,' I explained, feeling distinctly like Stan Laurel. 'Everyone follows the drum,' I said. The small boy translated then collapsed on the floor in hysterics.

The dancers looked uncomfortable at first, grinning at each other like unruly children at the Saturday morning dance class, but the drummer started to play, and they all moved aimlessly round the garden. Then the drummer stopped, then he started again. It was the Starting and Stopping Game. They were negotiating who should lead and who should follow. They would stop for almost a minute, just to raise the tension and keep each other on their toes. Then they started running and stopping. Then one person ran out from the group and took hold of a large water jug left on a table nearby. Instantly the others followed. The drummer raged on the drum and the group lifted the jug high above their heads and paraded it round the garden, and they got faster and faster until they were running at full tilt, and then they ran out of the gate and into the street. Instantly they were back but without the water jug. There was another tense pause whilst the drum laid down a soft pulse and the dancers stood in a tense group, like a cat stalking its prey. Who was going to go first: the drum or the group?

I could see at this stage that something wasn't quite right about these dancers. My interpreter was very still and quiet. Suddenly the dancers leapt forward. The drum raged again. Now they were all holding a chair. They lifted it high above their heads and ran round the garden faster and faster, and out into the street and the drum pounded away. This time as they stood at the gate there was something odd about their eyes. They weren't exactly focused and they looked determined and aggressive. I decided to stop the game. I signalled to the drummer to stop playing but his eyes were the same as the dancers. He didn't respond. I clapped my hands together like a strict schoolteacher. 'OK! That was great. Thank you very much.' Just as I started to speak, the drummer leapt into life and the group of dancers were holding a heavy wooden table. Oh no, now it was getting really out of hand. My interpreter looked terrified. He ran to get help. Meanwhile, the group had lifted the table high above their heads and were about to start their parade when my interpreter arrived with an elderly man carrying a bowl of water. He splashed the water in the drummer's face and then in the faces of each dancer in turn. The tension dissolved immediately, and we all sat round in an amiable and sweaty group. 'Free dance,' they grinned. 'Bagus, bagus.' (Which means: 'Very good, very good.')

Trance is a prerequisite for any performance that's going to be taken seriously in Bali. We don't value trance in our culture, and we distrust anything that looks out of control. Art for us is a conscious experience, while trance is the domain of the showbiz hypnotist. We respect inspiration, but for us this doesn't mean an out-of-mind experience. But then we're not involved in religious practices, and we don't have gods to feed. These dancers were only drawing on their habitual processes. All I was trying to do was to put their process into my context in order to get some idea of what was actually happening. Without the distractions of form and tradition it seemed clear to me that these dancers played in much the same way as I've seen choruses play in my own work. The only difference between them lay in their instinct for complicity. They knew all the games. They knew instinctively how far they might be able to push a particular moment and how far they might develop their intensity to a point where their engagement became 'taxus'. Trance isn't a natural product of complicity unless it's a culturally acceptable product. Had I done something like this in West Africa or Haiti or Sri Lanka, it is reasonable to assume that I might get similar results to those in Bali, because all these places value trance and use it widely. We don't. We play these mechanisms of imaginative engagement more consciously. Oh, we might feel liberated and elated, and we might even feel a sense of having delegated our responsibility for what might have happened in the course of the game, but to us that's just good imaginative work, and not the makings of rasa.

Complicity with Yourself

The dancers in Bali were using the force of complicity to inspire a state of trance. This is a cultural phenomenon and not a characteristic of complicity unless trance is an essential part of your culture. In Bali the best performances are always played in trance. In the West, complicity is a creative force for generating play, ideas and physical comedy. To be effective on stage, you've got to cultivate complicity with yourself, complicity with a partner and complicity with an audience.

The One Person at a Time Game

One person walks around and in between a group who remain still. As soon as that person stops moving, then anyone else can take over and become 'the walker'. The rule is that there should only be one walker at a time, so you've got to make silent negotiations at break-neck speed as soon as more than one person starts to walk. The object of the game is for the walker to prevent anyone taking his place – which is exactly what the rest of the group must try to do.

For those of us in the audience, our interest in the game lies in seeing how much you can trick the rest of the group into thinking that you're going to stop walking. That's all. In a good group, a subtle frisson of agitation will pass through everyone with the slightest change of rhythm. We want to see the rest of the group make mistakes. The game only becomes interesting when everyone in the group is really determined to get to become the walker, and for the game to work, it's got to really matter to the walker that no one in the group manages to take over. There's a hard contest here, and we want to see it played hard. The more I insist on only one person moving at a time, the higher I can keep the stakes, and the more amusing the game becomes to watch.

I once made the mistake of saying, 'How interesting can you be in playing this game?' The result was a disaster. People started assuming funny walks or started leaping about as if they were in a ballet, and all the games of teasing each other by stopping and starting and changing leadership were completely forgotten. They all became very boring, and everybody on stage looked more and more uncomfortable. Complicity with yourself is about being comfortable with yourself. When you're comfortable and you're playing just for the fun of it, then your pleasure in the game will be infectious and the audience will see you 'in the moment'.

If the game starts to become self-conscious, I find that it helps to play it faster. In other words, whilst still insisting on the 'one walker at a time' rule, I add a restriction to the person walking: that they only take one or two steps before stopping, and inviting somebody else to walk. The entire group will be agitated time and again as they all wrestle with each new negotiation. This version of the game makes you put all your attention on what's going on around you, rather than on what you're doing yourself. Now the game becomes fast, and full of mistakes and surprises. When there's no time to think about what you're doing, it's easier to feel more comfortable with big reactions than it is to do nothing.

I developed the following game in Hong Kong when I was directing a group of young actors who were having difficulty in building reactions.

The Cane Game

Set up a simple interaction with an aggressor and a victim such as: A steals something from B or A is trying to get off with B and C is furious. Watch the scene and on the point of the reaction – namely when the victim sees what's going on – slap the floor near to their feet with a bamboo cane and make them jump.

It sounds much worse than it really is. The idea is that they react instantly to the sound, and use that impulse to launch their reaction into the scene. Finding 'the cane moments' became very popular, and the company developed it by hitting the floor painfully close to each other's toes, but the reactions were excellent.

The 'Do Less' Game

Three or four actors run as fast as they can round the playing space. On my cue, they stop and face the audience as if they haven't been running at all and have just got out of bed.

This is a game of letting go of the huge amount of physical intensity that you invested in the running, and trying to just stand there, and do nothing. 'Do less,' I keep saying. In other words, drop your attitude. This game takes practice, but it's easy enough to repeat. I don't know a better game for convincing us that less means more. We become more interesting when we use the appropriate amount of tension for the job in hand. If you stand there rigid with tension, you'll be projecting a whole mass of information that is completely irrelevant. But if you 'do less' and try to eradicate the tension, you're instantly more interesting to watch. You're not comfortable – or complicit – when you're tense. You always look as if you have something else going on, but when your body is soft and easy, you look happy to be up there.

The 'I'm Not Doing Anything' Game

A small group of actors sit around on stage making themselves as comfortable as possible. On my cue, one of them starts a one-way conversation with the audience. Starting with the line: 'Don't look at me. I've got nothing to do,' and then improvising from there. 'I'm just sitting here . . . so there's nothing happening, so you might like to look over there or something . . . '

If there's the slightest trace of self-pity, sentimentality or anything that might be considered imposed or acted, then I get somebody else to play the same game.

It's the pauses and the level of personal comfort and honesty that we're looking for. To what extent can you just be yourself without trying to be interesting? The more boring you try to be, the more you try to do less, the more interesting you're going to become.

Some actors have an astonishing ability to be completely comfortable on stage even when they have next to nothing to do. The Spanish actor

Javier Marzan is one such actor. In *I'm So Big* (Told by an Idiot, 1995),
there was a scene when he was left at his brother's caravan on his own,
whilst his elder brother went to get some booze. 'What shall I do here?'
he asked in rehearsal. 'Oh, we'll find something later,' I said,
dismissively (we rehearsed this play with a number of little gaps, to
encourage the actors to play, but this was the only scene where we
hadn't planned a 'get out'). On the first performance Javier told Paul
Hunter, who was playing the elder brother , 'You should come on when
I say, 'My favourite yoghurt is the lemon one.' When it came to the
performance, Javier sat there, quite relaxed, having agreed a 'get-out
line,' and looked round at the audience, and settled into the 'I'm Not
Doing Anything' Game. 'Don't look at me,' he said. 'I've got nothing to
do. We'll just wait. He'll come on again in a moment.'

The audience loved the break in convention; it was obvious that he
didn't have anything to do, but he was perfectly happy and so were we.
In fact we were fascinated as to what he was going to do next. He was
sitting on a grotty old car seat made out of imitation leopard skin. 'This
isn't real,' he said, just to break the silence. 'It's imitation' – another
pause – the audience laughed. 'Look, I've got nothing to do. We wait.
Do you like yoghurt?' he said, trying to make conversation with us.
More laughter. 'My favourite yoghurt is the orange one.' Nothing happened. 'But I also like the blackberry one, the lime one, apple, straw-
berry, pineapple.' He'd completely forgotten what line they'd decided
on, and as his obvious anxiety began to rise, the audience laughed
uncontrollably. We could have watched him for longer but in the end he
remembered. 'It's the lemon one!' Instantly, Paul came bounding on,
and the drama continued. 'Thank God you came!' Javier said to Paul as
soon as he saw him. 'We were so bored.'

In conventional theatre terms, this incident would be the equivalent of
an actor forgetting his lines, and certainly nothing to be proud of. But in
the playful and spontaneous world of *I'm So Big*, the depth of pleasure
that Javier was able to sustain at this moment, the apparent absence of
acting, and his easy complicity with himself, managed to turn a genuine
mistake into a satisfying dramatic moment. We were laughing out of
empathy rather than mockery. In the audience, we read his panic at not
being able to remember the right yoghurt as being the rising anxiety of
an abandoned child. His text was a banal cover-up, and the more he

played the game, the more his predicament worsened, and his fretfulness grew. We loved him for it because he was totally honest about what he was doing. He was being himself, just talking to us frankly.

If acting is about reacting, as I've said many times before, then complicity with yourself is about letting yourself be open to those reactions. As a student, I'd often hear people saying things like, 'Oh, she's so expressive,' or 'He has an expressive face.' At the time I used to think it was a compliment. Today I'd be more inclined to see it as a criticism, and if you said I had an expressive face, I'd probably think that I'm doing too much with it. I used to think that acting was about being expressive, that feelings were a bit like steam building up in a pressure cooker and that emotions were released when the pressure was high enough. Today I see acting as a reaction to an action rather than an expression of a feeling. To be more precise, if I creep up behind you and make you jump, your reaction will look like an expression of shock to the audience but really it's just an instinctive reaction to what I've done to you. If I really make you jump, you'll look all the more expressive – but being expressive is the last thing you'll be thinking about. When I crept up on you in the first place it might have looked like an expression of mischief, but in reality, all I was doing was reacting to the fact that you were completely unaware of what I had in mind. You don't have to think about emotions, they look after themselves. And you can leave thinking to the academics. Your job is to find the game.

The Shoe Game

One person sits in a chair with their eyes closed. In front of them is a row of different pairs of shoes. Two other people choose a pair of shoes of the same sex as the person in the chair and slightly bigger than their normal shoe size. You need two people to put the shoes on because it's quicker, and the game won't work if the shoes are a difficult fit or if they're too tight. If you're in the chair, you keep your eyes closed all the time, and you observe how the shoes feel. Then you stand up, and feel the difference that the shoes make to how you stand and how you move about. 'Is your weight further forward or further back?' I might ask. 'Do you feel taller or smaller? Are you more athletic or more frail or just clumsy in those shoes?' Then, still with your eyes closed, I'd ask you to walk around the chair, and maybe across the space a little. 'How old are you?' I ask. 'Are you married?' Or 'Do you have a boyfriend or a girlfriend?'

The game can develop into a conventional 'hot-seat game' where I ask whoever is sitting in the chair a series of probing questions to establish who they are, how old they are, and their personal relationships.

Because you have your eyes closed and have no idea what the shoes look like, you're unable to make any visual judgements about the shoes. In other words, you can't say, 'Oh, those are trainers so I must be a sporty person'; you're forced to concentrate on how the shoes make you feel. You've got to let the physical impulse of the shoes affect your balance and the way you stand. Just try to be comfortable. Everything comes from this. You don't have to make anything up – just follow the logic inspired by how the shoes make you feel. You might well be wearing a flash new pair of trainers, but with your eyes closed you might feel clumsy and awkward in them and if you follow that logic you might think that you're an old lady in her nineties, or that you're somebody in hospital recovering from an operation. David Mamet's maxim of 'Invent nothing. Deny nothing' in his book *True and False* is particularly apposite here. In other words, don't deny how the shoes make you feel, and if you find yourself trying to make up some wild character from nowhere then you're inventing and imposing your ideas on the shoes rather than following a logical progression of ideas inspired by them. Of course it's all invention, but if I ask you, 'How old are you?', and you reply immediately, with no time for thought, and we all see that you're standing in an attitude that fits the age you say you are, then we'll all believe you completely. What seems an entirely logical reaction to you looks like a transformation to us. Beryl Reid, one of our greatest comic actors, used to say: 'I don't know who I am until I've found the shoes.' David Mamet, on the other hand, says that transformation is actors' superstition. That's nonsense, and he wouldn't say that if he'd ever played the Shoe Game.

You feel different in the shoes. That's to say you won't feel like you do normally and, to that extent, you'll feel 'transformed', but you won't lose yourself or be taken over by the shoes. It's not like in Bali where everyone believes with every fibre of their being that when they dance, a god enters their bodies and takes them over. It's more prosaic than that. You're finding the game of being somebody else, and it's liberating and mischievous and fun, and it makes us laugh because we all believe you've changed but we know it's only a game. Because we know it's a game, we believe it every bit as much as the Balinese do in their gods. That's the stuff of playing comedy. We laugh because we believe you in your game. We don't laugh because you're wearing silly shoes. We laugh because of what you've become in the shoes. Once you stop yourself from trying to make things up and give yourself permission to let things happen to you, then you can find the game of wearing a hat, or the game of having a new hairstyle. The game gives you a movement quality and as you move, you feel different and able to make more choices and find bigger reactions.

Play turns acting into a physical activity rather than some complex psychological process, and it enables you to approach acting more like sport than therapy. It's a waste of time rehearsing emotions or even asking yourself how you feel at this point. If the scene you're playing is sad and you enter in a state of sadness, then you'll be telling the story twice. The playwright has already dealt with all that. Once we know you're sad, almost anything you do will be interpreted as sadness. The situation tells us what you're feeling better than you can, so you can find other things to do. A writer can write a comic situation and carefully structure an incident and an action to wonderful climaxes but only you can make it funny. If you're uncomfortable, playing the best script in the world will be wasted on you.

In the audience, we want to see real people on stage more than anything else. We have a very short attention span for tricks and effects, but people fascinate us all the time. We see instantly what you're thinking and what you're feeling up there, and we'll all empathise with you the moment we recognise that it is you we're dealing with. The fake and the phoney really piss us off. We spot the phonies immediately because you're infinitely more interesting than anything you're going to make up. In his book *True and False*, David Mamet puts this point most succinctly:

66 *'And so,' we might ask ourselves, you and I, 'what is character?' Someone says character is the external life of the person on stage, the way that a person moves or holds a handkerchief, or their mannerisms. But that person on stage is you. It is not a construct you are free to amend or mould. It is you. It is your character which you take on stage.* 99

When you play the game as best as you can – when you're fully engaged just for the fun of it – then we see you in the moment. You won't have time to think about anything else. You'll be too busy reacting. Acting is a game, a game of reactions, and we want to see those reactions. If the text demands that you see a mouse in the kitchen so that you leap on a chair and scream hysterically, it's a waste of time saying, 'But I wouldn't do that. If it was me, I'd wring its neck and sling it in the bin.' It's not a question of what you'd do in that situation but the game of you being in that situation. In this case it's the *game* of being terrified, and you don't have to study hysteria in order to play it. Find the game of being hysterical. You'll know exactly what to do.

You and The Text

I met Athol Fugard at the Market Theatre in Johannesburg. He talked about writing and said that he only wanted to see his work on stage 'uncosmeticised': in other words, he wanted to remove anything that would, as he saw it, attempt to dress up what he had to say. He wants audiences to respond to his writing alone. A script articulates and orchestrates incidents, ideas and feelings into a satisfying and meaningful structure. That's all. Everything else is inferred or implied. Compared to a musical score, the written text is preposterously vague; it doesn't give us a definite key signature or tell us how fast or how slow we should play it – all that has to be found. It doesn't even tell much about the instrumentation or indicate harmony. That also has to be found. Edward Albee has said that all he would ever say to actors doing his work was, 'Do what you like but respect my intentions.'

Theatre is the most collaborative of all the arts. The writer isn't God. This is a trend that's only emerged over the past fifty years or so. The writer is part of a creative team, and the script is a provocation to everyone in that team. The process of making theatre is an entire chain of provocations to everybody involved, and most of those people won't believe in 'God'. Rather than acting in blind faith, they'll be working from their own impulses and their own judgements. The more you engage your personal impulses as to how to play something, the more you find ownership for what you do. Ownership is paramount if you're making physical comedy. If you try to play anything in a way that is uncomfortable or imposed, you'll be doomed to failure. The written text is inviolate but it's restricted to those things that can be expressed in writing. I'm equally concerned with the performance text which comprises everything that can't be expressed in writing: your physique, your personality, your intelligence, your imagination, your skill, and your personal taste. The written text can only give you dialogue and situation. It doesn't give you timing: that's your job. But personal ownership must always be weighed against the intentions of the writer, the designer and the director – and not necessarily in that order. We tend to follow the clearest vision in the room at that moment, and then all work together to achieve that vision.

I activate the performance text the moment I choose one actor as opposed to another. You activate the performance text the moment you stand on stage and speak the lines. To 'Invent nothing. Deny nothing', as Mamet puts it, is a plea to respect the text, and you do that by letting that text provoke you into working *with* it in the same way as we build associations with everything else. Physical comedy comes from what you do, how you play the situation and how you negotiate the interaction. All a writer can do is give you the ingredients to play with. The writer can't do the cooking, ultimately that's your job and you can only do that job in association with everybody else. We're all complicit in the final performance.

Complicity with Somebody Else

The Jumping Game

The whole group run about the space. They each make eye contact with a partner (partners are not pre-selected but 'found' as part of the game) and then both jump in the air together at the same time. The object of the game is for each pair to tease each other and genuinely try to catch each other out by pretending to jump but then pulling back at the last moment and not doing so. If they can still manage to jump in the air at the same time before running on and finding another partner, then they'll be playing the moment with complicity.

Complicity compels you to react. Acting, and physical comedy in particular, is more about reacting than anything else. There are basically two sorts of complicity games here: those where you know who the leader is and those where you're not so sure. They're both essential to generating robust and inventive physical comedy. The most open games are those where the leadership is hidden. Open games develop confidence and inspire invention. They put everyone in a more spontaneous frame of mind by taking the pressure off the individual and putting it more on the group. In this way, open games can be very liberating to play. Games like the Jumping Game, where the leadership is more openly contested, are more useful in inspiring detailed timing. Any dynamic action where two people are about to hit each other, kiss each other, grab something before each other or pretend not to see each other are ideal for generating interactive comedy.

So far I've spoken about leaders and followers, but that's not the most accurate way of describing this relationship. The roles are more dramatic and interdependent than that. The French teacher and practitioner Philippe Gaulier describes them as the 'major' and 'minor' roles and the contest between them will produce a rich stream of constantly changing rhythms and little surprises that are the substance of interactive comedy. The idea that play can be used to fuel theatre-making was inspired by the work of Jacques Copeau. His ideas were interrogated by the work of Jacques Lecoq, the architect of much of our thinking on play. However, the skills of play have been articulated by the pioneering teaching of Monica Pagneux and Philippe Gaulier. These two people, more than anybody else, have explored the disciplines of play and the role of game in making theatre. So where does this playful rigour come from and how can we use it in making physical comedy?

Major and Minor

The person 'in major' is the person whom we, in the audience, should be looking at. This is the person who's driving the scene and making the action at that moment. The person 'in minor' works in support of the major role ensuring that we keep focus on the person who we should be looking at. The minor role isn't passive – it's reactive. The pressure is off you when you're in minor. Your job is to go along with anything that the person in major throws at you.

The principle behind 'major' and 'minor' is that the roles are exchanged and not stolen. In other words, you keep the major role until you flop, then the other person takes over. This is the principle behind interactive complicity. It sounds like a restriction but it's not. It's a huge freedom. If you're carefully working up to some wonderful moment, and I steal the focus just before you get there and take the scene somewhere else, where's the freedom in that? The principle of giving the focus rather than stealing it is the hidden concord that makes us into secret associates rather than outright competitors. For example, take a simple game of Tag. A is required to 'touch' B. If we play the game hard, it will develop into a robust chasing game because, if you're B, the object of the game is not to let A touch you and if you are 'touched', the game is to touch somebody else as quickly as possible. If we play this game with complicity, then the fun comes more from the moments when you're about to touch somebody than from the moment when you actually do. That's the game we're after. We can play that one as hard as we like. If we play the conventional game of Tag as hard as we can, it's just a chasing game. We find the complicity in the way we negotiate the near misses. I might invite you to touch, I might tease you and provoke you. You might make me jump out of the way. The object of the game is not to 'score the point' so much as to play the moment. This is the secret concord of complicity. Of course, if you can't be bothered to score a point we'll lose interest in the game entirely, but you'll create a compelling interaction if you play the complicity game hard.

I'm So Big, the Told by an Idiot production mentioned earlier, was inspired by the film *Time of the Gypsies* (1988) by Emir Kusturica. The plot was about a young whore who was captured by two gypsies. They chained her up and kept her in a caravan living off her earnings, but in the end she became one of the 'family'. It was a brutal tale, but in spite of its theme, it was dripping with humanity, and at times very funny.

Occasionally, on a hot evening, this young whore would climb up on the roof of the caravan, where she could cool down and relax in the evening air. The younger of the two gypsies liked the whore and wanted to befriend her, but understandably she would have none of it. One hot night he spotted her on the roof and watched her as she took her sweater off and lay down. He climbed up to join her.

Instantly, there was a violent stand-off. The two of them faced each other like warring cats. He moved and she moved. He made a dash and so did she, her chain rattling about as she went. It was disturbing to watch. They couldn't have found a more precarious place for a fight. Nearly three metres up in the air, on a tin roof that buckled and rumbled underneath them. He stalked her round, forcing her dangerously close to the edge. She stumbled and just managed to keep her balance. The tension was almost unbearable, then he grabbed her discarded sweater. For a second we thought he was going to throw it at her and knock her off the roof, instead he put it on. He looked ridiculous, and made himself look even sillier by appearing to be very pleased with himself. He straightened his hair and put his hat on and climbed down. It was very funny. Even the whore looked as if she might raise a smile. With the tension gone, she relaxed again and watched him walk away.

When we made that scene, the only direction I remember giving the actors was for them to keep a fixed space between them. They didn't need any more suggestions. Their complicity was so assured that the scene on the roof of the caravan evolved from there. Clearly the roof was a huge physical restriction, but it defined an area that was big enough for a passionate love scene or a vicious rape. They were just far enough apart for them to spring at each other with some force whilst having just enough space to give them a chance to get away. The actors knew that for the 'sweater moment' to be a real surprise, the action before needed to be a desperate and dangerous struggle. Their skill in sustaining and developing the action on the roof, their ability to play the game hard, and to push the danger and the drama and the grim desperation of the scene, was all down to their interactive complicity.

The Fixed Space Game

Two people move about the room keeping a fixed space of about two metres between them. The game is to negotiate the exchanges of the major and minor.

This is a classic game of complicity and an excellent example of how liberating it is freely to exchange major and minor roles. It's a game that's as much about stillness as it is about surprise. Some of the most interesting moments are when neither person knows who's in major. You can provoke the game by testing each other's ability to switch roles. Inexperienced players will

turn it into a boring back and forth shuffle. To become interesting they have to learn to put each other 'in the shit'. They've
got to work very hard to catch each other out. This is where
the spontaneity comes from, and this is when the scene starts to
become really compelling to watch. Here is a clear example of a
situation where both of you are in control of the action all the
time, so it's up to both of you to build the action between you.

It could hardly be simpler, could it? Put this game into any situation,
such as A is going to help B tidy up the room, or A and B are trying to
decide where to set out the furniture or where to sit on a train or what
to look at in a store. The action will probably become very funny,
especially if neither of you seem capable of making a decision. Put the
same game into a situation like a honeymoon couple on the first night
together and the action will become farcical. Put it into two people
having a row or two people trying to leave each other, and the action
will become more disturbing or poignant. This game will generate
conflict in any situation, and providing it is played with subtlety, any
text will sit on top of it very comfortably.

Interesting things happen if we change the size of the fixed space. For
example, if we were to make a very intimate space of no more than a
handspan between us and play the Fixed Space Game then we'd both be
placed in a position of great vulnerability. It is almost impossible to
keep the fixed space accurately because it's too close for you to see each
other clearly. To play the game at this distance you'd both have to move
with great subtlety. If you go to the other extreme and play the game
with a fixed space of four metres then the stakes will be raised to an
immense height. Something truly significant must have happened
between you for you both to react so strongly at the mere sight of each
other. Now we're touching levels of intensity more appropriate to
Greek tragedy, but if the conflict was about being late for class then the
situation could be very funny indeed. A distance of about two metres is
ideal for vigorous action because you each have just enough space to be
able to get out of the way if you have to, and you have just enough
distance to be able to see each other completely from head to toe.

This is one of my favourite games for teaching complicity, and I never
tire of playing it.

Dressage for Camels

I start by explaining that dressage is a sport based on the skills of exercising the maximum control over a horse with the minimum apparent effort. I go on to say that we're going to do dressage for camels and that this is much the same, but, because camels are such ill-tempered beasts, we can only touch them with a single forefinger placed just behind the chin.

The idea is for one person to stand blindfolded, or with their eyes closed. They are the camel, and the other person is to lead them round the room controlling their camel by that single touch from the forefinger – it's a bit like leading an unruly dog on a lead at first. Once you've got your camel to stop and start, then try running, jumping, changing rhythm and going up and down – this is the most difficult, but perfectly possible with a little practice. Once the game is underway I indicate to the camel leaders that, unknown to the camels, they should swap camels. To what extent can the leaders smoothly negotiate their exchanges so that the camels don't know that they've been swapped?

Dressage for Camels examines how we give and take physical cues. All complicity games combine Stanislavski's holy trinity of concentration, relaxation and imagination into one dynamic game: Dressage for Camels emphasises this beautifully.

Concentration is fascination of the mind. If we're interested, we concentrate, and the more clear and specific the task that we're dealing with, the stronger our focus of concentration. It's helpful to differentiate between single-focus concentration and awareness. It's fascinating to be able to give clear commands just through the touch of your index finger, so you can focus on that single point very clearly. Whilst the camel leaders are doing that, they're also aware of what's happening all round them, namely who is just about to walk into them or who their camel is just about to walk into.

The level of concentration becomes very high in Dressage for Camels. You'll see this at a glance. Within two or three minutes, everyone will be locked into the game because the objectives are very clear and the skills are tangible.

There's a common misconception about relaxation: that you have to go to a floppy, rag-doll state before you achieve it and that 'tension' is a word that should be banned from the language. This is nonsense. The level of tension in our bodies goes up and down all the time depending on what we're doing. When we're 'relaxed', all that means is that we're using an appropriate level of tension for what we're doing, so that it looks comfortable and effortless. We know instantly that something is wrong when we see somebody move in an inappropriate state of tension. In order to concentrate either as the camel or as the leader of the camel, you have to relax, otherwise it's impossible for either of you to feel anything.

The simple question, 'How much control can I exert on my camel through the touch of one finger?' will immediately engage your imagination. We tend to think that being imaginative is all about having big ideas. It's not. It's about having a lot of very little ideas that eventually assemble themselves into something bigger. We're all immensely imaginative, on a very small scale, but everything tends to fall apart as soon as we try to think in bigger pictures. So play with your camel. What can you get it to do?

The Hand and Face Game I

One person puts a hand in front of another person's face – about a metre away from the face but directly in front of it. The game is for the person who's holding their hand out to move about in any way they like and the person with the hand in front of their face to follow them, trying to keep the distance consistent. The person with the hand is in major and the person following is in minor. The idea is for the major to work the minor as hard as possible.

This is really a game about engagement. How quick, how obedient and accurate, how reactive can the person in minor be?

You can also play this game in threes:

Then you have two people in minor, each controlled by one of your hands. Observe what happens if you clap, or rub your hands together or slam both hands on the floor. It sounds much more dangerous than it is. Complicity with somebody else demands sensitivity to each other. We develop that by provoking each other and becoming more aware of how we react to each other.

If you're in minor, to what extent can you throw yourself about accurately whilst being fully aware of where you are in space? The Hand and Face Game and Dressage for Camels reveal issues concerning complicity with yourself. How do you feel in the minor role? How comfortable are you?

The Hand and Face Game 2

This is a development of the game above and is played in exactly the same way, only now the person in major can drop the game whenever they like.

Dropping the game means that you just abandon it, relax, and look at the audience. This creates a brief pause in the action and opens up a contest between the major and the minor. Who's going to take the major? The first person to put their hand in place drives the scene.

It helps to cue 'the drop' at first because it's difficult to remember to abandon the game, especially if you're trying to play it with full engagement. A common fault when looking at the audience is to hold the pause too long and forget that there's still a game to be played with your partner.

A useful development of the game is to use 'the drop' to complain to the audience about your partner or even about the game itself. You can take the complaint even further by insisting that you're not playing the game any more, that it's stupid, only to snap your hand back in place at the most unexpected moment.

The Sweater Game

There are two teams of equal size standing in two lines facing each other, about three metres apart. Each person is given a number so that in the two lines, number one stands opposite the opposing number one and number two stands opposite number two and so on. One person stands at the end of the parallel lines holding a sweater in the air.

The game is this: the person with the sweater calls out a number. Let's say it's six. Both players with the number six rush forward to

*grab the sweater and try to run back to their place in the line before
their opponent touches them. The rule is that the game stops as
soon as one of the players is touched.*

If you play the game just to score the point it will soon get very
dull. The complicity lies in you playing the game for the fun of it
and not rushing for the sweater the moment your number is
called but playing the tension and teasing each other. There are
three sections to be played: approaching the sweater, grabbing
it, then rushing back to your place with it. Play the tension over
all three sections and the action will be kept alive. It's the
teasing, tricks and little surprises that we want to see. It's
boring just to win the point, given that there's so much scope
for audacity in this game.

It's more combative and more intense than any of the others that we've
looked at but its true value will only become apparent if you apply it to
a situation. I tend to set the game up as a simple two-hander with
clearly defined roles like a scene between doctor and patient, or
housewife and milkman, duck and gun dog, murderer and victim, or
two lovers in a romantic fantasy. Any simple relationship will do, as
long as you remember that you desperately want that sweater. You
probably won't know why you want it at the start of the game, but you
will do by the end.

Here's a doctor and patient scene. As far as I can remember it's from a
workshop at the Actors Centre in London:

Two players rush towards the sweater.

*A. Good morning, Mrs Jones. A blood test, isn't it? How are you
feeling today?*

B. Excellent, Doctor. (She moves towards the sweater.)

*A. Just come over here and I'll take a blood test. (He leads her away
from the sweater.)*

*B. I feel faint, Doctor. I need some fresh air. (Moving back to the
sweater again.)*

A. *Put your head down between your knees for a moment, you probably got up too fast. Take your time. There, is that better?*

B. *(She stands.) I'm so cold.*

A. *Here take this: it's my wife's. (He puts the sweater round her shoulders.) She won't mind, I'm sure.*

B. *Oh, that's very kind of you, Doctor. I couldn't. (Taking the sweater off.) I'm much better now.*

A. *Good. Now how long was it since last you were here?*

B. *I can't remember. I'm in a terrible hurry, Doctor.*

A. *Well, this won't take a minute. Just a little prick then it's all over.*

B. *I've changed my mind. I'm not going through with it.*

A. *Oh, for God's sake, it's only a blood test.*

B. *Don't you dare raise your voice at me!*

A. *I'm sorry, I was distracted. It's the sweater, you see. I keep thinking you're her and I can't stand her and I start to lose my temper.*

B. *Well, I'm not her. Here, take it back if it upsets you so much. (Doctor takes sweater.)*

A. *It's just that I have these fantasies about smothering her with this sweater.*

B. *Don't be silly, Doctor.*

A. *I'm not being silly, you're just like her. Come here!*

B. *Doctor, stop it. You're out of control. Help! Help! (The Doctor runs back into the line.)*

The desire for the sweater drove the scene on at a cracking pace. We all enjoyed him giving her the sweater because it raised the stakes and gave them both more action to play. You could apply that game just as easily to a scripted scene. How many dramatic situations are there about two people desperately wanting the same thing? Conflict like this is endemic in sitcoms. *Fawlty Towers, One Foot in the Grave* and *Porridge*, are replete with situations that are basically little more than the Sweater Game.

The Drum Game

Two drums are placed in the playing area. Two people find the game of _seeing who can pick a drum up first, clearly playing to the audience. The first person to take the drum taps out a simple rhythm and the second person joins in on their drum – all playing to the audience. The object of the game is for one of them to tap the other's drum. The game is over as soon as this happens.

This is a complex interaction game, demanding complicity with each other, and complicity with the audience. It's a stylised combat game that demands considerable skill to sustain effectively. I like to build it up gradually so that the various levels of skill have time to develop.

Working in threes, one person shouts out commands whilst the other two play the game, only clapping, trying to slap each other's hands, instead of using a drum. This version demands greater accuracy in scoring a hit, but it's more controllable.

Working in this way enables the third person to provoke the game in a number of ways. For example, they could insist the players clock the audience, or they could demand more surprises and sudden changes of rhythm, or they could insist that they both take more risks and be more daring. I find myself calling out 'audience – audience', then 'attack – audience – attack', or 'Drop it, and do something else – attack.' It takes practice to keep this game alive, and working in threes means that everyone can be given time to be provoked.

Surprise, audacity and complicity with the audience, and complicity with each other are the key components here, and these are the key components of physical comedy. On the outside, the Drum Game is a game of combat, but inside it's a demanding game of complicity that brings all the elements we've discussed together: engagement, lightness, putting each other 'in the shit', audacity, daring and surprise. We all think that there are more rules than there really are with this game. We all expect the game to be played according to the rules, and if we were playing for points in a competition that would be a reasonable expectation, but we're making comic action here. You can play this game at many levels. You can play it with great elegance and intelligence or at a level of visceral desperation. However you play, you've got to play it for real. So take a risk. Try grabbing both drums when you get up. The game won't be over. Or see what happens if you don't pick the drum up at all. If you have a skilled player to work with, the game will develop with an even greater intensity. You could even give your drum to your opponent and, if their skills of complicity are up to it, you'll still be able to play the game to the full.

Complicity with the Audience

The Clapping Game

The actor Steve Harper taught me this game. It's the best example of an audience-contact game that I've ever seen.

Put a random selection of objects in the playing area. Anything will do. One person leaves the room whilst the rest of the group decide what task they want that person to achieve. I'd keep it simple at first, like having to put a coat on and stand on a chair. This assumes of course that a coat and a chair are among the random objects. The object of the game is for the person on stage to complete the action that the group has planned, but the restriction is that the group can only clap their approval. No other means of communication are allowed, and the game is played in silence apart from the clapping.

So if I come in and put the hat on then nobody will clap but if I look at the coat, there might be a ripple of applause. If I touch the coat, the applause might build, and if I put the coat on, you'll all be on your feet in sheer exuberance.

What fascinates me about this game is the way you're forced to put so much dependence on the audience, and if you do this honestly and without a trace of acting, you will become eminently watchable because your thoughts become alive. You silently share a thought with the audience every time you look at us. It's as if you're in conversation with us: 'I know you didn't mean the hat,' you might think, or 'Oh, you like the coat, do you?' These silent comments keep the game comfortable for all of us. It's impossible to play this game effectively without relating to the audience. The moment you become uncomfortable and lose your complicity with yourself, you become agony to watch. You've got to feel good, and the applause is a huge confidence booster. Even the most timid actor can't fail to be affected by it.

It's basically the children's game Warmer/Colder but its great strength is that it puts you in the position of not knowing what to do on stage in the most painless way imaginable, and, in doing so, it reveals how you think and how you relate to us. All you have to do is to find out through trial and error what we've decided when you were out of the room. You're not required to be funny or to have brilliant ideas. Just to keep up that silent dialogue with us is enough.

If you approach the game by continually silently asking us 'is it that?' or 'that?' or 'that?' without letting yourself be 'in the shit' then you'll be about as interesting as someone on a checkout in a supermarket. And if you try to act or try to be funny, then our toes will start to curl. But if you embrace the game for what it is, be yourself and just keep silently chatting to us with those little communicative looks, then we'll be able to watch you up there for quite some time. The most interesting moments for us are when we all know that you haven't a clue. That's when you're 'in the shit', and we'll be delighted that nothing much is happening because you'll be infinitely more interesting than the props you're working with.

There are various developments of the Clapping Game and it's useful to be able to raise the stakes: if you're working with somebody who plays the game easily, it might be entertaining for the group not to choose an action at all.

A satisfying development of the game is for the group to prescribe a monologue for you to improvise once the physical tasks are completed. To do this, they need to give you things to do that will result in a telling image. For example, if they decide that they want you to play an heroic 'Once more unto the breach'-type speech, they can imply this by making a final image of you standing on a chair with a bucket on your head and brandishing a broom. You'll probably offer some kind of rousing speech from that image. It might not be heroic to start with but the audience could soon provoke one through the clapping. The final image inspires what you say.

The Clock Game

Little looks of communication from performer to audience are called 'clocks'. It's a word that comes from Cockney slang: the word 'face' is reminiscent of a clock face hence 'clock' which means to look, or in this context to turn your face to the audience. In a big auditorium a little glance of the eye will be too small.

We need to see your head turn and see your face, then the gesture will fill the room and share a thought. That's the technique. But like all techniques, if it looks as though you've been told to do it, it's going to be more of a hindrance than a help. Basically, you've only got three choices in playing a 'clock': you can look at the audience before you do something, whilst you're doing something, or after you've done something. But you'll know instinctively how to play a clock if you concentrate on the thought behind it rather than the action itself. It's astonishing how eloquent these little looks can be, and they add a whole new layer of meaning to what you do. In a brief glance you can comment on what you've just done, imply what you're going to do next, and show us how you feel at that moment regardless of what's happening on stage at the time.

For example, if I shake hands with you and, whilst I'm doing that, I clock the audience, I'd probably be signalling, 'Look at me, I'm shaking hands.' The clock will make me look stupid and probably debunk the action completely. Which could of course be very funny. Alternatively, if I shake your hand, finish the action and then clock the audience as if to say, 'What an idiot!' I'll probably be able to make you look stupid.

We radically manipulate meaning by the way we relate to the audience, but more importantly we radically change the context of the performance. Each little clock reminds us that everything we see on stage is happening in the 'here and now', and the more we acknowledge the audience in the room, the more we trash the old idea that theatre is an illusion. To try to play comedy without acknowledging the audience is like playing the piano with one hand. We always miss the other part.

Complicity with the audience reminds us just how live and how volatile theatre is. Theatre demands a more sophisticated level of engagement than either film or television. In film, we know the action is always in the 'there and then'. If the story is set on the side of a mountain, then it'll probably be shot on the side of a mountain. In television, things might be happening now but they're never here. They're always at the end of a camera lens and that could be thousands of miles away. In theatre we can't do that. Our attempts at verisimilitude or reportage are limited. But our facility in handling metaphor is second to none. We enter a curious split-mindedness when we watch a play: we flip from the 'here and now' to the 'there and then', and back again with consummate ease. If you were to come on stage as Hamlet, for example, we all know that you're only an actor playing Hamlet and our imaginative engagement will be trapped in the 'here and now', no matter how authentic your costume might be. But if your playing is credible and we get drawn into the world of the play, then we'll be drawn into the 'there and then' of the play for a few moments, only to flip back into the 'here and now' again when the person next to us starts fidgeting or taking their coat off.

We learn sophisticated levels of engagement like this through watching theatre, but as we all watch far more film and television than theatre, it helps us to declare that theatre is all happening in the 'here and now' right from the start. Then we're shocked into the actuality of the experience where we all know exactly where we are and what's happening. We don't 'willingly suspend our disbelief' quite so easily in the theatre any more. We've developed more refined tastes in realism than when Coleridge coined that phrase in 1818. But powerful human interactions are very enduring, and they stand the test of time better than popular taste.

In theatre everything happens in the same room, so it's honest to declare everything that happens on stage, and it's more enjoyable for us to see you cope with a mistake than it is to see you ignore it and pretend that it hasn't happened. Of course, how much you play the audience is a question of taste. But it's also a question of convention. The idea of 'the invisible fourth wall', where we substantially ignored the audience and left them sitting there like voyeurs into other people's private lives, evolved at the end of the nineteenth century and persisted throughout the twentieth. It was a theatrical innovation in its day but is something of a cliché now. All I'm saying is that we've got choices here, and ignoring the fact that there are people watching you, especially if you're trying to be funny, isn't a choice that's going to take you very far.

I tend to use the following game whenever I want to raise the level of play and make it more theatrical.

The Hands-Up Game

All it requires is for us to be completely honest, and to ask ourselves if we're bored. If we're bored we put our hands up. That's the game.

The important thing to remember is that solitary individuals don't make an audience. So no one should put their hand up on their own. Look round and see what the others think. Try to find a consensus. It's a game for making everyone aware of the flops. Everything flops eventually, and the first skill in making comedy is recognising each flop by name. Seeing a forest of hands going up and waving about doesn't mean the end of your career. It's just a wake-up call. All it means is that you've forgotten us and haven't taken us with you.

The Hands-Up Game isn't an incitement to play everything for laughs and milk each comic moment dry. It's just a reminder that your audience is part of the scene as well and that everything you do up there is conceived to have an effect on us in some way.

There's an uncompromising honesty about admitting that we're bored when we've got two people up there, trying to amuse us with next to nothing to work with. This game emphasises that playing an audience is a two-way relationship. In order to survive we must learn to watch each other, listen to each other and try to please and provoke each other in equal measure. As an audience we normally communicate with you through our laughter, our restlessness, our silences, or as Peter Brook observes, 'in those moments of stillness where all the question marks emerge.' Fortunately there's nothing ambiguous about putting one's hand up. Then everyone knows exactly where they are.

Our laughter and our silences are a vital part of the rhythm of any live performance. If you don't look at the audience you'll have no idea about how you're doing. But a few tries at being on stage with the rest of the group putting their hands up as soon as you start to flop, sharpens everybody's faculties and makes us all more sensitive to what's happening and how we feel about it. This mutual acknowledgement turns the game into a performance and the action into an event.

Theatre as Game

Theatre as game and acting as play are the two most radical ideas to hit theatre-making over the last twenty years, and they're still rattling the doors and windows of our most august theatre institutions. Games aren't 'icebreakers' or 'warm-ups' that you abandon when you decide to start work. The games *are* the work, particularly when you're making physical comedy. Games contain all the raw ingredients we need for generating material and evolving comedy of amazing richness and complexity. Games work because they give us restrictions. Rules, if you like. Not rules to live by, just rules to make things happen. If you don't like what's happening, you can always change the rules. By proposing a game rather than an exercise, or by finding a game rather than defining an objective, we keep the work playful and frivolous. Once you've found something and written something, then it can be rehearsed. But it's always easier to take risks and make choices when you can tell yourself that it doesn't really matter because it's only a game. We all want to be good, of course we do, but the pursuit of excellence is an appalling tyranny. It's liberating to know that sometimes it's OK to be crap. We don't learn anything when we're terrified. No matter how much we might thrive on adrenalin, there are times when we have to go to that vulnerable place with total impunity.

You can always tell if you're working in a place where acting is taught badly because the students talk about it as if acting were some arcane spiritual practice only to be understood by the initiated. Comedy thrives in an atmosphere of irreverence and pleasure: we need to think that we're in a space where we can do anything. Good acting needs exactly the same conditions. Play doesn't mean that the work is frivolous. Far from it. All it means is that we take play very seriously. Play warms the heart and cools the head. It's fun, it's liberating, it's empowering and it gives us that compelling combination of engagement and objectivity that enables all of us to generate meaning, take risks and find things.

Open Games and Closed Games

Play is fuelled by fun, complicity and contest. Every game has a contest; it might be between you and the theme, or you and the group, or you and somebody else. Contest fuels your engagement, and complicity contains the contest by manipulating your desire to win. In some games, the contest is in the forefront of what you're doing, in which case it reads as adversarial conflict, and in other games the contest is concealed, in which case it reads as subtext or dramatic tension.

To play with complicity you have to respect two things:

> 1. *Your partner is more important than you are, so that even in your most megalomaniac moments you never lose touch with the fact that your main job is to make other people react.*

> 2. *To play the game hard it's got to matter to you. You don't have to be particularly good at the game. We'll forgive you as long as you really care about it.*

You can't get much more simple than the Starting and Stopping Game or the Jumping Game. This is about as complicated as complicity games are likely to get. Play is an element of improvisation, but it's not as clever as improvisation. It deals with moments rather than scenes, and sensations and interactions rather than narratives. You can only play within a structure, so if you haven't got a structure you have to impose one on yourself with a game. Improvisation in the Keith Johnstone tradition tends to generate text. Keith originally evolved this work at the Royal Court Theatre in London to inspire writers rather than actors. Improvisation only comes alive within recognisable dramatic circumstances. In other words, it helps to know who you are, where you are, what you're doing and when. Play, on the other hand, generates action just for the fun of it. We only need the simplest of games to get us started.

Improvisation is like driving a car and not knowing where you're going until you've got there. Play is like driving a car and never looking beyond the end of the bonnet. Play keeps us in the moment and is likely to take us off in any direction. When we improvise we tend to be logical and causal, but play is more mercurial; this is its greatest strength because it stops us from doing the obvious. We can play with anything and within any dramatic structure. So if we were doing *Hamlet*, for example, I'd encourage you to play every interaction, to find games between you, and to find games within games. This would enable us to generate action and imagery, and the text will sit on top of all this, create resonance and generate meaning. Play is essentially meaningless, so we need a context before it can start to make any sense.

Playful games are 'open' games designed to make something happen rather than to make us come up with a clever idea. When we improvise we tend to use 'closed' games: these are more prescriptive and have narrower parameters. They're designed to make us come up with something. For example, my colleagues at Told by an Idiot went through a phase of playing the Alphabet Game. It's another Keith Johnstone game, and it's a brilliant one.

The Alphabet Game

This is the game of maintaining a conversation whilst having to start each new speech with the next letter of the alphabet. For example:

'Are you happy in those trousers or would you like to change?'

'Blue suits me, I think, so I'll stick with these.'

'Corduroys are nice, why not try these?'

'Don't tempt me, they're far too expensive.'

This is a classic closed game, and the restrictions can be narrowed even more by prescribing specific situations like giving bad news, or playing a love scene, while all the time still going through the alphabet. This puts more pressure on you to turn the inevitable pauses, whilst you struggle to remember what letter comes after 'T' for example, into action and atmosphere. These additional restrictions impel you to justify why you've stopped. In addition, of course, you to have to continue to generate an accurate and pertinent text.

Closed games are more formal in that the rules are evident to the audience. Our pleasure lies in seeing you be inventive within these rules. 'What's he going to do with that?' we think. It's the dominance of closed games that give events like Theatresports their virtuosity. They enable us to see just how clever you have been.

With open games the rules are often so inane that the audience tend to disregard them entirely. These games work more on the level of physical reactions. They're like children's games concerned with physical activities like chasing, dodging, hitting, creeping, being still, hiding or shocking each other. Just because they're not concerned with language or ideas doesn't mean they're naive or simplistic. These games are more about feelings than thoughts. As adults we only do things like chasing, dodging, hitting, creeping, hiding or shocking each other in the context of sport or else in the most extreme and dangerous circumstances. The stakes have to be very high indeed to get us to move with any speed or intensity as opposed to having long meaningful conversations or simply shouting at each other. Open games come into their own at a point beyond language where things are too desperate to be expressed in words. These games are open games because they involve intense emotions, just waiting to be put in a context. They'll only acquire meaning in a context we all understand. Physical comedy comes alive in extremis, and open games are a constant invitation to find possibilities.

The Object Game

Choose an object, anything will do as long as it isn't too fragile. In how many different ways can you use this object that it wasn't designed for? In other words, if you're playing with a chair, it can be anything other than a chair. So we might see a chair becoming a television, a horse, an open book or a window.

This is another closed game because you have to come up with one new idea after another. Its strength is that it makes you free-associate with the object. And the occasional idea might be satisfying. The open book might be more interesting than the telephone for example. But the weakness of the game lies in the fact that the ideas are unrelated. Consequently they're more likely to be conceived rather than found, with the result that there's no natural flow to the game.

> To turn this into an open game you have to remove the
> imperative of having to think of a new idea every time and just
> play with the object, move it about and look at it. Ask yourself
> how the object wants to move, what can the object do? Then
> the ideas start to come to you more naturally.

I remember watching an actor playing with a book. He balanced it on
its end and it fell over. He tried again, and it fell over again. He tried a
third time and the book stood up on its end, so he moved the book as if
he was opening a creaky door and he crawled through into a dark space
and 'the book' slammed shut behind him. Then the book became a
squawking bird that pecked his eyes out. He staggered round in agony
as the bird flapped and squawked about his head. He fought the bird off,
caught it and threw it against the wall and it lay on the floor, dead and
inanimate. His sight miraculously returned, as it does in these circumstances, he saw the book on the floor, and holding it at arm's length, he
dropped it in the bin.

What we see here is one open game leading to another. First he found
complicity with the book as a book and then he played the game of the
book being something else, then he found chasing and hitting games
and a few surprises just for the fun of it and, as one idea led to another,
a brief narrative started to emerge. Play puts us in a frame of mind
where anything can happen. Once we're in a playful mood we can easily
raise the stakes and make the games more challenging.

The most seminal observation concerning spontaneity that Keith
Johnstone made in his book *Impro* was his idea of the Yes Game. Basically
this entails us saying 'Yes' to any offer that's proposed to us and then
offering a related idea in return:

> 66 *There are people who prefer to say 'Yes' and there are people who prefer to say*
> *'No.' Those who say 'Yes' are rewarded by the adventures they have, and those who*
> *say 'No' are rewarded by the safety they attain. There are far more 'No'-sayers*
> *around than 'Yes'-sayers, but you can train one type to behave like another.* 99

Most of us say 'No' because we're scared. Scared of looking stupid. Play
takes us right to the 'Yes', and it's more a pleasurable sensation than a
formal contract. In play, anything and everything is a potential asso-

ciate. We're more concerned with prolonging the fun than proving that
we can play the game. Play is one big open 'Yes'. The main difference
between open and closed games is that in the former the invention
arises more through accident than design. Action is found rather than
dreamt up, and we find it because we were stupid enough to have
played the game in the first place. A funny text is a funny text. It might
be witty and insightful, but physical comedy emerges more from what
you do than what you say. Play and improvisation work hand in glove.
Impro is the glove that you can put on or take off again at will, but play
is the hand. It's part of you: it's your taste, your fun, your instinct and
your imagination.

Closed games are valuable, improvisation is invaluable, and the most
playful actors tend to make the best improvisers. It's a question of
recognising what the different games can do before deciding which
type of game to use. Sometimes we need to put ourselves on the spot to
make ourselves come up with something: if you're making a play from
scratch this will probably happen quite a lot. But most of us spend the
majority of our time being confronted with the task of playing within a
scene that has already been written. Open games rarely come into their
own when we're required to play the situation rather than write the
scene. Open games generate ideas, of course they do, but these ideas are
only given meaning through the context that we put them in. More than
anything else, open games are a constant invitation to be playful rather
than interpretive. We have to be constantly reminded to be mischievous
and daring rather than accurate and dutiful. It's not enough just to say
'Yes'; you've got to really enjoy saying 'Yes' on your terms.

Peter Brook once said that 'the function of rehearsal is to find the
meaning and make that meaning meaningful.' In my experience, we do
this by being playful and by constantly reminding each other to do
everything just for the fun of it. Lecoq once said: 'An actor can only
play when the driving structure of the [piece] allows him to do so.'

A written text is a carefully structured series of interactions. In this
structure, even if it's the wildest piece of comic writing, there will be
times when the text is in major; when the text drives everything
forward from incident to incident in an unrelenting rhythm. But no
text worth performing can do this all the time. There are always
moments that have to be negotiated, transactions that have to be won

or lost, atmospheres to be established and broken down, and these are the times for play.

Yoshi Oida, from Peter Brook's International Centre for Theatre Research, once told me that he could only be spontaneous if he knew exactly what he was doing. It's a conundrum but it's worth trying to unpick it.

All games, whether open or closed, inspire spontaneous physical reactions and they keep these reactions live. Games confine action to a simple structure; they impose limitations on us in order to make us do something; they restrict us and channel our creativity. Games are like plumbing; they're like the pipes that channel the flow of water: they control the pressure and the direction of that flow.

Hiding the Game

Here's a prime example of what I call a hidden game. In the film *Tootsie* (1982), Dustin Hoffman played an actor who was so desperate for work that he dressed up as a woman, as a result of which his career started to take off, with all the inevitable complications. There's a scene when he goes to meet his agent in a bar. Of course the agent doesn't recognise him, and the moment when Hoffman suddenly drops his female voice and tells his agent that it's really him in drag is arguably the funniest moment in the entire film. It took several takes to get this scene in the can, reportedly because Sydney Pollack, who played the agent and who also directed the film, couldn't get his reaction big enough. The story goes that after several unsuccessful takes, Dustin Hoffman reached under the table and grabbed Pollack by the balls, and that's the reaction that made it to the final cut. When we watch this sequence, all we see is the agent, suddenly flinching with a look of astonishment on his face. We're far too preoccupied with the situation in the film to have any inkling as to the real reason why he flinched. It's a 'hidden game'.

Like the games used while working on Jim Cartwright's *Two*, these are all games conceived to inspire physical reactions that only have meaning in the context of the drama. The more we hide the game, to the extent that actors are the only people who really know what's happening, the more you can play, with all the lively spontaneity of a game, whilst allowing the audience to read your action on a more psychological level. I'm not saying that the example I've just given is particularly psychological. It isn't. But if you hide the game, you have the capacity to play as psychologically as you like, with as much spontaneity as you like. In hiding the game, you can keep your play at a level that's so delicate and subtle that the audience will read anything you do as being your thoughts and intentions.

If I were working with inexperienced actors, I'd probably work with games that demand 'big' interactions: chasing, hitting, struggling, dodging, or games that demand stealth or perfect stillness. In this context, I'll be using games to provoke physical engagement and a genuine sense of play. It's easier to teach these things through bold physicality, where you're working with something that we can see and you can feel. Apparently crude games like these stop the work becoming too serious. They stop you thinking, and put you in a position where you've got to react. The determined chase in a game of Tag, for example, can be transformed in an instant into a harrowing emotional rollercoaster, if it's put in the context of street violence. In this context, a near miss or a lucky escape can become a huge shift in dramatic tension. An innocent game of Grandmother's Footsteps can be harrowing to watch, if it's put in the context of an intruder in a house. As soon as you put a game in a scene, the 'size' of play is negotiable.

If we take a simple children's game like Tag, we have a chasing game where the object of the game is not to get touched, but the fun in playing the game lies in the near misses. On one level of course it's a banal game: A goes to touch B and B tries to run away. So what? But on another level, Tag is an excellent example of action and response. All dramatic interaction boils down to this. I make an action – it could be anything: go to speak, shake hands, kiss you, stab you and whatever I do, you respond in any way that seems appropriate.

It's a simple enough transaction, but there are an infinite number of ways in which an action and a response can be played: it can be a complete surprise, it can ricochet back and forth between a group of people at a speed almost too fast to follow, or it can be played with a slow sustained build-up that can last for a matter of minutes. However it's played, action and response transactions must be alive, and you must find that life by playing for an objective. An objective is what you want in a scene. For example, the text states that I come into the room, lock the door and stab you to death. I might choose to play that action with the objective of looking relaxed and casual so as not to frighten you and avoid too much of a struggle. Let's say that you suspect my real intentions so you're tense and on your guard, and your objective is to get out of the room.

Games have the same function as an objective. The plot gives you the dramatic context but the game gives us the life of the interaction. Games give you a simple structure in which to play an objective – and you must play to win. The text tells you who wins, of course, so you both know who's going to walk out of that room alive at the end of the scene, but that doesn't inhibit us playing a real game. I'm not suggesting that you play the game afresh each performance. That's a brave choice, but you're more likely to recreate the game you played for real in the rehearsal room. A game like Tag will open up this action: you'll find strong images and exciting action sequences and the objectives will be played to the full. This will only work of course as long as the audience don't have the slightest idea that the real reason why you dive over the sofa or struggle precariously on the window ledge has no more substance than a game of Tag. So you have to hide the game.

The Slapping Game

This is the children's game sometimes called 'Slapsies'. It's action and response in its purest form, and it has innumerable applications.

A extends his or her hands forward, roughly at arm's length, with the palms down. B's hands, also roughly at arm's length, are placed, palms up, under A's hands. The object of the game is for B to slap the back of A's hands before A can pull them away.

Most children play this as a simple contest game but my reason for playing it is not to see you beat your partner to a pulp but to find a sharp reaction, like in the Cane Game.

I set up this game with the rule that B can also find the game of looking out to the audience at any time, and that A must also look out to the audience whenever B does. Now the game will be fully declared and the audience will be invited to share the pleasure of these little tricks and surprises, and the contest will be played to the full.

If you don't play to win the point, but to make a reaction, then B can distract A with conversation, flattery, romantic protestations of love, or by falsely assuring A that nobody is going to get slapped at all. These tactics are very close to putting the game into a simple dramatic situation. For example, B says to A: 'Where were you last night?' – SLAP. If an opening line like that is followed by a slap, A can use that physical reaction as the dramatic impulse for the reply. The impulse need not always be so aggressive. It could just as easily be: 'I love you' – SLAP. In this context that sudden twitch will mean something else entirely.

The Touching Game

This is another action and reaction game but it is much more subtle.

The game is for A to try to touch B inadvertently, and B's game is to try to avoid being touched as subtly as possible. The object of the game is to try to conceal these advances, and little retreats as much as possible. To do this, you have to play pauses and try to find different ways of advancing and retreating.

If you apply this game to a scene between two lovers, for example, and if the text is about them declaring their undying love for each other, then the pauses and subtle advances and retreats make an interaction of rich complexity full of dramatic tension. On the outside, we'll be absorbed in the emerging subtext as the hidden game develops, whilst on the inside, you'll have all the life and spontaneity of the game to work with, and providing the game is hidden, our interest will be focused more in the situation than the mechanism behind it.

Dramatic tension emerges as soon as we become aware that something is about to happen. If someone is about to be hit, or to kiss, or to jump off a high place, provided we believe that it's really going to happen, then a change occurs in the intensity of not only the two people involved, but also anyone watching. All contest games thrive on dramatic tension. The French call it '*élan*'. It's the tension that raises the stakes and keeps them high. The game will flop the moment that tension breaks. The stronger the dramatic tension, the more it spreads to everyone on stage. For example, if I accuse you of theft in front of every-one and you're clearly guilty, then your embarrassment at my accusation will spread through the entire group, and we'll create an atmosphere of embarrassment between us.

The Touching Game is a smaller version of the Slapping Game, and it gives us more scope for a delicate atmosphere to emerge. You can't rush this game. If we see the game, the drama will die. So you have to play the interaction with great subtlety. The person in major has to use any means possible to make contact with the other player. You could try inadvertently leaning on your partner, or casual brushing your partner's hand, or gradually closing of the space between you. Any of these strategies could be enough to push the dramatic tension to breaking point. The person in minor must use equal skill to hide their reactions. Perhaps they don't move away immediately, perhaps they smile affectionately before they move away. We see everything up there. The crude structure of the Slapping Game tends to produce crude external rhythms, with tense pauses and sudden surges of action. There's just as much a contest going on in the Touching Game, only in this game every action is so disguised that we read it as a change of thought and a shift of feeling. To hide the game, you've got to change the rhythm completely. Your surprises must now become secret strategies, and even your pauses must be disguised. It helps to use the text to disguise the pauses. In other words, having made your move, the more you focus your attention on the conversation as opposed to the physical action, the more it's possible to stay in fairly close proximity to each other. Your intention won't be lost – it'll simply become more delicate. You can bring the subtlest text to life with the Touching Game.

The Arm-Wrestling Game

We all know this macho pub game: two people put their elbows on a table, place their forearms together, hold hands, and try to wrestle their opponent's arm down to the table without lifting their own elbow off the table.

It's a game of strength and skill. If a large man and a small woman play this game it could hardly be called a fair contest but if they play the game with complicity, and play it to have an effect on the audience, then the game can be compelling to watch. All we have here is a sustained version of action and response.

If you hide this game in a scene of passion where A is trying to prevent B from doing something, such as preventing them from getting up and going away, or from taking a garment off, or making a phone call – any simple physical objective will do. If you play the same physical contest as in the Arm-Wrestling Game, with a view to having an effect on the audience rather than just trying to win, then you'll introduce a huge physical intensity into the scene that you can control and manipulate between you as much as you like. If you play your text on top of this intensity, that too will become passionate and urgent – as if you're almost out of control. The more you hide the game, the more you'll be inviting our empathy and the more you declare it, the more robust your comedy will become.

Hidden games not only invigorate objectives, they also generate subtext. The subtext refers to things that are never said but are implied by what you do, or in what you say. For example, your spoken text can be something as innocuous as, 'No, it's OK. I don't mind tidying up – I like tidying up. I'm fully aware of the politics of tidying up.' If your partner is thrusting a mop at you, and if you resist taking it completely by holding it at arm's length, you can both push on the handle of the mop in exactly the same way as if you were playing the Arm-Wrestling Game. The physical intensity of that game will make it very clear that what we see you doing is the opposite of what you've just said. If what you're doing is different to what you're saying, then we have subtext.

As a student, I remember being told never to play the subtext because if I did I would destroy it, and it would all become the 'top text', the spoken text. Hidden games generate subtext with ease. If rehearsal is about 'making meaning meaningful' then it's the subtext that does it. The greater the clash between what you say and what you do, the richer and more fascinating the subtext becomes.

Declaring the Game

I once saw a student production of *Titus Andronicus* at the National Student Drama Festival. This is a play with unremitting violence: there's rape, dismemberment, and eventual cannibalism. It's an ambitious undertaking for anybody. The question is how do you stage such relentless and graphic brutality without drifting into bathos and rendering everything ridiculous? This group had made a spirited attempt, and brought some imaginative solutions and considerable playfulness to their production, but in the end they gave us a turgid evening. The basic problem was that they refused us permission to laugh; in my jargon, they had refused to declare their games. Their costumes were an eclectic jumble of style and period. Some people were dressed in modern overcoats, others in lounge suits with laurel wreaths in their hair. Some were in modern battle dress, whilst others were wearing makeshift togas but with modern shoes and socks looking painfully incongruous at the end of pale, hairy legs. Titus had his hand chopped off on a modern bread board, with a cold chisel and a hammer, severed heads were wrapped in brown-paper parcels and dismembered hands were kept in freezer bags. These are outrageous design choices, and it's impossible to see these things without wanting to laugh. A good laugh would have made us all more comfortable. It would have enabled us to acknowledge their grotesque images for the jokes that they were intended to be, and we would all have felt more confident in the savage world they were trying to create. A suppressed laugh soon becomes a sneer, and once that happens, rather than sharing the joke of the shocking image, we're invited to read that image as a representation of reality, and we just didn't buy it. We all knew there wasn't a real severed hand in that freezer bag. So we mocked them for being inept, and were angry with them for thinking that we could ever be that stupid.

Because they seemed to take themselves so seriously, it became impossible to find a shred of credibility in their work. They rarely looked at the audience and, for the most part, failed to connect with us at all. When we did laugh, they ignored us, and carried on. Having made a potentially wonderful comic world for the play, they refused to let us in. Had we seen them, for example, at the beginning of the play, like kids with a dressing-up box, they could have declared the game of having such eclectic costumes. We might have enjoyed seeing them dressing up, and as a result found their design choices entirely credible and accepted them for the rest of the play. Similarly, had they presented their gruesome props – the severed heads, the bread board, the hammer and chisel – then, here too, they would have shared the game of what they were doing, and we could have shared the joke. It sounds as if I'm determined to wreck the drama with these suggestions, but I can assure you I'm not. Once we see the game and share the joke, at that moment we believe you completely. If you refuse the joke and ignore the obvious playfulness of your choices, our laughter turns into ridicule, and we'll want to mock you for being naff. Whereas if you're seen to be deliberately naff, then we'll accept you for what you are, and give you all the space you need to play the drama. Then of course, you'll have to be more interesting in the way you play your text. Once we believe in your games, and we can find equal credibility in the way you play both the situation and the text, then comedy and tragedy can sit together in relative comfort.

If you put on a badly fitting wig, in full view of the audience, then walk about in an appropriately different way, then you're declaring the game of being somebody else. If you tie a tennis ball to the end of a fishing rod and somebody serves the ball with a tennis racket out over the heads of the audience to an imaginary player, then you're declaring the game of playing tennis. If you're audacious enough to abandon the illusion of the tennis and just smash the ball about at random, then you're declaring the game for its own sake. If we're interested in the situation, and you're happy enough to be on stage playing, then we'll buy almost any game you care to play for us. Paul Hunter staged all these things in his Told by an Idiot production, *I'm a Fool to Want You* (2004). Games happen in the 'here and now'. They're real. Illusions happen in the 'there and then', and we all know that's not real. Theatre is curiously split-minded: we flip continually back and forth between the 'here and now' and the 'there and then'.

Theatre generates a metaphorical reality. When you 'play' in the theatre, you have the scope to do any part you like. Hamlet could easily be played by a woman, and has been on numerous occasions. Sarah Bernhardt even played the part when she had a wooden leg! If you're really keen, Shakespeare's Titus Andronicus could be a played by a child. That choice alone would be enough to build a complex metaphor that could have much to say about power, cruelty and revenge. Play will liberate you to a world of possibilities, and in declaring the game you blot out theatrical illusion, and invite the audience to imaginatively join in. We become participants in your game. There are far more possibilities in turning a chair into a horse, than there are in having a real horse on stage. To accept that a chair is a horse, the audience have to work harder, and the harder we work at it, the more we own it, and the more we believe it.

The Blagging Game

This is one of my favourite complicity games because it's based on a lie. 'Whom would you rather have dinner with?' Philippe Gaulier once asked me. 'Somebody who tells the truth, or somebody who'll tell you lies? Lies are more interesting.' The more obvious the lie and the more seriously you play it, the more you declare the game. Only in declaring the game, can you show us what's really happening.

I normally set up the Blagging Game by announcing (without telling anyone in the group that I'm going to) something preposterous such as, 'This group has spent the past few weeks rehearsing a tiny fragment of text in the original Ancient Greek. It's called The Libation Bearers. *We have very little of this text to go on, but they've chosen the most fascinating sections where the women come to the grave of the dead hero and perform their dithyramb of grief. Could you just do the last section?' I might add a stronger tone of authenticity and put them even more 'in the shit' by asking: 'What does that start with? I don't have the text in front of me.'*

In groups of five to seven, one person leads and all the others follow. The idea is that the leader is the only person to have been at the rehearsal, but the leader is as much in the dark as everybody else. The leader's task is to make the action, and the rest of the group are trying to look as if they know exactly what they're doing.

The object of the game is for the leader to provoke the others by dancing whatever he understands by a 'dithyramb of grief', the others strive to look as if they know exactly what they're doing but they can only see each other in their peripheral vision.

It's very satisfying to see people 'playing the lie' and trying to convince us that actually they do know what a dithyramb is and that, no matter what happens, this is precisely the way it was intended to be done. The Blagging Game has the unique potential to throw up some fascinating moments of physical comedy. I've seen some astonishing cannon effects, as a missed cue has passed from one person to another, down the line. Every mistake becomes the substance of comedy in this game.

The Blagging Game teaches us how vital it is that we take the action seriously. No matter how ridiculous you look or how stupidly you're behaving, it must never be stupid to you. We only believe you if you believe in the lie. If you think it's funny we lose interest. You know exactly how it must be done because you were at the rehearsal so the mistakes must be genuine. Play the game hard and let the mistakes happen. It's excruciating if you try to invent mistakes and impose them on us. Stay with the lie and try to brave it out. If you do that, the game will be declared and it will work for you.

I remember seeing *Antony and Cleopatra* at Shakespeare's Globe on London's South Bank. Mark Rylance was playing Cleopatra. He played her as a poor little rich girl, petulant and demanding. He was clearly a man dressed as a woman and not a very attractive woman at that – especially for such a potent sexual icon as Cleopatra. The game was clear right from the start. Here was a man dressed in woman's clothes, walking and sounding like a woman, with a face that was palpably that of a man. The key to his 'femininity' was a sable wig that he would occasionally brush away alluringly from his face. It was a rich and satisfying parody at first, and the early scenes of the play were very funny.

But at the end of the play, Antony was dead and Cleopatra had lost everything. Caesar came to her palace with his soldiers to take her to Rome, just to complete her humiliation. When Cleopatra came down to receive them, the wig was gone. Instead we were appalled to see ugly tufts of short hair growing out of a bald and bleeding scalp at odd angles. She'd hacked her hair off and deliberately disfigured herself in the violence of her grief. It was a shocking moment of witness. Even the soldiers were moved. A couple of them looked round at us as if to say, 'Do you see what I see?' We touched tragedy at this moment for the first time in the play. Now Mark Rylance was Cleopatra with all the beauty, power and dignity that the role demanded. We'd flipped from the 'there and then' to the 'here and now' and, for a few moments at least, this was for real.

OK, the gruesome reality of the surprise arrested our imaginations, but it's unlikely that we would have felt such a sense of loss had we not enjoyed the game of a man having the audacity to play such an iconic figure in the first place. By declaring the game, we shared the fun, and when the game turned nasty we shared in that as well. Declaring the game makes theatre theatrical. It breaks the illusion and reveals the metaphor. To see a man play the woman's part in one of the greatest love stories of all time highlighted the humanity of her predicament rather than the sex and the power. In the end, nothing could save her from herself.

Declare the game and the playing becomes more credible. Undermine the visual illusion of character and the more we see a person. The idea that actors might declare the game that they're only 'playing' at being somebody else is an ancient one going back at least to the eleventh century. There's a beautiful Japanese Noh mask called *Ko-omote* – it's the mask of a young girl in the bloom of youth. It's captivated us in the West since it first appeared during the Great Exhibition in 1851. Traditionally, this mask is played by a man, but a puzzling feature of its design is that it is too small for a man's face. It sits too far forward on the face to be believable. This is a deliberate choice. In order to highlight both the playing of the mask and the mask itself, the Noh masters deliberately declared the game by separating the illusion from the reality.

In the early fifties, the great acting teacher Michel Saint-Denis observed that there were two ways we could approach acting. We could either create a complete illusion of somebody else, and in effect become that person by capturing their appearance, the way they moved, how they spoke and how they looked at the world; or we could keep all that information at the back of our minds and use it as a 'second reference'. In other words, we could behave much like our normal selves but when the action demanded it, we could refer back to all that original detail and ask ourselves: 'What would they do now?'

Part Two

Messing About with Meaning

Storytelling reveals meaning
without committing the error of defining it.

Hannah Arendt

Introduction

❝ *It's a disaster! The masks the company have made are like huge crash helmets. They're far too big. They cover the entire head and face. They go down to the back of the neck at the back, and to a point way below the chin at the front. It's impossible for the actors to even look at the floor. They're very difficult to put on as well. You have to squeeze your head into them, and the rim of the mask scratches your ears. But once inside, it's even worse: your eyes are never aligned with the eye holes of the mask, so the best you can do to see anything is to squint down a nostril or through a group of tiny pinpricks puncturing the cheek. But then, because your ears are covered, not only is your hearing muffled, but your balance is affected as well! You end up tottering about like a patient recovering from an operation. In order to see an object, and to pick it up, you have to be completely still. If you're stupid enough to move too quickly, and have to breathe in — you get two jets of ice-cold air blasting into your eyes leaving you temporarily blinded, with tears running down your cheeks.*

We've spent all our money on these masks! It's too late to abandon them now. **❞**

I wrote these remarks in my notebook during the rehearsals of *Crèche*, our first production as Trestle Theatre Company, in 1981. I didn't realise at the time that those early attempts at making mask theatre, were going to be such a steep learning-curve, not so much in using masks, as in working with action. Let's say I was rehearsing a situation like a basic love triangle where A has just discovered that B is having an affair with C, and the action we'd thought of staging was that A was to snatch the car keys from the table, and storm out of the room in a rage. It sounds simple enough, but because of the physical restrictions of the mask, that action would have to change. The hapless actor probably wouldn't be able to see the car keys, so snatching them would be impossible. Inside the mask, A probably wouldn't even be able to see the table very clearly, so would have to guess where the keys might be. A would have to stand back, be completely still, then look round the table for the keys. By this time, B would also be standing back, and looking round the table for the keys, in an attempt to help – just keeping the action moving on. B might even end up having to hand the keys to A. By then of course, when it came to A trying to storm out of the room in a rage, the exit would be preposterously naive, and very funny.

The physical restrictions of the masks had a regressive influence on our behaviour on stage, and continually took our ideas in a slightly different direction. We had to constantly restructure the action in order to accommodate what the actors could do in them, so we developed a pragmatic approach to action. Working with those crude, home-made masks gave us a very literal understanding of Stanislavski's idea of 'the given circumstances of a scene'. We learnt to accommodate what was possible, in preference to what we wanted to play. Ironically, after all our compromises, the end result would more often than not be more interesting than what we'd thought of doing in the first place; the action would be less obvious, more oblique, and would probably generate more subtext.

Whenever we tried to speak wearing a full mask, it sounded muffled and ridiculous, so by necessity our work was completely silent. This meant that for the simplest action to make any sense, the audience had to be looking at the right place at the right time. Nothing could be left to chance, and everything had to be tightly choreographed. But we wanted to make comic dramas – not little mime sketches – and to do that, we had to learn to give the smallest action the sort of analysis normally reserved for a line of written text. We evolved a process that required the actors to speak their thoughts throughout the scene. When you're working in a full mask, your movement is always slightly slower than in real life, and, in the absence of text, every little movement counts. You simply can't afford to waffle, or not know what you're do-ing. Speaking your thoughts in a mask keeps your attention on what you want in the scene, and how you're going to get it. By focusing on the thoughts, the timing of an action would start to develop naturally, and by changing the thoughts, you change the action. But it also works the other way round: by changing the action you have to change the thoughts. We developed a rehearsal process where we'd rehearse out of mask for much of the time, so we could break down and question everything we did, moment by moment. Every pause, look, walk and turn came under our scrutiny; every detail of the scenario would be taken apart, and put back together again – then repeated with complete accuracy. It was a tough training ground. Our stagecraft blossomed, but I missed the playfulness and spontaneity. The fun started to fade.

I approach action very differently today from the way I did in the eighties. I no longer start with analysis; I prefer to find things as we go along rather than trying to work everything out beforehand. Today I rarely ask actors to speak their thoughts, because I'm no longer working with such lumbering limitations as those badly made masks. Once you can see and hear, you react quicker than you can think, and you can be instinctive. But I'm eternally grateful to those testing times; my appreciation of action, and my approach to meaning is very much the result of those experiences. The appalling restrictions imposed by those early Trestle masks taught me that the term 'action' refers to anything you do on stage. Even if you're just sitting and breathing, it's an action replete with potential meaning. Pauses, stops, changes in speed and direction, moments of stillness or frenetic energy are all, in the appropriate context, eloquent expressions of thought and feeling. All we were doing on those early Trestle plays was messing about with the action in order to accommodate the restrictions of the masks, but action proved to be far more resilient than any of us first imagined. The only thing that action can't do very easily is to articulate abstract thought. We need language for that. In everything else, in establishing our intentions, telling a story, revealing feelings, changes of thought, dramatic intensity, and the atmospheres we build up between us, language is of secondary importance. Anything you're likely to say just sits on top of what we see you doing. As Gaulier would say: 'The text sits on top of the movement like the sauce on top of the meat – not like that 'orrible nouvelle cuisine, where the sauce sits under the meat.'

Psychologists tell us that more than ninety per cent of all our communication is non-verbal. So when you're on stage, how you hold yourself, how you move, when you move, what you're wearing, what you're carrying, what you smell like, and the context in which we, as an audience, see all these things, convey more meaning in the end, than anything you're likely to tell us verbally. I value the written text as much as I do the performance text, but ultimately it's the action choices that determine whether we believe what you're saying or not. So, if your credibility on stage is determined more by what you do than what you say, and if what we perceive as 'character' is also determined more by what you do than what you say, then what is action? What is it composed of?

If we scrape away written text, narrative, and situation for the moment, if we put meaning on hold, what are we really playing with when we're messing about with action? Almost every acting teacher since Stanislavski has said that action is a perpetual cycle of impulses and reactions. In other words, if you drop something, that's an impulse; and your reaction might be to pick it up. Of course how you 'pick it up' depends on what 'it' is in the first place, and what you feel about 'it'. Even when all these circumstances have been decided, there is a multitude of different ways of playing the simplest action, and if you're trying to make comedy, you need to develop a taste for finding these variations because the written text won't be of much help. Action is at its most robust, its most audacious, and its most surprising in physical comedy. But in exploring variations in action, there are only a limited number of things we can use. Once the original impulse is clear, precise meaning is expressed by how tense you are when you first react to the impulse. This tension influences your rhythm, and this rhythm expresses what you mean, but precise meaning is articulated by the way you time that movement; in other words, by the way you play with the rhythms. It sounds far more complicated than it really is, and if you try to think about all those things at the same time you probably won't even be able to stand up. We do all these things instinctively. If you were playing a game, you wouldn't think about them at all, but if something isn't working, or if what's happening isn't giving you any ideas, it helps to know what else you might be able to do. Basically there are only three things to play with in trying to find different variations of an action:

1. *The State of Tension*

2. *The Rhythm*

3. *The Timing*

States of Tension

Jacques Lecoq developed his work on the states of tension over many years. I first learnt this work from Simon MacBurney in about 1982, who'd recently finished training with Lecoq. Soon afterwards I learnt them from Lecoq himself, and they were slightly different. Lecoq also discusses the states of tension in his book, and they're different again. Lecoq's work was in a constant state of change and development; things were never set in stone for him. He'd always tell his students to 'do what you do, and not what I do'; so there are innumerable interpretations of this work. Like so much of his teaching, it's entered an oral tradition. Here is my version:

We can define a range of physical states of tension, gradating from the minimum level of tension in the body, to the maximum level of tension. These different tension states have no meaning in themselves; meaning is conveyed by the context. And on first sight they look as if they're best seen as a linear scale, but on closer examination they look more like a cycle because both the minimum and the maximum states of tension are levels of intensity where action is impossible. It's a cycle that traces an emotional journey – from death to death.

1. 'Exhausted'

This is the lowest state of tension in the body. In its most extreme form it's a bit like being deeply asleep, and when you're provoked into movement, you graduate from a state of complete inertia to one that looks as if you're intoxicated or ill or seasick. Exhaustion is my preferred metaphor for this state. Of course it doesn't mean any of these things but it's easier to have something to work from.

To find the physical definition: lie in a comfortable position on the floor. Make sure that your whole body is supported so that you can 'let go'. Scan around the body and try to relax each part. The out-breath predominates here, so use your out-breath to soften your body onto the floor.

Keeping your attention on the out-breath, start to try to bring yourself to a sitting position. Try breathing out at the start of each movement. Stop every now and then and feel your body fighting with gravity. This tension state is a perpetual fight against gravity; its direction in space is down to the earth. Start to bring yourself to standing, and take the image of your belly being full of lead, so that it's particularly heavy.

To apply this state of tension: try walking round the room. Notice that every step is an effort. You have to lean forward, to shift your centre off-balance to make yourself take a step or else you'll fall over. Try smiling. Try to dance for joy. Try a sexy dance, or a display of aggression.

Before we go on, I must clarify what I mean by the word 'centre'. We all have a physiological centre of balance in the body, situated in the region of the abdomen, about three quarters of an inch down from the navel. Depending on how skinny you are, you might be able to feel a vertical ridge of muscle running up your abdomen, and about three quarters of an inch below your navel, you'll find a little indentation. That's your centre. If you were going to balance horizontally – face down on the end of a broom handle – that is where you'd put the broom. This is the point of balance we have to get at right angles to the ground if we're to stand up on our two legs, or if we're planning to ride a bicycle.

The Centring Game

Balance on your heels, and give yourself the intention of falling back onto your bum. If, at the last moment, you change your mind, and thrust your pelvis forward, you'll be deliberately putting yourself off your habitual centre. If you've ever tried wind surfing, you'll be well acquainted with the problem.

Walking unaided on two legs is probably the greatest physical feat that the vast majority of us will ever accomplish in our lifetimes. The acting teacher Michael Chekhov proposed the idea that we can invent imaginary centres that have little effect on our balance, but give strong physical and imaginative impulses when we focus our attention on them. For example, if you place an imaginary centre in your lips, and simply think about your lips, without feeling the need to demonstrate what you're doing, you'll feel different, and you'll move in a slightly different way than if you were to put an imaginary centre in your crotch, or your chin.

Each tension state has an imaginary centre. In the 'Exhausted' state the centre is below your pelvis, somewhere in the region of your lower thighs, or even your knees. Lecoq used an image to define it when I worked with him: 'Imagine that you have a great lead weight in you belly,' he said. In exploring these states of tension, go for either: an imaginary centre, an image, a description, a breath, or a physical rhythm – whatever you think works for you, but don't try them all at once. The tension states are a very simple idea, which is why they're so useful.

It's helpful to try to clash the tension state with the action, as a constant reminder that we're not dealing with literal meaning here. It's more interesting to see somebody running for a bus in 'Exhausted' or to see a general briefing his troops in 'Exhausted,' than to see somebody getting out of bed in 'Exhausted'. If you try to sing or to deliver a speech, notice that the voice is barely activated. It's almost impossible to sing or to speak in this state of tension. If you try to declare your love for somebody from the 'Exhausted' tension state, it takes on a huge emotional resonance – as if your feelings are beyond your control. This is when tension states really come into their own: when the clash between what the text is saying and what your body is saying opens up a rich vein of emotional engagement that takes everyone by surprise.

2. 'Laid Back'

This is a very indeterminate state of tension; it can be so casual that it appears ambiguous and unpredictable. It's got the diffidence and the cool of an adolescent.

> *To find the physical definition: try standing with your weight on one hip so that your pelvis is slightly tilted to one side. Now put your*

weight onto the other hip, and tilt your pelvis the other way. Now alternate between the two. Try tilting your pelvis forward and backwards. Now move your pelvis in a small circle. This is a state of tension that works around your centre. Keep the movement light and gentle and observe what's happening in the region of your chest and your neck. Soften your face. This state of tension is casual to the point of being insolent. It's carefree, uncommitted, disinterested or disaffected depending on the context.

The breathing in this state of tension is light and shallow. Try a light, unsustained sigh. The out-breath is the dominant impulse here, but it's not as heavy as in 'Exhausted'.

If you speak in this state of tension, your body is invariably too relaxed, and apparently disengaged for us to think that you believe in what you're saying. It's as if you're saying everything as a casual throw-away; as if you were saying, 'Oh, I think I'll go to bed now.' If your text is something like: 'I love you and I want to spend my life with you,' then 'Laid Back' is going to create a splendid clash between your physicality and your text.

3. 'One Movement at a Time'

The dominant quality here is that of being preoccupied, as if you've got something so pressing on your mind that moving is the last thing you're thinking about. Every single gesture is direct and clear, and finishes in a fixed point.

To find a physical definition: stand or sit in a comfortable position and find a simple objective, like looking at something in the far distance. As you play the objective, restrict yourself to playing one movement at a time. So you might tilt your head as the first movement, sit upright for the second, lift your hand up to shield your eyes for the third, and so on. Make sure that each movement is clear and direct. Try moving around the room, and treat each journey as if it were a single thought finishing with a fixed point. Your movement will follow a clear, direct, and uninterrupted line. You'll be comfortably on your centre of balance here, and the more you repeat the movement, the more you'll find poise and precision here.

It's difficult to speak in this tension state without breaking up the flow of the text. Those single movements finishing every time in a fixed point will soon interrupt your flow of thought. It's very difficult to give detailed instructions to somebody in this state of tension; you'll invariably become distracted.

The breath, like the movement, is interrupted. Try holding your breath for short periods of time. This has the effect of giving the fixed points greater emphasis, and gives the movement a brittle quality.

The obvious application of this tension state would be two people about to have an argument. A more interesting clash between the action and the movement quality would be two people trying to dance together.

4. 'Neutral'

This is one of the most famous aspects of Lecoq's work, and because he taught this state of tension through a specially designed 'neutral mask', it's generally forgotten that neutral is simply another calibration in a cyclical range of tension states. There's probably more confusion about neutrality than any other aspect of Lecoq's teaching. In the glossary of his book, *The Moving Body*, neutrality is defined as:

66 *The state prior to acting or character creation where the actor is in a state of perfect balance, presenting nothing but a neutral generic being. A character has a history, a past, a context, passions. On the contrary, a neutral mask puts the actor in a state of perfect balance and economy of movement.* **99**

Neutrality is moving with no story behind your movement. If you watch somebody walk across the room, and if you can use an adjective to describe how they're walking – for example, you might say that someone looks determined, anxious, carefree, or distracted – then there is an inflection, or colour to their movement that clearly isn't neutral. Contrary to popular belief, 'Neutral' doesn't mean neuter or uniform. Basically it's a state of tension that we all go to when we're not in conflict of any kind, as when simply walking across the room in a comfortable and equable frame of mind.

Neutrality is a study in power and economy. It's a classic case of less meaning more. In other words, if somebody were to insult you, and knock you to the ground, and you simply got up, without comment, and walked away again – without a flicker of response – we'd scrutinise every gesture, and every little movement for the smallest reaction, but if you were in 'Neutral' we'd only see the bare facts of the action. There'd be no story, no colour, and no emotional reaction to what has just happened, so in the absence of anything else you might have given us, we start to impose our own story and our own emotional response to what we've just seen. That's what I mean by economy: the power of doing as little as possible in order to achieve the maximum effect. But playing neutral doesn't mean that you never react to the impulses of the drama. Remember neutrality is a choice – not a golden rule. There are no rules, but if you never touch neutrality, your work will be in danger of becoming two-dimensional or frenetic. 'Neutral' is an essential level of engagement because it gives depth and contrast to all the other tension states.

Keith Johnstone's idea of 'high status,' as described in his book, *Impro*, is essentially the same idea as Lecoq's neutrality. Both concepts are trying to articulate how playing an action without comment, or playing an action without conflict will draw us in, and engage our imaginations at a more profound level than bolder or more physical levels of engagement. In the same way that anybody who's incapable of dropping their status would be regarded as behaving abnormally, so anyone stuck in 'Neutral' all the time could hardly be described as a balanced human being. Neutrality, like high status, is a state of tension that comes into its own when seen in the context of a whole range of different status levels, or of different tension states. The main difference between Johnstone's 'high status' and Lecoq's neutrality isn't the idea, so much as the presentation. Keith Johnstone puts high status at the top of his scale of engagement; implying that high status is a sort of pinnacle of power – which in a sense it is – whereas Jacques Lecoq puts his neutrality in the middle of a range of tension states that are cyclical rather than linear.

I once heard Lecoq describe 'Neutral' as like having an empty jug: you can put any liquid you like into the jug, but if your jug is already full of milk, then you can't put anything in it. 'Neutral' is the state of tension we play before something happens, a state of pre-expressivity; it's the place we depart from, and the place we return to. In other words, if we train ourselves to play the action rather than worrying about the feeling, then we're in a better position to absorb anything the play throws at us. This is an important idea because it turns the conventional way of looking at acting on its head. Popular wisdom would have it that we must train ourselves to be expressive, whereas Lecoq would say that we should let the world make its impression on us. Rather then letting feelings out, we should let them in. Lecoq taught that pre-expressivity is ultimately more expressive because it keeps our attention on the fact that something is about to happen. The less we do, the less conflict we have, the less resistance we put up against the world, the more reactive we appear to be to everything around us. This is the real lesson. By putting 'Neutral' in the middle of the range we can see that neutrality is delicately poised between using far too little tension, or far too much. Use too little and your work will become more heavy and less focused; use too much tension, and it'll become too hard and unrelenting. Economy is a hard lesson. It takes time and practice, but if you want to clown effectively, or be a good performer, or a powerful actor then study neutrality. You'll learn the art of only doing what's required, and no more.

There are two obstacles to neutrality. One springs from your personal holding patterns as demonstrated in the way you habitually move and the way you hold yourself. The second obstacle is your natural instinct to 'act', and your desire to express your feelings. Any alignment discipline like Alexander Technique, Feldenkrais Method or Tai Chi will help you with the first, so I'm going to concentrate on the second.

I like to approach neutrality by using masks, but this isn't essential. I use masks because we read each other's faces instinctively, and by covering the face we're made to read the body instead. Whether you're using masks or not, in looking for neutrality we've got to ask ourselves: Is this person simply doing the action, or are they bringing a story to the action? If adjectives start to spring to mind, implying what they're feeling, then they're not neutral.

The Good Cop/Bad Cop Game

A (the bad cop) and B (the good cop), are giving C a series of commands and instructions designed to irritate or intimidate C. The game is for C to try to maintain his or her neutrality in spite of the provocations to do otherwise. It's easier to play this game if C remains completely silent. You can introduce text once the physicality is more assured.

A. Stand up!

B. Take your time. We're not in a hurry.

A. Get over there. Come on. You're very pissed, aren't you? Take your coat off, and put it on the chair.

B. Would you mind walking over here, please?

A. Now do you see that white line on the floor? Walk along it without wobbling. Now!

The game is for A and B to try to make C react in a way that isn't neutral. For example, if C looks insolent, irritated, or hesitant, then C's neutrality is compromised, somebody else becomes C, and the game continues. C must try not to be tricked into reacting to the provocations of A and B. The idea isn't to ignore A and B, but rather to do everything they ask in such a way that doesn't comment, or show an emotional response. To do this you have to take your time, and give space to your actions. But if you move too slowly you'll look disengaged, and if you move too quickly, you're in danger of looking anxious or distressed. It takes practice to play this game well, but it's not impossible.

The idea is for A and B to get C to do things rather than to answer questions. The more assured C becomes in playing neutral, the more robust A and B can be with the provocations. C's job is to do the action as well as possible, without rising to any conflict. A and B's job is to make conflict and to try to confuse C. If you're playing C and the instructions come too quickly, do nothing. Wait until you're clear. Be still. And when you do something be direct with your action and complete every gesture in a way that feels comfortable to you.

You'll probably find that the roles will change very quickly at first. Neutrality is lighter and more comfortable to play than you think. A and B can really provoke in this game. Try vigorous action like running and jumping. Try dancing in neutral. Stillness is important insofar as it keeps you in control of the action, but stories will soon creep in if you rely on it too much. Be comfortable. If you find yourself moving about like something from *Doctor Who*, you're really missing the point.

The Corpse that Wouldn't Lie Down

This is a short scene inspired by Peter Shaffer's play, *The Royal Hunt of the Sun*. I use it to explore the relationship between neutrality and comedy. If you do more or less action than is absolutely necessary to play the scene, then it will become comic. If you do exactly what's required and no more, then the scene will have a haunting tragedy about it. If the entire audience erupts into laughter as soon as you start, it doesn't help anybody to see this as a failure. Accept what happens for what it is. I use this game to examine the idea of power and economy.

It's a scene for two people, and I'm writing it here in the form of simple action lines, with no adjectives, in such a way that it only provides the essential information – just as I'd present it in the rehearsal room.

A stands in the space, and looks out towards the distant horizon.

B enters carrying a short length of rope. B looks at A.

A continues looking out to the distant horizon.

B holds the rope at both ends, preparing a ligature.

B walks towards A and puts the rope round A's neck.

B strangles A.

A stands still at first, then starts to struggle more and more.

B wrestles A to the floor.

A continues to struggle, then dies.

B stands up, leaving the rope round A's neck, and walks away. B stops.

A stands up.

B turns round.

A and B look at each other.

A walks towards B.

B runs out of the room.

A stands in the space, looking out towards the distant horizon.

It's up to you how you use the space, how fast or how slow you play the action, how much you struggle during the strangling, and how B plays the exit at the end. It can be astonishing how many different ways there are of playing this apparently simple scene, and how many different qualities and different resonances can be brought to it, whilst remaining neutral. It's all about choices.

Awareness of neutrality makes us mindful of all the other choices open to us. The challenge of having to do as little as possible reveals just how huge and clumsy our habitual choices tend to be. But remember: neutrality isn't an ideal you've got to aspire to in the pursuit of some notion of excellence. It's just another choice – that's all. If you make us laugh, that's great. There's potential skill there. Now ask yourself why we laughed, and play the scene again.

Every action has the potential for comedy in this game, and the more seriously you try to play the scene, the funnier it's likely to become. Neutrality isn't the same as being serious. I've seen audiences reduced to helpless hysteria with this game, whilst the two actors on stage have tried to muster every ounce of presence they could find to try to keep the scene credible. It's a mistake to think that being serious is going to stop us laughing. If you want to do that, you've got to play with the appropriate amount of engagement for the action. Any more or any less than is genuinely required is going to be hysterical to watch.

If B comes in too quickly there's a danger of looking like Eric Morecambe, or of becoming melodramatic and ridiculous. I've seen people come on stage more like the Terminator than any human being that I've ever met. If A's action is too slow at the beginning, it's likely to become sentimental. But the strangling is the most difficult action to play. This takes some rehearsal. B has to find a way of controlling the rope so that it looks as if it's being pulled tightly all the time. There are several ways to do this. One actor I know found a way of pushing his fists together behind A's neck which made it look as if he were applying all his strength. In reality he was pushing quite hard but none of his efforts were being applied to the rope which remained comfortably loose round A's neck. B has to be quite passive here and to be able to follow A who has to do all the work leading the fall and playing the agony. B has to convince us that the rope is being pulled with the maximum pressure against A's throat. You have to work out how A is going to struggle, so that you can repeat the same sequence in the same way every time, or it's going to be dangerous to play because the strangling has to be convincing. Our comedy sensors will be twitching violently with the slightest hint of a phoney death. We need a strong death struggle if the event is to have any meaning or empathy for us.

I'm reminded of that excellent strangling scene in *The Godfather* (1972), which takes place in the front seat of a car. The victim is strangled from behind, and his feet move about so violently that he kicks out the windscreen of the car before he dies. When teaching neutral mask, Lecoq would say 'the neutral mask becomes what it sees'. In this context, A has to *become* 'Agony', and that rhythm of agony has to be played to the full, or we'll feel cheated.

The other difficult moment is the concluding section. How do you play A's return from the dead? How do you play the stand-off? And finally, how does B exit? Any attempt at 'ghost acting' is out of the question, unless you want to turn the scene into a clown show. The key lies in finishing each unit of action before you play the next one. Don't rush the details. Find the moment of the death. A must become still before B turns to leave or we won't see that A is actually dead. When A sits up, if it's too slow, those comedy sensors will be twitching again, and if it's too fast, they'll be bouncing round the room. There's a hair's breadth between playing a level of intensity that is perfectly appropriate to what you're doing, and one that isn't. You have to experiment until you believe what you see.

'Exhausted', Laid Back', 'One Movement at a Time' and 'Neutral' are the levels of physical intensity most commonly used in our everyday psychological interactions. With the exception of 'Neutral', they're all different levels of preoccupation really. 'Exhausted' implies a weighty preoccupation, 'Laid Back' is more evasive and cool, and 'One Movement at a Time' tends to look very calculating, but 'Neutral' is more about just doing something. If you're playing at the level of psychological realism, these four states of tension will predominate. They sound crude and over the top when explained in isolation, because I'm trying to emphasise their direction in space, and nudge them towards being seen as a movement quality rather than a psychological state of mind, but if you graduate, quite randomly, from one to another, it soon becomes apparent that you can play these different levels of intensity very subtly indeed. In life, we deftly slip from one tension state to another in the middle of a sentence. Sometimes our voices are at one tension state whilst our bodies are at another. Watch how people go about their ordinary lives, and observe to what extent you can identify the state of tension they're in at any given moment. Look at your own states of tension. I might think, 'Oh, I've got such and such to do', and breathe out, and immediately I'm going towards 'Exhausted', then I might meet a colleague, and become 'Laid Back', then become distracted in our conversation as I search for my car keys, and go to 'One Movement at a Time'; then get in my car and drive off in a state of neutrality. You'll soon see how subtle the changes are from one to another, and much of the subtlety in these lower, more minimal states comes from the breath.

Breathing and Tension

In life, we tend to internalise our states of tension, and change from one state to another by manipulating the breath. 'Manipulating' is too strong a word because this isn't necessarily a conscious act. Most of the time it's instinctive, but the breath is one of the most powerful impulses in influencing our mood. Practitioners of Yoga, we're told, can train themselves to manipulate their breathing to such an extent that they can change their metabolism, and stay alive for days on end whilst buried underground. On a more mundane level, we try to control our breathing when we're nervous, or trying to get to sleep; we control our breathing to change the way we feel. Antonin Artaud, author, actor, and visionary, maintained that there were three types of breath: the 'in-breath' (feminine), the 'out-breath' (masculine), and 'the held breath' (neuter). Only the French would try to determine the gender of breathing, but in examining subtle transitions between these states of tension, Artaud's three breaths help us internalise a state of tension into a breathing pattern. On first thought it sounds as if the in-breath is optimistic, and the out is the opposite, but this is far too simplistic. Try a short in-breath – first with a smile, then with a frown. Now do the same with the out-breath. Even these simple permutations open up a vast range of possibilities and are a strong reminder that the breath, like the tension states, is only a vague impulse; it's only the means of change and not the definition of what that change might be.

'Exhausted' is predominantly, but not exclusively an out-breath. If I were to ask you 'Whose job is it to clean out the lavatory?' and you put your hand up in admission, you'd probably breathe out as you put up your hand. This out-breath is an instinctive reaction to the distasteful job that's being proposed. If you're grinning at somebody in a 'Laid Back' kind of way, your breathing will probably be equally balanced between the in and the out, and will probably be quite shallow, short and light. If you're trying to remember where you put your car keys, and playing 'One Movement at a Time', you're probably holding your breath occasionally. If you're about to walk across the room in a state of neutrality, you'll probably breathe in on the impulse to move, and out again whilst you're walking, which is our customary breathing pattern in a situation where there is no conflict to deal with, when your breathing can match your activity, and you can remain equable and calm.

You can settle yourself into 'Neutral' if you break each movement down into comfortable units of breath such as when you're about to stand up, breathe in; then when you stand up, breathe out; and when you're about to walk, breathe in again; and as you're walking, breathe out. It's a comfortable thing to do because it's what we do in life, but if your breaths are too big, your movement will become slow and ponderous, and if it's comfortable and light and shallow, it will feel natural, and you'll look neutral. Simply listening to your breathing will stop your mind racing on about all the other things you've got to do, and keep you 'in the moment'. Unfortunately there are no reliable recipes for playing anything. But by playing with the breath, you will at least start to find greater economy.

Having established what we do naturally, it always more interesting to dispense with it for the moment, and look at the opposite of 'the norm'. So if you breathe *out* on the impulse to stand up, and *in* as you walk, this impulse will make you feel very different indeed. We can make this feeling stronger by putting it into a basic interaction:

The Breathing Game

A stands opposite B, about two metres apart. A looks into B's eyes, and breathes out. A then walks towards B whilst breathing in.

B's job is to notice the changes in the way A walks towards B. To what extent does A look more threatening, angry or intimidating than before? A's job is to observe the changes in feeling that the in-breath provokes.

The act of looking into someone's eyes is generally enough to make you find a reason for your action. If you look into somebody's eyes, breathe out, and then slowly breathe in as you walk towards them, you'll be projecting much bigger changes in your feelings towards them than if you were to breathe in the conventional pattern.

Once we start to move away from 'Neutral', we quickly reach states of tension more typical of physical comedy, and more typical of an intense dramatic situation. This sounds an unlikely combination, but these levels of intensity only occur in moments of extremis – when the stakes are at their highest. Comedy and drama are both preoccupied with all those things that we would least like to happen to us, or to anybody we know and love. All the tension states, with the exception of 'Neutral', are different states of conflict. Comedy, in particular, takes conflict to preposterous proportions, to levels of intensity so high that they become self-generating rhythms.

5. 'Is There a Bomb in the Room?'

This 'bomb' is a metaphor for a state of tension that implies a passion of some kind. It could be fear, love, joy, embarrassment, guilt, eroticism – anything you like, really, but whatever it is, you play it with the same intensity you'd have if you really were looking for a bomb in a room. It might go off at any moment. Every action is urgent and imperative. You've got to find it now! Where is it? This state of tension can be very painful or very funny, depending on the context, but the rhythmic intensity remains the same.

Move about the room looking urgently for a bomb. You must look everywhere. The bomb could be anywhere – in anything. Anybody could be carrying it.

Now apply that rhythm to a different context:

An over-anxious host, at a posh garden party is trying to make casual introductions and impress the guests with lavish hospitality, to keep the party flowing.

In this state of tension, the 'crisis' is always just about to happen. Put an imaginary centre at the end of your eye-line so that you're drawn towards wherever you happen to look at. You're pulled forward into the space, and because everything is done at a high level of anxiety, you're constantly making mistakes, and having to make adjustments. These adjustments only make the situation worse, and one thing leads to another. For example, you might approach a chair with such urgency that you knock it over, which disturbs one of the guests, which alarms you, and increases your anxiety, so you move even faster round the room, bumping into people, and eventually falling over. You make hasty apologies, go to leave, then find it impossible to open the door, which is even more embarrassing, because now everyone is watching you, so you break the door down in a frenzy to escape.

On one level, this is a classic comic build-up, on another, it's the 'And . . . And' Game that we looked at in Part One, but the driving force behind both these things is a preposterously inappropriate level of physical tension that radically affects how you breathe, how you think, how you move, and how you react. It's much easier to play either the 'And . . . And' Game or a comic build-up if you've got the rhythmic agility to sustain such a level of intensity. Playing an inappropriate rhythm like 'Is There a Bomb in the Room?' will make any situation frenetic. Literally anything, from getting dressed in the morning to choosing a library book, can be turned into a comic sequence simply by playing an inappropriate rhythm.

It's the world of John Cleese, Brian Rix, Laurel and Hardy, Brighella, Pantalone, or Arlecchino. The majority of the principal masks of the *Commedia dell'Arte* are played at the level of 'Is There a Bomb in the Room?' and with the energy of farce. The self-generating properties of this tension state enable the simplest action and the most mundane situation to be developed from the basic comedy of recognition, where we laugh at your typicality, to the comedy of the bizarre, where your actions take us to the furthest extremes of human behaviour. The simplest task like drinking tea becomes impossible to handle when you're as frenetic as this, and the more mistakes you make, the worse you feel, and so the level of intensity goes on growing. But what is it that makes it self-generating? Basically it's the rhythm itself. Just running round the room asking yourself: Is it here? Is it here? Is it here? – which is really all you're doing in this state – sets up a strong rhythmic definition that the body can repeat quicker than your imagination can justify. Like all simple repetitive rhythms, it gets faster and faster the more you repeat it, until it falls apart, or until you haven't the strength to continue. It's a rhythm that puts you almost out of control, which is both scary, and liberating at the same time. To find yourself doing something without thought or premeditation is exhilarating, and if you play this rhythm for any length of time, and then stop, you'll notice that it takes you some minutes to calm down again.

5a. 'Virgin Mary Acting'

Imagine going down the street, and suddenly you have a vision of the Virgin Mary. There she is, levitating in front of you. You're momentarily transfixed in awe and wonder. You might experience similar feelings on meeting somebody close to you whom you believed had died some years ago, or in meeting a celebrity, or someone you're madly in love with, or on receiving the cheque when you win the lottery. It's basically the same state of tension as 'Is There a Bomb in the Room?' and you can play it with the same imaginary centre at the end of your eye-line. The only difference is that in this instance the level of intensity is played slowly. Now the tension is sustained. Now your breathing is slower and deeper – both on the in-breath and the out-breath. It's as if you're being reeled in, like a fish on a line – only too willing to be caught – and pulled closer towards your 'vision'.

This is a very dramatic state of tension, but it's more widely used than you might think. An old woman desperately searching for a bargain in a bring-and-buy sale, for example, might be thrusting her way through the crowds at the level of 'Is There a Bomb in the Room?', when suddenly she finds a personal object of great sentimental value that she'd lost years ago. That impulse could easily inspire 'Virgin Mary Acting'. It's a state of tension that implies immense emotional engagement, and as such it's used extensively at moments of intense drama, tragedy or melodrama.

6. 'There *Is* a Bomb in the Room!'

Imagine walking into a room and seeing an escaped lion sitting there on the living-room carpet. Or imagine finding a deadly poisonous snake in the shower. Or you open the door to a psychopath brandishing an axe. Unlike the previous two tension states, this one is pulling you back. Now the urgency is in the room with you, and you want out of there. Like 'Is There a Bomb in the Room?', this tension state can be played as fast or as slow as you like, but if you play it slowly it doesn't change its level of intensity. 'Is there a bomb in the room?' is the only tension state that does that in the entire range.

The only difference between this, and 'There *Is* a Bomb in the Room!' is the direction: you're being pulled back as opposed to being pulled forward, but the physical tension remains the same. It's this shift from forward to back that moves the dramatic tension up a notch. Now it's imperative that you're not in this room at all. If you play the change quickly, it becomes a 'reversal', a common device in comic timing, which I'll look at in more detail later in this section. For the moment, imagine creeping up on someone with whom you're absolutely furious, tapping them on the shoulder, only to find that when they turn round, they have the face of a lizard. You'd move from 'Is There a Bomb?' to 'There *Is* a Bomb!' quicker than you can think. If you sustain the tension state by trying to have a polite conversation with the 'lizard', then the clash between wanting to run away, and the desire to be charming and relaxed becomes very interesting to watch, and is capable of generating yards of subtext.

This sustained intensity in your movement away from the point of focus is characteristic of melodrama. It's a counter-movement. In other words, a movement that goes in the opposite direction to the dramatic intention. For example, if you say 'Embrace me', and keep walking backwards, and away from the person you've said it to, your movement will be in direct opposition to your text, which will have the effect of heightening

your intention. Contrary to all expectations, you'll look more engaged
and more moved. You can imagine how it works: the husband pulls back
the covers and sees that his young wife is dead in bed; as he moves back
from her body, and across the room, he says how peaceful she looks. Or
the jilted lover has taken deadly poison, just as her true love bursts into
the room; as she retreats across the room, and back against the wall, he
tells her that she's made a terrible mistake, and that he didn't mean
what he said after all. Either of these examples could take you to 'There
Is a Bomb in the Room!' and yet they're both potential counter-
movements.

In sustaining a level of intensity like this, whatever you do – as you
stumble backwards over the furniture, intentionally or not – will be
read as a physical embodiment of the emotion. If you're pulled back
across the space, and sent sprawling across the floor, and if you keep on
going, until you reach the wall in true Lillian Gish fashion, we'll buy the
whole journey, providing we believe the dramatic impulse in the first
place. More importantly, we must see that your physical intensity is
credibly sustained throughout the entire journey across the room.

7. 'The Bomb is About to Go Off!'

This is another metaphor. Imagine defusing a bomb, or carefully immo-
bilising a booby trap, or delicately tapping a safe, or creeping upstairs
late at night so that nobody can hear you, or going to kiss somebody
with great tenderness with the fear of being rebuffed, or having to tell
somebody of the death of their child. Now the level of intensity has
gone up yet another notch. This tension state is created by sustaining a
slow, but painfully light movement quality – as if any sudden movement, or the slightest sound, could cause an explosion.

Grandmother's Footsteps

*A faces the wall, and everybody else has to creep up behind. The
object of the game is for A to stop the others from touching the wall.
To do this A will suddenly turn round, whereupon everybody freezes.
If A sees anybody moving, that person has to go back to the starting
line. A faces the wall again and the game continues.*

> This classic childrens' game captures the state of tension we're talking about, and it's much lighter and far more delicate than you might think. Here, your centre is just below your feet. It's as if you're so light that you'd really like to be flying, so your contact with the earth is as light as possible. Every movement is in a continual state of suspension because it's simply too dangerous to move either backwards or forwards. You're caught in the moment here. Perhaps something terrible is going to happen – perhaps not – all you can do is to continue. Your breath is light and shallow, and the in-breath is probably the most dominant. I say 'probably' because there are no hard and fast rules here. Try it for yourself.

This is a highly dramatic state: it's the highest level of intensity at which you can still move. The stakes could hardly get much higher than this. It's the calm before the storm, the stealthy turning of the key in the lock before making your escape. It's the painful approach to the passionate embrace, or the moment of temptation before eating the cream cake.

8. 'Rigor Mortis'

This is the state of tension that you go to when all further movement is impossible. If you throw yourself to the floor, or at the wall and stick there, like a piece of wet clay, or curl up into a ball like a brittle cinder, or you embrace somebody so passionately that neither of you are capable of any further movement – then you'll hit 'Rigor Mortis'. It's the moment when the unfortunate messenger throws himself on the floor at Cleopatra's feet. It's the moment when your worst or your best fears are suddenly realised. This is where your movement comes to its final fixed point. If you're against the wall you must be so flat against the wall that you simply can't move any more. Nothing further is possible at this tension state. You can't move, you can't speak, and you're holding your breath. 'Rigor Mortis' is the end of the cycle.

Like 'Exhausted', this is a point of death. Unlike 'Exhausted', this is a rigid death: carbonised and brittle. 'Rigor Mortis' is death from a total excess of tension, as opposed to the heavy floppy death of 'Exhausted', which is due to the total lack of tension. So the cycle goes from death to death. Too little tension is just as impossible as too much tension.

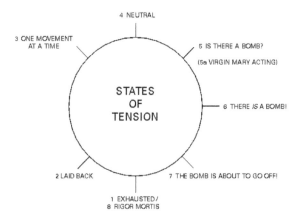

Lecoq's scale traces the basic calibrations of tension from one extreme to the other. Any farce or high drama will cover the entire range, in an infinite number of combinations. But different tension states dominate different theatrical forms: 'Exhausted', 'Laid Back', 'One Movement at a Time', and 'Neutral' dominate psychological realism; 'Is There a Bomb in the Room?' is predominant in farce and physical comedy; 'There *Is* a Bomb in the Room!' and 'The Bomb is About to Go Off!' are predominant in melodrama, but most plays of any real dramatic range encompass them all. The important thing to remember is that when you're using tension states, meaning is rarely literal. You can provoke any action you care to think of, simply by changing the tension state.

The tension states are a cycle of different levels of physical intensity, that indicate different states of mind but essentially they're just clearly defined rhythms given more clarity by their direction in space. You can vary the speed and the force of a tension state, but you can also clap or breathe the rhythm of a tension state. You can hum a tune that excites a particular tension state in your body, you can copy and exchange tension states from one to another. The more familiar you become in working with tension states, and the more you explore their detail and their subtleties, the more you'll find your body capturing the appropriate rhythm of a tension state. You'll develop a sort of physical short-hand that will enhance your ability to change from one state to another very quickly. When you change tension states at speed, you generate different rhythms.

Rhythm

Rhythmic Agility

Our interest in physical comedy relies on your ability to play clear, credible and rapidly changing rhythms. We want to see how you're feeling, and we delight in seeing huge changes in feeling – one after the other. Lecoq's cycle of tension states encompasses all the rhythms you're going to need to play any aspect of human experience! Now there's a bit of hyperbole for you, but I can make this extravagant claim, safe in the knowledge that one rhythm can absorb an astonishing variety of different meanings, because rhythms are ambiguous. When you play a slow transition from one state of tension to another, or if you like, from one rhythm to another, you pass through other innumerable other rhythms on the way. Tension states are the equivalent of an athlete stretching and warming-up before an event. The idea is to prepare the body so that movement is the last thing on that athlete's mind when contemplating jumping over that bar, or finishing that race. After the event, the strongest impression of the performance will be a rhythmic one, and subsequent analysis will start by examining rhythm.

The tension states are not a means of 'acting by numbers'; they're not 'emotions'. I value them because they enable us to make bold choices independent of the dramatic context. They take us to the extremes, and teach us the stamina and the flexibility to be able to sustain those extreme choices. In isolation, the tension states are meaningless, because meaning isn't contained in rhythm alone. Rhythm is only a vague indication of meaning. But making meaning through rhythm isn't the problem at the moment. The initial challenge is to make the rhythms with some degree of accuracy, and having done that, to be able to flip from one to the other instinctively, so that you can sustain those rhythms in a clear line of movement into the space, or to internalise them, so that you can play each rhythm with the same clarity, but barely moving at all.

It's a tall order but it isn't impossible. It just takes practice and experimentation, and once you've learnt it, you can forget about it, because you'll probably find yourself doing it anyway. It's just like learning any other physical skill, be it boxing, typing, dancing, juggling, or wearing stiletto heels: we train our bodies to behave in such a way, then trust them to remember what they've learned. There's no technique or method here – just a useful starting point: something to learn, then put at the back of our minds until something goes wrong.

Here are a few agility games:

The Big Journey Game

A walks from one end of the room to the other whilst B calls out each tension state in order.

The game is for A to move as smoothly as possible from the rhythm of one tension state to the other without stopping, in a continuous journey across the room. B's job is to prompt, and to make sure that there's enough space allotted to each different rhythm in turn as A moves across the room. Having tried this a couple of times, A can change from one state to another at will. B's job now is to call out the name of each tension state as it's recognised.

It's worth noting that B's recognition isn't for the audience, but for A. 'Oh, he thinks that's so and so, does he?' you might think. Nobody goes to the theatre to recognise states of tension but to identify with familiar rhythms. All that matters here is that A knows what's being played and that A and B between them know exactly what they're doing. We, in the audience, are not remotely interested in rhythms in the abstract. We're only interested in the scene and the situation. The tension states are a detailed personal reference for an easily recognisable rhythm so if you lack the accuracy and the agility to play these rhythms at will, you won't have any reliable reference points to play with in the first place. You'd be like a musician unable to play a scale.

Rhythmic Tag

This is a conventional game of Tag with one person 'on', trying to 'tag' or touch somebody else. The game here is to play exactly the same game, whilst sustaining a chosen tension state.

This is more demanding than you might think because there's a tendency to let the tension of the game flop whilst you're preoccupied with the rhythm. Some rhythms like 'Is There a Bomb?' are easy to apply, whereas 'Exhausted' or 'The Bomb is About to Go Off!' are more difficult. 'Neutral' is a challenge. But a game of Tag emphasises the fact that you can run and move very quickly in a state of neutrality. You don't have to run with 'aggression' or 'anger' or 'terror'. 'Rigor Mortis', of course, is impossible to sustain.

The Ever-Changing Love Scene

A and B devise an affectionate conversation – something that they can sustain, and repeat with some degree of accuracy. C calls out each tension state in turn. The idea is to go through the whole cycle in order, whilst A and B try to sustain their interaction, with their original text, as accurately as they can.

C's job is primarily to prompt and provoke the changes, as A and B move deftly from one state to another. C must keep A and B moving on, and tell them if they're waffling. They've got to hit each state accurately, but don't think – the changes in rhythm read as changes in thought. 'Exhausted' is a much slower rhythm than 'Laid Back'; a quick move, from one to the other, in the course of a conversation will generate meaning. Take a simple line like, 'I didn't think that you'd be here today. I thought you'd gone on holiday.' If you play the first sentence 'Exhausted' and the second 'Laid Back', the line will instantly accumulate subtext, and conjure up an entire back-story. As the scene progresses, and the rhythms change through the whole cycle we'll start to see an entire arc of emotional intensity regardless of the original text. In fact, the text will be of little consequence; you could be saying anything. I've even played this game with A and B speaking different languages, and it's worked perfectly.

You can use tension states in exactly the same way you might break down a text into different units of thought. All you're doing here is playing contrasting rhythms under the text, which makes your thoughts bigger, and gives them the status of emotions. This isn't necessarily better, or more appropriate; it's just another choice.

The Forgotten Lie-in Game

A and B are in bed. A nudges B out of bed to make the coffee. B wanders off to the kitchen, and notices the time. B runs back to wake up A. They are both in a blind panic – rushing about trying to get dressed. They run to the front door and see the Sunday papers on the mat. They realise what day it is, and go back to bed.

That's the bare bones of a scenario inspired by a Franca Rame play. You can play any one of the events in a variety of different ways. You could play the most obvious and predictable states of tension, which would be something like: A and B are in bed ('Exhausted'). A nudges B out of bed to make the coffee ('One Movement at a Time'). B wanders off to the kitchen ('Laid Back') and notices the time ('Is There a Bomb in the Room?'). This would be a literal reading of the action. But you can throw this scenario in the air, and really provoke the situation so as to make something more interesting and more surprising. Try being more random in your choice of tension states: A and B are in bed ('Is There a Bomb in the Room?'). A nudges B out of bed to make the coffee ('One Movement at a Time'). B wanders off to the kitchen ('The Bomb is About to Go Off!'). And notices the time ('Exhausted'). In this game, your job is just to put the cat amongst the pigeons and to provoke each other. If you're excited enough by the provocation, you'll come up with something that's going to take everyone by surprise, and between you, you'll find a different reading of the scene that's way beyond the obvious.

Now you're messing about with meaning. These physical reference points that you're throwing round the room are only vague implications of different levels of emotional engagement. They're not emotions, and they don't have any meaning until they've been placed in a dramatic context. The next stage in the above exercise is to complete the dramatic context of the scene. In the Forgotten Lie-In Game, all you're doing is using different rhythms to inspire different readings of the same action. You can apply the same process to a piece of text, and open it up in much the same way. You can provoke some audacious choices this way that are impossible to find in any other process. But the most liberating thing about working like this is that if you don't like one choice, you can always change your mind and try another. You might be fully engaged, but you haven't spent any time on it. There hasn't been weeks of research or hours of analysis and discussion, so it's easy to disregard a bad idea in favour of something else. But this is only the start. The discussion and the analysis will come later. This is a process for generating surprises and possibilities.

The best actors of my acquaintance have an extraordinary rhythmic agility, and I'm not just talking of young actors here. Even those who can no longer throw themselves across the space and have never heard of Lecoq, and whose idea of a warm-up is a quick fag and an anecdote, can often demonstrate phenomenal ability to flip from one rhythm to another without even moving from a chair. How we arrive at the various rhythms in the end is down to personal process.

The Thinking Game

A sits on the floor, resting against the wall, so that the back and head are fully supported and comfortably still. The game is for A to go to any tension state that B requests with as little movement as possible.

It's easier than you might think; it's astonishing how expressive the eyes, the breath and the set of the face can be. There's the potential for real intensity here. In fact, most people playing tend to work too hard at first. The lesson is not to worry about how you're going to realise a particular tension state, but rather to trust that you can. The thought of 'Is there a bomb in the room?' is enough to trigger the rhythm in your entire body without any conscious intervention from you. After all, you're only doing something that you do every moment of your waking life. All you're doing here is playing different tension states to order.

If you start from trying to see how little you can get away with, there are a number of ways B can provoke you. In the first instance, B can challenge the speed of your transitions by hardly giving you any time to dwell on one state, before going to another, although it helps if B gives you a signal that one state has been established before moving on. This game is more satisfying to play if B provokes A with rapid changes whilst A is explaining how to make an omelette, or giving some other detailed instructions. Now there's a lot more to play with. Now B must listen to the text, and find appropriate moments for each transition. As always, there are choices. B can either help or hinder; either the provocation will be a logical development of what has gone before, or it's going to be a huge challenge. As A, you should try to react rather than to justify what you're doing. Once you've got a text to play, all your choices are put in a context. Now issues of credibility are much more pronounced; you have logic and subtext and meaning to contend with, and if your physicality was crude before, it won't be any better now. If your work looks imposed, you've blown it, but keep going. There are always going to be good bits and bad bits.

Another variation of the game is to try to amplify each rhythm:

The game starts as before, only in this version B gets very close to A when provoking the transitions, as if they're engaged in a very intimate conversation, with A whispering to B. As the game progresses, B moves further away from A who remains still against the wall. There comes a point when B can't see A's transitions very clearly, so A is compelled to speak louder, and to move slightly more.

The game can be played to the point where A is strutting about the space in full voice, and B is right over the other side of the room, still provoking one transition after another. Of course if B starts to walk towards A, then the reverse happens, and the rhythms start to get smaller and smaller.

If you approach acting and theatre-making from the outside in, as I do most of the time, then Lecoq's cycle of tension states is a bit like a compass to a navigator. If you're making a scene from scratch, the more you have to play, and the easier it is to generate ideas and develop action. The tension states give names, definitions and descriptions to key rhythms that we all employ at every moment of our lives. If you have little experience in playing with rhythm, then this cycle is an excellent means of finding a clear connection between rhythm and feeling. So much physical comedy arises from playing inappropriate rhythms, or from making huge transitions, such as from 'Exhausted' to 'The Bomb is About to Go Off!', or from 'Neutral' to 'Rigor Mortis', or 'Is there a Bomb in the Room?' to 'There *Is* a Bomb in the Room!' Tension is the substance of rhythm, and rhythm is the substance of physical comedy. To play huge rhythmic transitions like these, you have to be able to play with tension creatively. We'd have a much more physical tradition of acting and theatre-making if our drama schools taught us how to play with tension, and how to manipulate it, rather than seeing tension as the universal enemy of effective acting.

Rhythm is another one of those universals that runs through every aspect of our lives. Our sensitivity to rhythm is part and parcel of our skills in non-verbal communication. It's a skill that's wired in to our brains, and it's part of our built-in survival package. Rhythm carries thought and meaning. It lulls us to sleep, and it wakes us up again. It informs us that all is well, and warns of impending danger.

If you're alone in the house and a friend or a member of the family comes in, you'll know, within seconds, who it is by the sounds they make as they move about the house. If you know them well you'll also be able to tell what mood they're in. Your ability to do this boils down to your sensitivity to rhythm. Of course, rhythm isn't the only clue. I don't suppose that there are that many variations of who might come into your house, unannounced. If you heard a stranger open the front door and come in, the unusual rhythm would put all your faculties on red alert. You'd be alarmed because you'd have no image in your head of who that person might be.

But if it's someone you know, their familiar rhythms as they move about will conjure up a picture of them doing something in their particular way. In your mind's eye you'll see them throwing their bags down and hanging their coat up. In this context, rhythm is shorthand for evoking images, and the feelings associated with knowledge gained from past experiences. The more background knowledge we bring to the rhythms we hear, the more eloquent those rhythms become. If the detail is patchy, then we have an immense capacity for filling in the gaps for ourselves. I can recognise every member of my family by how they run down the stairs or open the fridge. Even the way they come into the room will tell me what mood they're in.

In the film of *Moby Dick* (1956), with Gregory Peck as Captain Ahab, our first encounter with him is by means of a rhythm. The sight of the worried sailors cowering in the forecastle, listening to the step, thump, step, thump, as Ahab paces the deck above them with his peg leg, offers a chilling premonition of the man before we've even seen him. With no images to put to this outlandish rhythm, we conjure up a monster in our minds as soon as we hear it. If we were to hear him suddenly slip and fall over, of course, it would be hysterical. Then the monster in our heads would become idiotic, and our laughter would come as a huge relief. In drama as in life, rhythm encapsulates meaning, but in comedy, rhythm manipulates meaning ruthlessly.

Internal and External Rhythm

I distinguish between two types of rhythm: internal and external rhythm. External rhythm is anything that you can clap, or consciously move about to. Internal rhythm is any rhythm that you feel, and unconsciously move about to. If you dance to a musical beat or walk like a robot, we'll see the rhythm you're playing, so it's an external rhythm. Of course, internal rhythms also inspire movement, but in this case the movement is not so obvious. For example, if you go into a bar, and there's raunchy rock 'n' roll playing, you'll probably find yourself standing in a slightly different way than you would if the bar were playing Bach or Mozart. If you go over to the bar, in the rock 'n' roll pub, you'll probably find that you'll walk slightly differently, and place your order in a slightly different way. These changes are unlikely to be the result of a conscious choice – you just find yourself moving like this. This is the effect of an internal rhythm. You're not dancing – so much as walking with an attitude, and it's the music that's given you that attitude. All music has the capacity to change our élan, in the sense of a change in your state of physical intensity when you're just about to do something. It could be anything: an athlete on the blocks, just before the gun goes off at the start of a race, or a diver just about to leap off the high board to do a triple somersault. Both these examples have a level of physical intensity – an élan. It's sometimes referred to as pre-expressivity, a quality of intensity that implies that something is about to happen. It's a moment that's particularly watchable because it's full of anticipation and potential meaning. Somebody standing on the deck of a ship, feeling seasick, would have a very different élan from an angry mother threatening to slap her child, or somebody about to sneeze, or to smile, or burst into tears. Internal rhythm is expressed through subtle changes in our physical intensity. External rhythm is more obvious. We can see it, we can clap it, and it's much easier to copy. Here are a few games in using external rhythm.

The Counting Game

Take an action like making a phone call in a public telephone box. A does the action and B claps a regular rhythm (about a beat per second). As A, the game is to restrict yourself to one gesture per beat, without losing the logic of where you are in the action.

Here we see an action dominated by an external rhythm. Each beat is marked by a fixed point in the movement, that breaks up the natural flow of the action – a bit like silent-movie acting. The more you play this game, the stronger each gesture becomes, and the more economical the action becomes. The restriction of the beat leaves you no time to do anything irrelevant to the job in hand, and the action becomes clear, simple and direct.

An interesting variation is to play the game in threes, with one person clapping the rhythm and the other two playing about to start a fight, or one person trying to console the other. Now every fixed point will define an image: the situation will appear heightened, and the narrative will be clearer. Another variation of the same game is for two people to play contrasting rhythms.

I once made an interesting scene about an old lady being taken out for a walk by her helper. The old lady moved in a slow regular rhythm that, in rehearsal, she counted out for herself: 1-2-3-4-stop. 1-2-3-4-stop. Whilst the helper moved in rapid little triplets of 1,2,3, stop, 1,2,3, stop, 1,2,3, stop – every time the old lady reached her fixed point. So, the effect was something like: 1-2-3-4-stop (old lady) – 1,2,3, stop, 1,2,3, stop, 1,2,3, stop (the helper) then 1-2-3-4-stop (old lady). All they were doing was putting her coat on and going out for a walk, but the crude external rhythms created images of dependency, pain, and discomfort, as well as giving the action a parodic quality. It was a bit like a cartoon: the action was funny, and engaging at the same time.

Regular rhythms lull us to sleep. We need surprises in the rhythm to keep us awake. Surprises make us think, and sharpen our awareness. The most dramatic rhythms are irregular. In the scene with the old lady, we found surprises when we broke the rhythm, and I invited them to find the game of only having one person moving at a time, whilst continually trying to catch each other out. Occasionally the old lady might play: 1-stop, and the helper would be thrown into confusion, and play: 1,2,3, stop, 1,2,3, stop, 1,2,3, stop. Then, in response, the old lady might play: 1-2-3-4-5-6-7-8-9-stop.

Imagine the rhythm of a frightened horse being led into a horsebox. It's a disturbing arrhythmic sound as the hooves stamp the boards of the trailer. Arrhythmic rhythms keep our attention and keep us alert. They're unpredictable and occasionally alarming.

I learnt the following game from Monica Pagneux. It's an excellent game for developing complicity in a large group, but I use it to teach rhythm.

The Rope Game

Two people swing a rope, between them like children playing a skipping game. Only here the game is to run under the rope without touching it.

It is as much about listening as it is about watching. To safely clear the rope, you have to run immediately after the 'tap' of the rope on the floor. It generally doesn't take long to get a clear round with the whole group running under the rope one by one: once everyone has tuned into the idea of listening to the rhythm of the rope slapping the floor and established a 'tap – run' response. In other words, you run on cue, rather than trying to think about it. Once you've found your complicity with the rope, there are innumerable variations. Try running under the rope in pairs, try holding hands with one of you running with their eyes closed, try both of you running under the rope with your eyes closed. This always sounds a bit of a challenge at first, but this is the part of the game that takes us to the substance of working with external rhythm. Once you try the game working with a partner, you not only listen to the rope, but you've also got to become aware of your partner at the same time. You've got to find complicity with each other. With every tap of the rope you'll feel a shift in intensity in your partner, in their stillness, and their breathing will change. Your job is to interpret those changes in relation to the intention of running under the rope.

The more sophisticated development of the Rope Game at this stage is for two people to play an argument about going under the rope. The game becomes more intense if you genuinely tease each other, whilst listening to the 'tap, tap' of the rope on the floor, and try to trick the other person into running under the rope before you do:

A. *After you – go on.*

B. *No, after you. I'd hate to rush things.*

(B *makes to run under the rope. A follows, then B suddenly stops.*)

A. *Come on then – go!*

(A *makes to run, then stops.*)

B. *OK – after you.*

The text will probably be the last thing you'll be thinking about. Now you've got to watch the rope, and watch each other at the same time. You're looking for the slightest physical clue; the slightest change in élan indicating that your partner is going to make a dash for it, and catch you out. The next development of this game is to tease each other but end up with both of you running under the rope at the same time. This is an excellent test of rhythm and complicity.

The Entrance Game

This is a game that applies the skills of the Rope Game to a dramatic context. It's about timing an entrance.

Set up a fairly robust dramatic situation such as A and B are about to have a fight, or they're trying to steal something from a room. Once the scene is underway, I set up the Rope Game to the side of the playing space. The job of the people swinging the rope is to tap out the rhythm of the scene. This is much easier to do than you might think. Just listen to the scene, and keep experimenting with the rhythm until you find one that fits. C stands ready to run under the rope to make an entrance into the scene and either stop the fight or prevent the theft.

It's C's entrance that I find particularly fascinating in this game. After running under the rope, C bursts on and a new surge of energy fills the stage. The 'tap – run' principle makes C enter on the off-beat, which has the effect of lifting the élan of C's entrance if, as C, you discard the rope, and clap the external rhythm of the scene, and then make your entrance on the beat, you won't come bursting on, the energy won't lift, and you'll have a more gentle presence in the scene. Off-beat entrances tend to have a stronger élan than those made on the beat. I think it's because an off-beat entrance is more of a surprise for us, offering a syncopation in an otherwise predictable pattern.

Internal and external rhythms are easily transposable. You can watch a sad scene and clap the appropriate rhythm. This is an external rhythm. Alternately, you can clap the rhythm, then stop clapping and still hear it in your head. This would be an internal rhythm. When you play an external rhythm, you're using the specific beats to drive you along: to make you move faster or slower than you would normally. You have to be ruled by the rhythm completely – to the point where you're almost out of control. In playing with internal rhythm, you've got to be prepared to let the beat inform your feelings, and you're not so much governed by the beat as exploiting it as you like. If you play the Counting Game where a driving 1-2, 1-2, 1-2, 1-2 rhythm is being tapped out for you, and the set-up is a situation where two people are just trying to be polite to each other, you'll soon feel the external rhythm beginning to push you a little too far. Conversely, if you try to play a chase scene to a slow waltz time, the slow incongruous beat will compel you to fill each gesture with meaning. If you try to play the rhythm without any meaning, you'll find yourself slipping towards dance. In life, we use internal and external rhythms all the time but our rhythm is only externalised in moments of crisis, or of great significance. Here are a few games involving internal rhythm.

The 'About to Dance' Game

Music is playing. It could be anything from Satie to Slade. A and B stand two metres apart. Their game is to maintain eye contact with each other and slowly approach each other with the intention of dancing to the music. The game is for A and B to rivet their whole attention to each other whilst the music is playing away in the background.

This isn't a game about dancing. Don't try to dance. This is a game about two people approaching each other with the intention of dancing. You don't even have to dance in the end. Just focus on your partner and put your partner's feelings before your own, and don't worry about the action. Just gradually approach each other and listen to the music.

It's a game of complicity: complicity with each other, and complicity with the music. If you listen to the music whilst playing a simple action like this, you'll have all the time you need to negotiate how one another feels, and to know it's OK to move closer, and when it's OK to touch and to start to move together. It's astonishing how emotional such a simple game like this can be. The audience knows your intentions, while the music implies an interpretation of your intentions. We all expect you to go for an external rhythm and to start dancing, but you don't move, and your movement appears to have nothing to do with the music. We see that you're more interested in each another, but the more we watch you and listen to the music, the more it looks as if the music is driving you together, and as if it's expressing what you're really feeling. In moving so minimally whilst sustaining a clear intention to dance, you make us work much harder. We watch more and we listen more.

The Delegation Game

The game is to play some music, capture the internal rhythm of the music, and to improvise a speech, or to say a monologue, whilst sustaining the internal rhythm of the music.

Listen to the music and, without any conscious thought, let whatever impulses emerge. It might be little more than you breathing in a slightly different way or no more than you looking languidly round the room. Once you experience the subtle changes inspired by the music, if you keep listening to the music, it will give you a feeling of buoyancy, enabling you to keep afloat – to keep the action alive and interesting without doing very much at all. Now you can take your time, and let the action emerge in the way that seems fit.

These are basically delegation games where you give the responsibility for your actions over to the music. If the scene doesn't work, it's the fault of the music, and nothing to do with you.

I once had a group of acting students who really took to this work. They'd work in twos. A would play the music and B would let the élan of the music influence their physicality, and take them into the text. Once the text was being spoken in the manner inspired by the music, A would turn the volume down. If B were to lose the quality, A would turn the volume up again.

These students came up with some courageous choices. The game gave them great assurance. Suddenly they had time to pause, and find space in the action to play to the audience. The literal meaning of the text emerged quite effortlessly, and we discovered that Scott Joplin had some unique insights into Hedda Gabler.

The Musical Information Game

Some years ago when devising the opera, Arcane for Opera Circus, I was working with a company of performers, some of whom were musicians and some of whom weren't. In an attempt to level the playing field between those who could read the dots and those who couldn't, I invented a game that aimed to push this notion of internal rhythm about as far as possible.

A small group of non-musical performers stood blindfolded in the space, with strict instructions to wait until the music actually tells them what to do. 'Don't waffle,' I told them. 'Treat the music as a series of instructions. Just listen to what you think it's telling you to do and don't move until you are quite clear.'

Then, out of earshot of the performers, I told the musicians that they should tell the performers 'in music' that they are in the sea, and that there is a great storm, and they all drown, and go to heaven. 'Try to communicate the information as clearly as possible,' I told them emphatically, 'without resorting to illustrative quotations. Just keep repeating your directions until the performers understand. We want verbs rather than adjectives.'

The performers waited in their blindfolds, and the musicians started to play a short phrase, which to all of us watching spoke clearly of the sea. Gradually the performers started to move. One or two of them seemed to respond instantly, but others were slower off the mark. But the musicians were insistent, and played the phrase over and over. Eventually, the performers were all swirling about in a nautical storm. The 'dying' motif, and the 'going to heaven' motif, seemed to come more easily, probably because the texture of the music changed so dramatically, and maybe the sea music had already set up a logical storyline.

Once the game was over, the innate ambiguity of this musical language became more apparent. Those of us watching all shared the same context as the musicians, and we interpreted everything in the light of what we knew, but not all the performers thought it was about the sea. Some of them thought it was about mental breakdown. Others thought it was like being under an anaesthetic. We all agreed on the broad emotional strokes however: the feelings of foreboding, anxiety and desperate panic culminating in a sudden and blissful calm.

The ability of music to cut through our chattering minds is well documented. Philosophers tell us that music is the one art form most at peace with its own irreducibility. In other words, music can never be a report or an account of anything because it doesn't exist in relation to anything else that can be adequately discussed or described. Music is to be experienced for itself alone. This is why music is generally held to be the purest of the arts, and the closest to the sublime.

For the performers, the Musical Information Game was a lesson in responding instinctively to the music. Rather than worrying about 'getting it right', and following the score, and trying to calculate what's possible in the writing, this game puts you in a position where you've got no alternative but to react to what you hear. If we know that the music is trying to tell you that you're in the sea, then we'll read the slightest change in your physicality as your reaction to being in the sea. All you've got to work with is your personal response to the élan of the music, and it's astonishing how specific that élan can be. It's not unusual for three out of eight people, all working in blindfolds, to be doing remarkably similar things to the same musical phrase, at the same time.

Internal rhythms are more abstract and more ambiguous than external rhythms. Nobody really knows what they're doing in this game: the 'information' is the last thing on your mind. This is the disarmingly simple process of listening, and allowing your body to move. When I played the game myself, my 'interpretation' only struck me as being in any way significant to the game when I was asked what I was doing. Before then, I had no time to think about what I was doing. I was too busy doing it.

Music is the most atavistic language we have, and its power is spellbinding. It can make us rampage about the stage one minute, and go to sleep the next. It can soften like melting butter, and in the next instant, make us stand still with bated breath.

Once we really listen to music it becomes the strongest presence in the room. We can go with it, or we can deliberately work against it, but on stage, we ignore it at our peril.

Most meaning in our non-verbal communications is carried through the continual interaction of internal and external rhythms. In life, internal rhythms predominate. We spend most of our time absorbed in the subtle ambiguities, and delicate inferences created by equivocal moments of stillness and fleeting gestures. The delicate interactions played out as the couple tried to approach each other in the 'About to Dance' Game, for example, are absorbing because of their verisimilitude. It's the music that gives the scene its theatricality. The predominance of the internal rhythm and the preoccupation that the couple seem to have with each other makes us think that the couple have abandoned the music completely. This is something that takes us by surprise, so we start to build our own connections between the action and the music and to generate our own meanings.

If 'the husband' or 'the wife' of one of the two people involved were to enter the scene, the spell would be broken, the stakes would be raised, and the situation would become more tense, more volatile. Then external rhythms would predominate. External rhythms are clear, direct and unequivocal. They're more like a top text, and they speak to us directly, whereas internal rhythms are more like a subtext. On stage, and particularly in conventional farce and physical comedy, external rhythms predominate. Look at any clip from *Fawlty Towers,* and you'll see Basil Fawlty strutting about with his customary air of ludicrous self-importance, Manuel looking hesitant and confused, Polly with her usual intelligent efficiency, and the potty old Major, always dignified and bewildered. These are all external rhythms, and we read them at a glance. The atmosphere of *The Office* or *The Royle Family* is, by comparison, very different. Because they're billed as comedies, we expect the conventional shorthand of the bold rhythmic statements to tell us what's going on, but we don't get it. Instead, the internal rhythms of mundane dullness are allowed to predominate, and to the uninitiated, it looks as if nothing much is happening. In reality it's a simple case of there being more subtext than top text.

Young actors, in my experience, have no difficulty with external rhythms. It's much easier to get them to run about like axe-wielding psychopaths than it is to get them to do nothing, and just let the situation breathe. This is why the use of music in the Delegation Game, and the 'About to Dance' Game is so useful. Internal and external rhythms work together, antagonistically, rather like the muscles in the body; we need both types of rhythm because they're complementary and mutually supportive. Most comic timing comes from the manipulation of external rhythm but most of the substance, the empathy, the depth of content, and the humanity in any interaction comes from the way we use internal rhythm.

Rhythm and Emotion

Psychologists have been fascinated by emotion since the early nineteenth century. At the turn of the last century, two psychologists, working quite independently – William James in America, and Carl Lange in Denmark – reached the same conclusions in their study of human emotions. They both agreed that we know very little about emotion, and that it's only the symptoms of an emotion that we can talk about with any degree of certainty. They cited the example of someone stepping off the kerb into the path of a passing car, and suddenly leaping back out of the way. They argued that these feelings of shock were experienced after the jump, and they concluded that 'the jump' provoked the symptoms of shock as much as the incident itself. And so the 'fright-flight syndrome' was born.

Whilst working in Bali, I remember watching a masked dancer playing to a group of children in the street. He would dance to the music of a gamelan blaring out of a battered old ghetto blaster. His masked face would look very shy and coy, so the children would tentatively advance towards him, some giggling, some crying, and others literally trembling in fear. Then, without warning, he'd rush forward and capture one of them. Of course they'd all scream and scatter. But the ones who ran the fastest, and got away, always looked more frightened than the child who got caught. The victim was given a penny, then he'd run back to join the others, and the game would begin again. It was a 'fright-flight syndrome' game. Those kids loved the sensation of being scared to death, and then being rewarded for their efforts. According to the James/Lange theory, the action of running away made them more frightened than the sight of a man in a mask running towards them. If you display the symptoms of breathing heavily, and making rapid eye movements, and looking tense, I might recognise these characteristics as being the symptoms of fear, and if I were to imitate your symptoms, I could generate the similar feeling of 'fear' for myself.

What psychologists call symptoms, I call rhythms, and to a theatre-maker like me these ideas are particularly dynamic because I don't need to know anything about your background, and I don't need to ransack any painful emotional memories, in an attempt to recreate your symptoms. I've just got to copy your rhythm as accurately as I can. So, if you're smiling mischievously, and I copy your mischievous smile, I too will begin to feel mischievous. Similarly, if you're sitting quietly, and feeling near to tears, and I copy your stillness, your breathing pattern, and your facial expression, I too will end up feeling near to tears. Copying induces empathy, and we have an immense capacity for putting ourselves into other people's shoes. Watch any audience during a tense dramatic scene, and notice how many people are mirroring the tensions and facial expressions of the actors. Copying can make an emotional response contagious.

Over the years, other psychologists have concluded that emotional response is more complex than James and Lange would have us believe; the idea that our emotions have their roots in physical symptoms doesn't constitute a full picture. After all, their theory was proposed while investigations into the transmission of nerve impulses were still in their infancy. By the 1920s it was observed, for example, that paraplegics still experience emotional responses although they might be devoid of any feeling in the muscles, and be unable to move at all. It was also observed that emotional experiences tend to affect us quicker than physiological changes do, and also that many of the same physiological changes occur in a number of different emotional states. In the sixties, Stanley Schachter observed that we tend to recognise a particular emotional state as much by its context as its characteristic rhythm. In other words, I might see that you're looking tense, and sweating, and breathing quickly, and displaying rapid eye movements, but I would only conclude that these were the symptoms of 'terror' with any confidence if I saw that there was somebody pointing a gun at your head. The sight of the gun to the head establishes the context: the context would tell me you were terrified, and the symptoms would only confirm my interpretation. Similarly, if I observed the same symptoms except that this time I were to see a note and an empty bottle of pills on the table, I might conclude that you were attempting suicide, and that it was the drugs you had just taken that had induced your symptoms.

Schachter called this phenomenon 'cognitive labelling'; in the context of playing comedy and making theatre, his idea has very important implications. It's pointless, for example, trying to work out how to play jealousy if you're playing Othello. The play tells us that this is the story of a man consumed with jealousy so we already know all that. The situations and the plot label anything Othello does as an act of jealousy. So if he enters looking laid back and casual, for example, we'll read those 'symptoms' as an attempt to hide his true feelings with a show of cool. If Othello looks agitated then we'll probably conclude that he's losing his self-control, and perhaps he's going mad – with jealousy. In short, the writer has done everything for us. In *True and False*, David Mamet expresses this idea perfectly:

66 *When the performance is made truthful, the work of the writer is made something more than the words on the page, not by the inventiveness, but by the courage of*

the actors. Yes, it might seem like a good and attractive idea to embellish — it's your job to resist that attractive idea; for you cannot both 'guide' the performance, and keep your attention and will on accomplishing your objective on stage. The impulse to help it along, 'to add a bit of emotion' or 'behaviour' is a good signpost — it means you are being offered — in resisting it — the possibility of greatness. Invent nothing. Deny nothing. Develop that hard habit. **"**

This is an honest and refreshing look at acting that demystifies what's going on, and keeps things firmly within the realm of common sense. He could be talking about neutrality when he says, 'Invent nothing. Deny nothing', but this isn't the full picture. This is the opinion of a writer in a writer's theatre. I've spent most of my life working in an actor's theatre, where things are made from scratch. If we have a text to work from, we treat it as a provocation, and not the Ten Commandments. David Mamet isn't particularly interested in making comedy, farce or 'stylised' dramatic literature. He writes acutely observed American dramas firmly rooted in their time and place, and if you want to go beyond this level of recognition towards the visceral and the bizarre, then you have to find stronger levels of engagement, and display more serious 'symptoms' just to meet the demands of the written text. Physical comedy transcends personal experience, and it's rarely, if ever, all contained on the page.

Schachter's cognitive labelling, and David Mamet's insistence on the absolutism of the text are seductive ideas, particularly if you're a playwright, and particularly if you're preoccupied with writing plays that are like life, as opposed to being better than life, worse than life, or not like life at all. I agree with David Mamet that it's simplistic and reductive to talk about playing emotions. Regrettably, most playwrights aren't as good as he is. Surprisingly few new writers, in my experience, are capable of writing a script where the text is saying one thing, whilst the action is saying something else. The vast majority of new writers are oblivious to the importance of action in the first place. I prefer the ambiguities of the situational approach, and I'd rather deduce what your feelings might be from my reading of the situation, than run the risk of you demonstrating what I should feel. We find more credibility in our own conclusions than in anything that's spelled out for us. Ambiguity is often more dynamic than precision and accuracy. If I read what you do as terror, and you call it passion, then that to me is an acceptable degree of latitude. At least we'll have something to talk about at the end of the play.

Emotions run very high in comedy. Physical comedy and intense drama deal with similar extremes, with situations that take alarming twists and turns, where, as a performer, you have to learn to 'turn on a six-pence' and be kicked from one extreme to another. You might be supremely confident one minute, and quaking with fear the next, then jubilant, then full of remorse, then completely dumbfounded. It can be an emotional rollercoaster of boldly clashing external rhythms. At its best, comedy pushes life to the limits, but if we're going to laugh then we've got to believe it. So what constitutes theatrical credibility?

The 'I've Got a New Lover' Game

This is the game of playing a rapid sequence of contrasting rhythms without pause or reflection – one after the other.

A says 'I've got a new lover' over and over again, with a different external rhythm every time the line is spoken. For example, A might start by saying the line with the rhythm of pride, then saying it with the rhythm of fear, then terror, then joy, then reason, panic, eroticism, agony, despair, pleasure, aestheticism, violence – the list can go on and on.

This game probably goes back to the *Commedia dell' Arte*. We can hardly describe these brief physical states as being different 'emotions'. They're crude physical rhythms – that's all. Yet in the context of that single line of text, the crude physicality comes alive. There's ambiguity here. We're not being given everything on a plate. We have to work, to draw our own conclusions. We won't empathise with you particularly, but we'll admire your skill and enjoy the surprises.

This is little more than a game of agility, and our interest lies in seeing the different rhythms played one after the other in a continuous flow, and the effect is bizarre, and curiously uplifting. But the game is only effective if each rhythm is fully engaged. There's no room for subtlety here. This is a game that you can play with almost any sentence you like: 'I'm going to die', 'I'm changing sex', or even 'I'm going to my mother's.' It works in almost any context.

If you're fully engaged with the rhythm then we'll read that rhythm as recognisable human behaviour, but you could hardly call it verisimilitude. It's decidedly worse than life; it's a cartoon representation of a state of mind, but it's still emotionally credible. David Mamet's epigram 'Invent nothing. Deny nothing' doesn't apply here. Those contrasting rhythms, and that physical intensity, are all 'invented'. We're dealing with performance here, rather than dramatic literature. This game probably evolved before plays were written down.

Rhythmic agility enables us to play vast changes of 'emotion' with more alacrity. It doesn't rule out the work of the playwright at all; on the contrary, it gives the writer a bigger canvas to work on. Rhythmic agility gives you the ability to skip effortlessly from one rhythm, or one emotion, to another; it enables you to transcend personal experience, and ultimately play on a much bigger scale, without losing your credibility. The text does the labelling, leaving you free to play the rhythms.

In his book *The Act of Creation*, Arthur Koestler said that there are only two types of emotion: 'active emotions' and 'passive emotions'. Rage, joy or euphoria, he would describe as 'active emotions'; he'd describe feelings like nostalgia, or aesthetic appreciation as 'passive emotions'. He could just as easily have been talking about internal and external rhythms.

Timing

Punctuating the Rhythm

I was running a development workshop for a new play, *Happy Birthday, Mister Deka D.* by Biyi Bandele (Told by an Idiot, 1997), and we were exploring a moment in the play when an old man, sitting stock-still, in a dilapidated old pub, not having moved, or spoken a word to anybody, suddenly got up, stumbled across the bar, and went into the gents. That's all the action was. One of the cast played his version, and we all laughed, then another member of the group got up, and played another idea, and we laughed again. Then the first person had another idea, and then somebody else had another. It was hysterical. 'We only need one idea for the moment,' I remember saying, but by now the blood was up and they were experimenting with the walk, with negotiating the steps, and with the toilet doors. 'Does he know where the gents' toilet is?' they asked. We must have spent over an hour, exploring different permutations of how this old man might get up and walk over to the lavatory, and thinking about the implications that each idea might have on the scene.

All these actors were expert in their use of timing. An outsider would think that they were playing for laughs, I'm sure – but in reality they were bashing the meaning of that scene round the room with the skill and commitment of a tennis player. In the end we didn't use any of the ideas we came up with that day, because we found others later in rehearsal. Comic timing is the sort of thing you learn on the job. It tends not to get taught at drama school, but then comedy gets a pretty bad press in most of our institutions. Timing is the sort of knowledge that's passed on through an oral tradition: 'That was a fantastic double take,' someone might say, and you sort of know what they mean, or: 'If you do a reversal there – you'll get a laugh,' some old hand might tell you. Esoteric jargon? Perhaps, but timing devices like these are invaluable, not just in making comedy, but in making theatre in general. We articulate meaning through our timing, and we time a line or an action by deflecting, stopping, or changing the rhythm. It's all about stops, turns, interruptions, and sudden surprises; delicate punctuation marks that articulate what we really mean.

The Fixed Point

If you're walking round an art gallery, and an exhibit takes your attention for some reason, you'll probably go to a fixed point. In other words you'll stop moving because you're lost in thought. Alternately, if you've just said something emphatic in an argument, or if you've lost your temper completely, and you slam the cupboard door, or drop your briefcase on the floor, you'll probably finish with a fixed point for emphasis. A fixed point is a brief stop in your movement – it might be little more than half a second in length – but that's an adequate amount of time to make your meaning clear. A fixed point is like a full stop at the end of a sentence. You'd use it if you were giving someone detailed instructions, or if you were trying to justify your actions to somebody. We use fixed points instinctively in all our non-verbal communications. They mark the end of a unit of information, or the start of a significant action. They tell us when something is important.

We use fixed points more consciously in the theatre than we do in life, because in theatre we're more conscious in our manipulation of meaning. Occasionally we use them to visually underline the importance of an object. For example, if you were giving a huge bunch of flowers to someone, you could hold the flowers at arm's length, towards the person who is to receive them, then keep the bouquet at a fixed point, and bend your arm, as you walk towards them. This isn't a natural gesture at all, and by keeping the flowers at a fixed point, you'd be giving the flowers themselves more significance than the act of giving them, and in the right circumstances this could be a good choice. Once you know the function of fixed points and the effect they have on what you say or do, they become indispensable tools in the way you make meaning.

The Fixed Point Game

A and B meet, shake hands, and take off their coats as they enter a café. Either of them, at any point, can stop and look at the other, then continue with the action. The game is to see to what extent A and B can build an atmosphere between them, in complete silence, just using fixed points.

If you go to a fixed point whilst looking at someone, that person will probably set you thinking: 'What's happening here?' You won't know what it is, so you'll probably end up getting very irritated, and so an atmosphere will start to build up between you. If you play the same game with exactly the same action, only this time it's two romantic lovers, or an assassin and victim, or a whore and her client, then the fixed points and the atmospheres will take on an entirely different meanings.

The Suspension

If a fixed point is like a full stop, then a suspension is like a comma. We use them when we're interested in something, but not so interested that we actually stop. Take the art exhibition example again: if you see something that interests you, just as you've decided that it's time to leave the gallery, you might glance at it and you might almost come to a stop, but your preoccupation with leaving the gallery is stronger than your desire to stop and look at the exhibit. That inclination to stop is a suspension. We punctuate most of our daily interactions with a combination of fixed points and suspensions. A suspension is an indication that the thought you've just had might be interesting, but it's not important enough to warrant a fixed point.

The 'Find the Scene' Game

A and B approach each other, maintaining eye contact all the time. There is no conflict between them. If A goes to a suspension – goes to stop, making a subtle break in the rhythm – then B does the same. The game is to negotiate the suspensions between the two of them as they approach each other. When they get to about a metre apart, they keep a fixed space between them, and walk round each other in a complete circle, again with either person going to a suspension whenever they like.

There may be no agreed conflict, but the suspensions say otherwise, and the movement pattern of two people slowly approaching each other, circling each other, and reacting to each other all the way, implies a definite conflict between them. In life, two people will only approach each other, and circle each other if they're about to fight, or if there's a sexual intention of some kind. Having circled round each other, they're free to move about the space in any way they like. The game is to try to prevent the action from peaking to a confrontation, and to avoid a fight. The suspension implies that something is about to happen, and it's generally more interesting to maintain this suspense and this ambiguity than it is to submit to violence, which marks the end of the interaction and the subtle play between you.

A series of suspensions, like a series of fixed points, will build up a very strong atmosphere. The main difference between suspensions and fixed points is that fixed points tend to be more definite and confrontational. As the game progresses, fixed points will probably creep in, but it's more difficult to resolve the conflict if you rely on them too much.

The Comic Stop

If your body twitches in a sudden short jolt, as if you'd just experienced an electric shock, and then you recover, without comment, you'll have played a comic stop. It's an elaborate fixed point, but it's far too big and over the top to be taken seriously. It's not so much a stop as an abrupt surge of tension, and it's funny because it shows us a brief moment when you're out of control. You can't plan or choreograph a comic stop. It's too bizarre for that, and it's pointless trying to copy anybody else's way of playing it. It's a device that requires you to put yourself out of control for about a second at the most, and then to continue as if nothing had happened. The impulse is so sudden, and so intense that it appears to take you unawares, and it seems to work at its best when it looks as if you don't even know that you've done it.

I tend to introduce comic stops by getting people to play sudden violent twitches on command. The game is to twitch the whole body every time I clap or bang a drum. It's astonishing the number of variations you can find on this theme. Some people can generate such a powerful jolt that it makes them leap in the air; others are more subtle and contained. We're looking for instinctive movement here; we'll know immediately if your movement is pre-meditated or imposed. The game is to try to catch yourself unawares, so that your body is relaxed, or preoccupied with something else, when you move. The more relaxed the body is before that stop, the greater the impact of this sudden bizarre physicality is likely to be.

The Name Game

A and B have a conversation. Every time either of them says the other person's name, that person has to play a comic stop. So a line like, 'Oh, John, John, John, John. What are we going to do with you, John?' would inspire a series of comic stops which make John look ridiculous by emphasising the significance of his name, to the extent that it might look as if John was really a false name and that he's an impostor.

Comic stops are an excellent device for emphasising anything. There's another version of the Name Game where you play a stop every time your partner mentions sex, or money – anything that might make you feel angry or guilty or uncomfortable. I remember the actor Richard Kats using this device to great effect when playing the evil Abanazar in *Aladdin*. Every time somebody mentioned 'the lamp' or 'Aladdin', no matter what he was doing, or who he was talking to, he'd play a comic stop. It ludicrously clarified his intensions, making him look stupid in our eyes, and his duplicity so transparent.

The Drop

This is the biggest stop of all: here you stop everything. A fixed point is a brief moment of stillness that indicates a significant change of thought. A comic stop indicates an excessive personal reaction to an incident that is so extreme that it looks bizarre. The drop is an abrupt abandonment of everything about the scene. It's the strongest interruption possible in an action. It's a brief abandonment of the scene and draws our attention to you, the actor, looking at us, the audience; and it's an opportunity for the action to start afresh. There's an audacity to the drop if you use it well. Use it crudely, and we'll hate you for it. Clowns use this device a lot, as a sort of rescue strategy, when their attempts to make us laugh come to nothing. But the drop isn't the sole preserve of the clown; it's the strongest means of indicating a realisation.

At the press night of *Happpy Birthday, Mister Deka D* at the Traverse Theatre in Edinburgh, about five minutes into the action, the actor Paul Hunter walked downstage and casually scooped a cigarette lighter off the table – at least it would have been a casual scoop had the lighter not slipped out of his hand, slid along the floor, then fallen down between the floorboards and out of sight. Press nights are always rather tense and self-conscious affairs, and a blatant misfortune like this didn't help anyone, but as soon as we all heard the lighter clunk to the floor under the stage, Paul just relaxed, stood there, and looked at us, as if to say: 'Can you believe it?' He was playing a drop. There was no acting here; he simply acknowledged what had happened, and his honesty broke the tension. It was an audacious thing to do, to step out of the play for a moment and look at us like that, but it worked perfectly. The audience erupted in laughter and applause, everybody was let off the hook, and Paul was able to carry on with the play. If you use them sensitively, drops can be very powerful because they're a frank declaration of what's happening, but they're not always funny. I remember researching the theme of domestic violence for a play, and we made a scene where a woman put a plate of food on the table for her husband, but the food had gone cold. The husband just felt the plate, played a drop to the audience, then punched her in the face. Drops are an intimate moment of complicity with the audience, and when used in a violent context like this they can be profoundly shocking.

Comic Timing

Timing is the art of convincing us that you're changing your mind, and you do this by playing games that activate two opposing dynamics: the 'Yes' Game, and the 'No' Game. All timing can be broken down to how you play with these polar opposites. For example, let's take a simple complicity game.

The Jumping Game

The game is for a group of people to run about a space, and every time two people find eye contact, they both have to jump in the air at the same time. We looked at this game when exploring complicity, but it's also very useful for investigating 'Yes' or 'No'.

To turn this into a simple timing game, you've got to try to put each other 'in the shit', and to do that, you'll to have to maintain your eye contact, go to a fixed point, then one of you will play a 'Yes, we're going to' movement, and the other will copy it tentatively, then immediately play a 'No, we're not going to' movement, and from then on, both of you will negotiate the various feints and surprises until the moment of the final jump. If you play the game hard, and genuinely take each other by surprise, the interaction will have an actuality all of its own, and be completely credible.

The dynamics of the 'Yes' and the 'No' are the two most important elements we have to work with in comic timing, and they're remarkably eloquent.

The 'Yes' Game

Suppose you want to play a simple action such as: you walk to the centre of the stage, look at the audience, and then walk off again. If you give that action the intonation of 'Yes, that's quite comfortable', or 'Yes, I feel quite good about that', by saying the line in your head as you do the movement, then your rhythm will become assured and direct, and you'll probably end up playing the movement with considerable neutrality.

If you change the intonation of the movement, and change the line to 'Yes, I quite like that. It's rather good,' then an element of conceit will creep in; a sort of confrontational jokiness, the way Stephen Fry might do it. If you change the intonation to anger by saying 'Yes, of course that's right. That's perfect. Yes. Like that, and that, and that!' in your head, then you'll end up strutting about the stage like Adolf Hitler.

Whatever your intonation, playing the 'Yes' Game is affirming, and empowering, and the closer it is to neutral, the more powerful it is. The closer you get to Stephen Fry or Adolf Hitler, the more we'll be waiting for the proverbial banana skin to take you down a peg or two. The movement inspired by the 'Yes' Game is invariably linked to our feeling of anticipation that something is going to happen. If you play it at the level of Stephen Fry or Adolf Hitler, you're just tempting fate, but at the level of neutrality, your movement will be so simple and direct, the 'Yes' Game so equitable and so balanced in its execution that we'll read the movement for what it is.

Kissing Aunt Mary

We've all had this experience as a child: an elderly relative comes to the house, and somebody says 'Go and kiss your Aunt Mary', and you dutifully do so. This is invariably a reluctant 'Yes'.

A walks towards B with the intention of kissing B on the cheek. The game here is to negotiate the 'Yes', and to see to what extent you can play this action with no story behind your movement.

The slightest hint of sexuality, or kookiness is instantly amplified in this game. The idea is to play the 'Yes' Game as comfortably as you can, right through to the conclusion of the movement. It's the start and the finish that are the most troublesome, and the slightest variation from neutral will be very amusing to watch because the more economical you are, the more obvious the slightest nuance of meaning is going to be. There are an infinite number of different intonations to the way you can play the 'Yes'.

The 'No' Game

Now play the same intention as before, only this time play the 'No' Game. In other words, as you walk to the centre of the stage, look at the audience, and walk off again, you say to yourself: 'No. I shouldn't be doing this. This is wrong. I shouldn't be here at all. No, this isn't for me.' Now every gesture will be dripping with conflict. Your rhythm will be irregular, and you'll look troubled, or vulnerable, or apologetic – anything but comfortable and assured.

The more you provoke somebody into playing the 'No' Game, the more they're likely to look psychotic. In life, anybody who plays the 'Yes' Game all the time, or the 'No' Game all the time is definitely peculiar, because one tempers the other. The 'No' Game reveals your doubts, your fears, and your insecurities, and when played against the 'Yes' Game, it can be read as endearing and empathetic. In other circumstances, the 'No' Game can also reveal your reasoning and your logic, but for the most part, it articulates conflict. Try running across the room, whilst playing not having a clue why you're running, and you'll encounter a huge conflict here. The run implies a very big 'Yes', but your lack of engagement in the run poses serious questions in our minds. Seeing these two dynamics, one against the other, is very funny. Here's an example:

A does the most innocuous action, like adjusting clothing, or moving a chair. The smallest action will be the most effective. B's game is to criticise everything that A does.

(A moves a chair.)

B. Don't do that.

A. (Moves the chair back.) Oh. All right then.

B. Look. Stop it. And don't look at me like that.

A. (Looks confused.) Sorry.

B. You're hopeless. Stand up straight. Look at you. I don't understand how you get through the day.

The important thing here is that A must play some reaction to every criticism; these reactions normally take the form of a small move back. There's always an element of the retreat in the 'No'. It's another example of 'There *Is* a Bomb in the Room!' It need not be much, but we want to see that A has taken the comment on board in some way, and the quality of the retreat implies how seriously they are taking it. B must be relentless with the criticism. The game is to reduce A to an inadequate mess.

The 'Yes/No' Game

A and B establish eye contact and start to play a simple action together such as going to shake hands or going to embrace each other. In the middle of the action, one of them says 'No', and the other immediately says 'No' as well. They might repeat saying 'No, No, No,' as if such a thing like embracing each other is completely out of the question, until one of them says 'Yes,' and the other says 'Yes', and so the action continues.

Saying 'Yes', and 'No' out loud is a good way to start, and it helps you to read each other's intentions, but the game is more interesting if you internalise the 'Yes' and the 'No'. If you both move forward on the 'Yes', in an attempt to play your objective more keenly, and back on the 'No' as if you're agreeing with each other's change of mind, you'll make your intentions very clear. It's a game of brinkmanship really. How far can you push either the 'Yes' or the 'No'? And to what extent can you surprise each other by switching suddenly from one to the other, or by both changing your minds at the same time?

Clearly there are two versions of the game. If you start by agreeing with each other, you'll build complicity between you. But the game will get even more interesting if occasionally you don't agree; then there are more opportunities to catch each other out, and to put each other 'in the shit'.

In moments of crisis, when something appalling has happened, and we're in a quandary, not knowing what to do, we veer between the 'Yes' and 'No' so quickly that we seem to oscillate between the two extremes. This movement becomes a self-perpetuating rhythm called 'Yes/No'. It's ambiguous and indeterminate. It can be deeply moving, or profoundly irritating, depending on the context. Somebody trying to inform a parent about the death of a child, for example, will probably drift into a 'Yes/No' quality just as easily as a person not knowing where to sit in a restaurant.

To play 'Yes/No' effectively you have to catch yourself out. If you could play it with an inner monologue it would be something like: 'I'll just sit there. Oh no, maybe there. Yes. That's better, but there's good, or there. No. Not there. There. No – yes – no – yes, there. No there.' It's an irregular rhythm. In fact irregularity is the key for playing 'Yes/No.' But to be able to oscillate between the two, you have to react sharply at the beginning of the action. The physical reaction is always so much quicker than your mental reaction that, in the end, speaking the thoughts won't help you here.

The 'Yes/No' Chorus

A good way to learn to play 'Yes/No' is to try it as part of a small chorus. As the chorus slows down the pace of the game, it reveals more fully how it works.

The chorus is seated on stage in a row, facing the audience. The game is for the chorus to determine, without any text, how polite it is for them to remain sitting in our company.

The more they try to work the problem out between them and us, the more the each new decision will start to run, in canon, up and down the group. A 'Yes/No' chorus is never stable, and never sure of itself, the irregular rhythm just keeps on going, and the action goes on developing its own logic.

I remember one group who couldn't decide if they should sit in our company, and they became increasingly embarrassed about it. Eventually, they got rid of the chairs, and then they felt that removing the chairs was even more discourteous to us, so they brought all the chairs back. Then they sat on the floor. Finally, they lost their temper, and tried to leave the stage, but they could never quite manage it. That's 'Yes/No': volatile in its indecision.

The Reluctant Lovers

A and B sit together side by side. Their objective is to make passionate love to each other there and then. The only problem is that they're both too nervous to do anything of the kind.

This is an excellent situation for 'Yes/No'. The objective is strong and clear, and so are the obstacles in the way, but to play the game well, it's important not to retreat too much. In other words, if A is going to kiss B on the mouth and pulls back too far, then the tension will drop. But if A only pulls back a little, the tension will hold, and since both mouths are so close together, the image is sustained, and the tension keeps rising as the action develops. When this game is played well, no action is ever completed, but both players push the action as far as they possibly can. A common fault is getting stuck in repetition. If this happens, I'd probably remind you to move the action on.

You might never be able to complete an action, but you can always find a way round to playing the next logical development of the action. It's as if you're so embarrassed at the prospect of making love that you're only going through the motions. Our interest lies in seeing a constantly evolving series of awkward and painful images. It's the pain of the situation that's captivating – not the sex. We laugh because it hurts, because it looks ridiculous, and because it's credible.

The Reversal

The reversal is the most basic device in comic timing, and it's one of the simplest to play. In fact, most timing devices have an element of the reversal in them. They crop up everywhere, in one form or another. Even Bergson's famous banana-skin incident is basically a reversal. The comic stop is a reversal. If you nonchalantly lean on a wall and suddenly get an electric shock, you'd do a reversal. If you were to inadvertently sit on a drawing pin, you'd do a reversal. It's an abrupt switch from the 'Yes' to the 'No', but a reversal only works if there's a real surprise to it. It's the clash between the comfort and the agony that takes us by surprise. The more comfortable you look when you go to lean on the wall, and the more violent your leap back when you get the shock, the more we're going to laugh. Most reversals are played from 'Yes' to 'No' because pain is more effective in generating comedy than pleasure. Pain tends to be more empathetic than pleasure, so going back to the idea that laughter is an 'OK signal', if we think one minute that you're genuinely hurt, then realise that there's nothing remotely wrong with you the next, and if your pain has touched us in some way, then we're likely to laugh even louder.

Rhythms indicative of pain like shock, agony or terror, tend to be more visceral than the more euphoric rhythms of joy or ecstasy.

The Reversal Game

Imagine that you're looking for something small and very valuable. You open one drawer after another in a state of great agitation. 'Is it here? No. Is it here? No. Here? No. Here? – No. No!' Then immediately, 'Yes!', and you leap about in sheer joy. For that reversal to work you're going to have to hit the 'Yes' very hard indeed to reach

*a rhythm that's going to be strong enough to contrast the 'No'
rhythms you started with. That 'Yes' will probably have to be
ecstatic. If you jump up and down with such euphoric delight that you
break the object you were looking for in the first place, that second
reversal would be much easier to play because the contrasting
rhythm is easier to find. It's very effective to play a reversal from 'No'
to 'Yes' if you're trying to conceal your euphoria. For example, if
you're looking for your immensely valuable object secretly and don't
want the person who's in the room with you to know what you're
doing, you can't just leap for joy when you find it. You have to
sublimate your euphoria, your 'Yes' rhythm will be more intense, and
will make a stronger contrast to the 'No' rhythm you'd started with.*

A reversal is a short sharp shock – an abrupt switch in feeling.
It's a reaction that we enjoy watching over and over. For
example, if you lean on the wall, and get an electric shock, then
immediately touch the chair, and get a shock from that, then
step back from the chair, and get a shock from the floor, you'll
make a short sequence of reversals; and, providing your reactions are credible, and you don't lose the contrast between the
'Yes' and the 'No', each repetition will be even more amusing
than the one before.

These chains of reversals are harder to play because you haven't time to
really play the 'Yes' between each shock for fear of losing the
momentum of the sequence. But if we don't see even a hint of the 'Yes',
you'll lose the contrast in your reaction.

The Slight

If a reversal is a sudden change of intention from 'Yes' to 'No', or from
'No' to 'Yes', then a slight is a subtle elision from one to the other. It's
a slide from one feeling to another. Sometimes it's hidden: like being
given a present which you think is going to be something you'd really
like but when you take the wrapping off, you realise that it's something
you don't want at all, but you don't want to hurt the feelings of the
person who's just given it to you. On other occasions it's declared.
Then we want to see you play the slide from 'Yes' to 'No'.

The Kissing Game

A and B play the intention of kissing each other passionately on the mouth. If you know that you're not actually going to kiss, then you can commit yourself to that intention completely.

The game is to play the approach to the kiss, and at the last moment, to subtly change your mind; not to retreat, as you would if you were playing a reversal, but to continue in the same direction as before, and instead of recoiling you let your lips just slide past your partner's lips, as close as possible, without touching.

That 'slide' from 'Yes' to 'No' is a slight. Like watching a conjuror doing a card trick: we accept the first part of the action, yet the outcome surprises us because we didn't see the change. We might have been watching all the time, but we're still astonished at how it ends up, and we're left to work out how it happened.

The Hitting Game

A looks away from B. B goes to hit A, and when A looks round at B, B turns the aggressive blow into an affectionate touch.

That word – 'turns' – is the slight. If you're going to hit somebody with real aggression, and then turn that gesture of aggression into one of affection, we want to see that change of feeling. A slight isn't a sudden snap from one thing to another, there's a slow and painful transition here; 'aggression' to 'affection' is a big jump, and our interest lies in seeing you negotiate that jump. Your job is to take us with you in your change of feeling. The more engaged you are in the original hit, the more passionate your gesture of affection will be in the end.

The easiest way to handle a slight is to look for the action. If you're going to kiss somebody, then you've got something clear to play. When you fail to kiss, for example, give yourself something else to play, like admiring the sunshine, or remembering that you have to make a phone call. They're obviously lies, but as long as you don't snap from one action to the next, and as long as you let us see the lie, you'll be able to play the slight more easily.

The Mistaken Identity Game

A is sitting in a street café. B is sitting some tables behind A. Across the road, C is waving to try to catch the attention of B. A thinks that C is gesturing to him or her and feels very flattered. C walks over the road, straight past A and into the arms of B. A plays a slight from being flattered at the thought of talking to this person, to having to cover up their embarrassment.

It helps if A is placed in a direct line between B and C, so that C's path is as close to A as possible, and A can really be put on the spot. I remember an actor playing this game: she stood up as C came towards her, and as he passed, she played quite a gentle slight from a delightful greeting to a carefree stretch, then she sat down with such force that she caught the table, and knocked her water over. Then she was so quick to pick up the bottle, that she knocked the table over as well, and in the end she made such a noise that A and B turned round and looked at her in amazement, so she was forced to acknowledge them – and looked mortified with embarrassment.

Engagement is the key in all these timing games. What you're doing has got to matter to you; you've got to take it seriously. If you're relaxing against a wall, be genuinely relaxed. If you're about to hit somebody, be really aggressive. Don't try to plan how you're going to get from one feeling to the other, just make the jump, and let your body sort itself out in the air. The best reactions when playing a reversal or a slight come from when it looks as if you've taken yourself by surprise, and that happens when you're so engaged with the first part of the action that the second part comes as a real shock. Effective timing is more about inspiring instinctive reactions than executing accurate choreography, and for the most part, the greater your engagement in the action, the more likely we are to believe you, and to empathise with you on the way.

The Double Take

A double take is basically a delayed reaction. You're sitting on a bench in the park, and your next-door neighbour, who died some time ago, sits down next to you. If you look at that person, and say 'Hello', then look away again, then snap your head back in a state of extreme anxiety, you'll have played a double take. The first take would be your initial acknowledgement of the person next to you. This first take goes for nothing; in other words, there's no reaction, and this non-reaction lulls us into a state of calm, or excites our anticipation, depending on the context. But the calm of the 'first take' amplifies our reaction when we see what you're doing in the 'second take', and giving it more significance, and making it look bigger than we might have anticipated.

The Helpful Victim Game

A comes home to see B carrying a television out of the house. A helps B out of the house with the television, and holds open the door of the van, and B drives off. Then A goes to switch on the television and realises that it's been stolen.

Helping B with the television is the 'first take', and realising that the television has gone, is the 'second take'. The problem here is how long a gap to leave between the first take and the second. Lecoq used to say that there should be an equal number of beats between the start of the action, the 'first take', and the 'second take'. In other words, if there are ten beats in a scene, and if you walk on stage for four beats, play the first take on the fifth, then you can play another four beats, and play the second take on the tenth beat.

Lecoq maintained that the first take should be equally distanced between the start of the action and the second take. I'm not convinced that this is always the case, but it soon becomes clear that if you leave the second take too long after the first, there's a danger we'll forget the first take completely, so that the second take will look like another incident rather than a delayed realisation. Sometimes it's possible to keep our attention on the first take in order to delay the reaction for far too many beats to fit into Lecoq's rule. In *You Haven't Embraced Me Yet* (Told by an Idiot, 1996) two characters were caught in a compromising embrace by a third character. She saw the couple embracing each other almost as soon as she entered. That was the first take, and the guilty couple watched her in grim anticipation as she walked, quite contentedly, across the room, and up a spiral staircase. She was just about to reach the top, when she turned and ran back, all the way down the stairs, and across the room to where the couple were sitting, still in their embrace. That was the second take. The delayed reaction worked in this instance because the embracing couple assumed the role of a chorus, and kept our attention on the woman all the time, and didn't let us forget what was going on. The second take was explosive. I don't think I've ever seen a double take held for quite so long as that.

The Double Take Game

This is the best game I know for exploring double takes. It's a simple situation that's crying out for a delayed reaction, and it can be played in a multitude of different ways. The scene is set out in such a way that makes it easy to count the beats to see just how long you can hold the delay.

A selection of ordinary objects and personal effects like bags, coats and shoes are arranged in a long line across the playing space. Somewhere in the middle of the line of objects, there is a table, and somewhere on the table is an upturned cup concealing a small sweet. The sweet is a stand-in prop for an eyeball. (I use a sweet so that you might have no objection to putting it in your mouth, and swallowing it, if you want to — but everyone in the room knows that it's a stand-in prop.)

The situation is this: you are searching for something small and valuable, like a precious piece of jewellery. You look everywhere, so each object is inspected and turned over, all the way along the line on the floor and along the table, but under the upturned cup, there's a human eye. That's the first take. The second take can happen whenever you like after that. The game is to see how many different double takes can be played in this situation.

We all know the set-up so the stand-in eyeball will have no surprises for us. Our interest lies in how credibly you play a double take to surprise us, and this simple device can be played in a multitude of ways.

The first thing that most people pick up on in playing double takes is the importance of that initial rhythm, before you play the first take. It establishes your mood, and it sets up a potential contrast with your impending second take. You can play this as fast or as slowly as you like, providing you can find a strong enough contrast once you've realised that there's a human eyeball under the cup. The rhythm after you've played the first take is also very important. This is where we savour the delayed reaction, and build our anticipation, and it's generally the same rhythm that you started with, at the top of the scene. We need it to be like that to know that the presence of the eyeball hasn't registered yet.

That 'human eye' gives the game an excellent hot spot, and the closer you get to that hot spot, the more intense the drama becomes. If you see the eye, replace the cup, and continue looking through the objects, then go to a fixed point, when you realise what you've just seen, that can be a very effective double take. But if you were to see the eye, pick it up, and put it in your pocket, your second take would be more intense. If you were to see the eye, pick it up, and put it in your mouth, then play your second take, it will be even more intense. But if you were to see the eye, pick it up, put it in your mouth, and chew it a bit then swallow it, then you'll have taken the hot spot just about as far as you can, and your second take will be truly amplified.

Making Choices and Shaping Action

Miss Rose's Lesson

We had an art teacher when I started secondary school who was called Miss Rose. She was a potter, with short stubby fingers, and she would slam a piece of clay down on the bench and pummel it about a bit, and say:

> 66 *'What does that remind you of?'*
>
> *Silence.*
>
> *'Come on. What do you see? Make a choice,' she'd say.*
>
> *'It's a hat, Miss,' someone might say.*
>
> *'OK — yes, I can see a hat there. It's a hat. Excellent — so we make a choice,' she'd say, and she'd tweak and twist the clay about a bit, and the crown and rim of a Stetson hat would emerge on the bench.*
>
> *'Then we make it bigger,' she'd say, and the rim would get broader and curl up at the sides a little, and the crown would get taller with a deeper dent in it.*
>
> *'Now,' she'd say, 'we tidy it up a bit. And there you are — a hat.'* 99

That was the lesson: we make a choice, make it bigger and tidy it up a bit. It's a good lesson, and it's stuck in my mind since I was eleven. You can make a choice with a story, a scenario, a scene, a situation, or even a single action. You ask yourself, 'How am I going to play that?' And you have to make a choice. It's astonishing how choices proliferate, particularly when you're not sure. There's something insidiously inhibiting about being told that you can do anything you like. Whether you're sure or not doesn't matter. Try the first thing that comes into your head. It might not be the right choice — in fact, it probably won't be the right choice, but you can always change your mind, and at least you'll know what you don't want to do.

MAKE IT BIGGER: it sounds extraordinary to be told to exaggerate, but it's not an instruction to take everything 'over the top', so much as an insistence that the choice you make is a clear choice. If you choose to play a scene as minimally as possible then 'making it bigger' means that you make it even more minimal. Few of us are as bold as we think we are. Having made your choice, you've got to be committed to it and we've got to be in no doubt as to what you've chosen. If you're not fully committed you'll probably try to change your mind halfway through, and then you'll be even more confused and won't know where you are with it.

TIDYING IT UP A BIT: Having made your choice and committed to it, then that choice needs to look effortless and comfortable to achieve. Lecoq used to define style as being the easiest way of working between certain fixed parameters. Not unlike playing a game really. 'Tidying it up a bit' is a plea for economy. Get rid of anything that gets in the way of that original choice, and keep it simple.

This is a fairly conventional model for creativity. Arthur Koestler proposes the 'same idea' in his book *The Act of Creation*, where he talks about 'the trinity of selection, exaggeration and economy'. It's an idea that emphasises that art is the product of conscious choice, that it isn't as spontaneous as birdsong and that we must be responsible for our choices. But scientists tell us that even birdsong isn't spontaneous. Birds learn their songs, apparently, from other birds, and practise them. They just sound spontaneous. Koestler's 'trinity' is an excellent model if you know exactly what you're going to make, and it's an excellent model for looking at your work in retrospect, and examining its composition. The problem is that in play we rarely know what we're making until we've made it.

This is precisely what Miss Rose was trying to teach us: the game was to let the clay suggest the subject and making it bigger and tidying it up a bit was a process for making us develop an original subject. The trouble is, of course, that action isn't like clay. Action is more causal; more a flow of events that twist and turn, and keep our attention with the promise of continual surprises. In this respect, action is more like music and a musician colleague once told me that his version of Miss Rose's game would be to make a choice, mess about with it, and then do something completely different.

There are only three things you can do with an idea: you can repeat it, you can find little variations of it, or you can do something completely different. It sounds simplistic but it works:

> **❝** *Hello! Hello! I'm over here, on the rock.* [Basic idea] *The tide's coming in really fast. Hello! I'm on the rock. The tide — Hello! It's coming in. Hello — Over here and I'm — really fast — on the rock and over here. Hello! Hello!! — Hello!!* [Repetitions of the original idea] *— Oh — I didn't see you down there, in the water. Is it cold?* [Variation]*I'm afraid I can't swim.* [Something different] **❞**

There's more scope for spontaneity and play in this model. You can make it up as you go along. The variations accrue meaning as they go along, and the new idea at the end launches the action onto something else. This is nearer to what happens in a game, but there's something even simpler than this that deals with action itself rather than ideas in the abstract.

Yoshi's Clapping Game

> **❝** *We sit in circle. We close eyes. We all clap at same time.* **❞**

I wrote Yoshi Oida's cryptic instructions in my notebook in the late seventies after taking part in a workshop that left me inspired and baffled at the same time. Yoshi was a founding member of Peter Brook's International Centre for Theatre Research in Paris. He was originally a Noh performer who came to the West as part of an International Theatre Festival set up by Jean-Louis Barrault in the sixties. That's where he met Peter Brook, and that's why he stayed. For me, Yoshi opened up a personal investigation into the relationship between movement and acting which still preoccupies me today. Yoshi was a man of very few words. I don't remember him ever explaining anything to us. His English was too minimal for that. So instead he confronted us with raw experiences, and the result was edifying.

At the time I thought his clapping game was some kind of arcane concentration exercise but months later, as the different pieces began to fit together, it became clear that his clapping game was a lesson in *Jo-ha-kyu,* a seminal idea in ancient Japanese aesthetics. In *The Noh Theatre,* a highly readable book by Kunio Komparu, the *Jo-ha-kyu* of rhythm is described as follows:

“ *Jo-ha-kyu governs all the rhythms of Noh, based on the assumption that Jo-ha-kyu is the natural rhythm of human life, that all thought and verbal modulations proceed not at an even pace but with time on an incline, so to speak. The idea is that the most natural human way of being and doing is to begin slowly, and gradually build to a rapid climax, to stop and to begin again.* **”**

If you try Yoshi's game for yourself you'll see that at first the clapping will be sporadic and messy, then gradually, the group will settle into a rhythm and, as that rhythm is repeated, it becomes more confident and then it starts to get faster and faster until eventually you're all clapping so fast that that everything falls apart and you're back to the sporadic mess of the beginning, whereupon the whole cycle starts again.

Jo-ha-kyu is a natural law – like gravity. The concept goes back to the teaching of a twelfth-century playwright, teacher and theorist, Zeami Motokiyo (c. 1363-1443). Zeami was the main creative imagination behind Japanese Noh Theatre, and his theories are still the foundations of Japanese aesthetics today. *Jo-ha-kyu* is one of those elemental ideas that are baffling in their simplicity.

In his book, *Conference of the Birds*, John Heilpern describes how Peter Brook used *Jo-ha-kyu* during his experiments in Africa in the seventies. To clarify the idea, he describes a typical moment from an old Western film, when we see a long shot of a lone horseman galloping across open country. The film cuts to a rifle barrel being tilted into position behind a bush. The gun goes off and the rider sprawls into the dust. We cut to the dusty boots of the gunman as he walks towards the rider's body. Just as the gunman approaches, the rider jumps up and shoots him dead.

The galloping rider is the *jo*, the sequence with the gun barrel in the bush, the shooting and the slow walk are all continued in the *ha* and the final shooting is the *kyu*. This is the incident that turns the action, and launches the next cycle of action, namely the next *Jo-ha-kyu*.

There's no literal translation of *Jo-ha-kyu*, but in life, all natural rhythms seem to fall into these three component parts. Not a beginning, middle and end as you might think. Because, according to Zeami at least, there is no end. The *kyu* of the first action immediately becomes the *jo* of the next, and action evolves in a perpetual cycle.

In the gunman incident, the *jo* is as fast as a galloping horse, the *ha* is slow and sustained and the *kyu* is short and abrupt. All we're doing in identifying these three stages of an action is finding the potential for making effective choices. We're trying to distinguish between the promise of something about to happen, the force of the happening itself, and the change of feeling after that.

The three parts can be of any length. They can be fast or slow, abrupt or sporadic. You can talk about the *Jo-ha-kyu* of a single action, a scene, a play, an entire festival of plays or even an entire tradition of dramatic writing. You can also break down each of the components themselves and talk about the *jo* of *jo*, the *ha* of *jo*, and the *kyu* of *jo*. These terms are a bit arcane for me. If I'm trying to get you to do something amusing with an ironing board, the last thing I want to do is to embark on an explanation of ancient Japanese aesthetic theory. In rehearsal I need something more immediate, so I talk about the anticipation, the release and the pay-off of an action.

These terms are self-explanatory. They keep us mindful of the original idea whilst letting us use the original concept without having to explain anything.

Imagine that you're about to sneeze: this is the anticipation of the action. Now sneeze: this is the release of the action. You feel relieved after the sneeze: that's the pay-off. You look for a tissue: that's the anticipation of the next action. You find your tissues and blow your nose, that's the release. You feel more comfortable: that's the pay-off. You look round for a waste bin: that's the anticipation of the next action. And so the cycles of action perpetuate.

The anticipation and the release are straightforward enough. It's the pay-off that seems to baffle people. Notice in the sneeze how the final phase of the action was always marked by a change of feeling. You feel relieved after the sneeze, and you feel more comfortable once you have blown your nose. The significance of any action is determined by the way we feel once that action has been completed.

The Action Game

Working in threes, A and B take any action that involves physical contact between two people, like shaking hands, kissing, embracing, or threatening violence. Or you can be more specific: two people trying to leave a restaurant without paying, two people trying to steal something from a shop.

A and B play the scene and C calls out each of the three phases as they're played.

A and B repeat the action and try to provoke C by coming up with as many different variations as they can.

You'll soon discover that you can vary the length of each part of the action. For example, you can have a long anticipation, a short release and a short pay-off. Or you can have a short anticipation, a short release, and a long pay-off. It helps to abbreviate the action to long-long-short, or short-long-long, or short-short-short if you like.

The game really comes alive for me when it's played without the planning. If you find the complicity between you, rather than planning what you're going to do, then the action will become more alive, more volatile and more credible. If you put a spoken text on top of the action – providing you're not talking about what you're doing – then the subtext will grow with the action.

Zeami has given us an invaluable analytical tool here that enables us to become aware of exactly where we are in the action, moment by moment. It's astonishing how these three elements enable us to manipulate meaning. If you shake hands with a long anticipation and a short release and a short pay-off, you'll be saying something very different than if you play a short anticipation, short release and a long pay-off.

It's a simple idea, but it's invaluable because it keeps our minds focused on the emerging incidents so that all our choices are action choices; now we can play with the situation itself, rather than with ideas in the abstract. By preoccupying ourselves with the 'here and now' we're able to play with possibilities whilst still keeping our options open. The guiding principle of anticipation, release and pay-off enables us to stay 'in the moment', and by emphasising the importance of the pay-off, the action is always being driven forward.

It helps to keep Zeami's three-point action plan at the back of your mind, but if you insist on playing the anticipation, release, and pay-off all the time, then the very thought of it will become inhibiting and irritating. I wouldn't bother to analyse an action unless I think there's something wrong with it. It's the lack of an effective pay-off that invariably causes problems, but then not every action is going to have a pay-off. We often play a series of actions that simply don't reach a pay-off at all, which is perfectly fine and normal, but if we never get to know what you feel like in the end, it's generally unsatisfying. We tend to think that physical comedy is only about action, but it's not. It's primarily about huge changes in feeling, and those changes are primarily contained in the pay-off.

In rehearsal your interest lies in recognising these changes in feeling. If you don't play the pay-off of an action, then that action will remain unresolved and left in the air. Of course this might be exactly what you want to do, if you are building suspense in a scene. All I'm saying is that you should be aware of what you're doing. You can keep us on tenterhooks for as long as you like, but ultimately it's the pay-off that we're all waiting for. Any action will become interesting to watch if it has a good pay-off. In comedy it's the pay-off that invariably makes us laugh, and it's the pay-off that gives the action its significance for us, and turns the story. As a general rule, the more we invest in the anticipation, the bigger the pay-off.

The Long-Lost Lovers Game

Two people have just alighted from a train. They see one another along the platform. They recognise each other. They each thought the other was dead. They run and they embrace. That's the situation.

Two people stand opposite each other – about three metres apart. They find complicity in both running at the same time and embracing each other. Then they slowly let themselves relax in each other's arms. Then they let their arms drop to their sides and they look at each other.

Here we can see a clear anticipation, release and pay-off, but if the lovers run into each other's arms on a cue, without finding complicity to launch their run, the anticipation of the action will be much weaker. Complicity raises the stakes, the anticipation hits the roof, and the pay-off at the end of the embrace wins our engagement. In this context we read the intensity of the anticipation as emotional intensity, and it can be very moving to watch. But if we put the same sequence into a comic situation this rule is even clearer.

The Mistaken Embrace Game

Set up the same situation as before and the two lovers fly into each other's arms but this time they realise, at the most crucial moment, that they don't know each other from Adam.

Now we've turned the situation into a huge reversal. The question is, of course, where is that most crucial moment? Is it in the anticipation, the release or the pay-off? My money would go on some point towards the end of the release – at the last possible moment – just before they complete a passionate embrace, and before the expected pay-off. That's the hot spot of the scene, and that's the strongest impulse from which to play the reversal. If you put a reversal here, it would be such a surprise. It would spin us all round back to the anticipation again, only this time the stakes would be even higher. Now we'd hit an appropriate level of intensity to play comedy, but the next stage is more difficult because it's much easier to generate the required intensity than it is to sustain it.

If this incident were a scene in a sitcom or a farce, this mistaken embrace would be the set-up for the real meat of the scene, which would probably be about how these two people cope with each other if they both had to wait on the same platform together for the next train.

Build-ups

If you were to set up a scene where you were sunbathing on an anthill, you'd probably end up playing a series of reversals: a constant chain of twitching, scratching and wriggling about. An effective way for you to sustain our interest in such a scene would be to orchestrate these little chains of reversals into an ascending spiral of intensity, ranging from a languid irritation at the start of the scene to a demonic dance of agony at the end. Any action that's repeated in such a way that it appears to get worse and worse, or better and better, so that the final rhythm is the polar opposite of the rhythm you started with is a build-up. You can play a build-up with almost anything.

The Numbers Game

The hardest thing to learn about build-ups is that ascending spiral of intensity. You've got to be able to identify the level you're playing at the moment, and be prepared to take it that little step further.

This is a game for a chorus of five people. All you have to do is to count from one to fifteen or twenty. You probably won't be able to go much further. The idea is that each number is an obscenity, so that one is slightly obscene, two is worse, but three, four, five, and six are getting increasingly daring and disgusting to say in public.

So the first person in the group looks at the others, and then at the audience and says: 'One'. Everybody giggles, then the next person does the same with 'Two', and so on. It's important to relish each number and to enjoy the game of being obscene. The giggles are also important because if the build-up is going to work you've all got to be at the same level of intensity and the giggles help you to identify what that level is.

Once again the key is to be engaged. Each number must have an effect on you, and that effect must be amplified throughout the group; that amplification is expressed in movement so you have to copy each other and learn to keep together.

You can play a build-up with almost anything. The group could be trying to tell the audience that they're going to die, or that they find them sexually attractive, or that they need some money, or that touching the floor makes them feel euphoric; almost anything can be built up. Any incident, any simple statement of fact can be pushed to the extremes, to a bizarre distortion of human behaviour. It's like a child throwing a tantrum, or Basil Fawlty banging his head against a wall. It's the moment when you flip, when you really lose it. Played at a frenetic rhythm, a build-up is the stuff of farce and cartoon comedy, but in different circumstances, a build-up can be very dark and disturbing. I once used a build-up in rehearsing a chorus who were required to pray at a surreal version of the twelve stations of the cross. I set the rule that the intensity should go up every time they went to the next station. I asked them to play at a frenzied rhythm at first, to find extreme images of desperation and despair, and then I asked them to play the same action and to find the same images, only this time to play at a slower rhythm, which gave everything they did an increasingly dark, expressionist quality that was both moving and surreal at the same time. However you choose to play a build-up, we want to see how far you can go – that's our principal interest once you've established that ascending spiral of intensity. You'll probably find that in the early stages you'll be able to speak and to control your actions, but once the intensity really starts to kick in, you'll soon reach a point where it becomes impossible to speak or make any noises at all. It's then that your work starts to become increasingly bizarre and tips into wild fantasy or inarticulate anxiety as your desperation builds.

The Five Steps to Heaven Game

Imagine a group of people are robbing a shop and a security guard hears them and slowly approaches the scene of the crime.

We can trace the gradual build-up of dramatic tension in this situation through the following five steps:

1. The security guard calls but the thieves don't hear anything. The initial cause for alarm is only for the audience.

2. The guard calls again. This time the thieves hear something but carry on with what they're doing. The tension has now moved up a notch in our imaginations, but the robbers remain unmoved.

3. The guard calls a third time. The robbers hear it this time. They go to a fixed point, and then resume what they're doing at twice the speed. At last our anticipation is being channelled into action.

4. The guard calls again. The guard is closer now. Again the thieves go to a fixed point, and then they go as fast as they did before, only now the tension is getting to the robbers, and by this time it's probably spreading to us as well.

5. Now the guard calls from the door. Again the robbers go to a fixed point, and they hold it for as long as they can, then erupt into a mad panic. Now 'There Is a Bomb in the Room!' – all order has broken down. Everybody's running about all over the place banging into each other, attacking each other and trying to escape. It doesn't matter what happens here as long as the frenzy is sustained. The scene finishes the moment it flops.

This is a build-up with an external control, and it's surprisingly effective. It can be adapted to almost any situation, once you've identified what the trigger is going to be. In the situation I've just described, the call of the guard triggers the rise in intensity.

I once used the Five Steps in a scene where a vet was telling a distraught pet owner that his dog would have to be put down. Every time the vet said the dog's name, the owner's reaction would go up a notch. You could develop 'the mistaken embrace' incident using the Five Steps. Their reactions could get more intense every time the couple look at each other. I've also used it in a scene where a group of racists beat a man to death. Every time he looked at them, their reactions went up a notch. Build-ups are only comic if the situation is comic. They work best as a choric device. If you were rehearsing *The Bacchae* or *Medea*, a control on the intensity of the chorus would be essential if you're to build the climaxes, and generate the imagery. Build-ups can take us to images of ecstasy, chaos, and right into the heart of the nightmare if you like, or they can help us find comedy in a grieving pet owner. All we're doing here is moving in Lecoq's tension cycle.

Set-ups

If we apply these principles to the bigger picture of the narrative then the anticipation becomes the set-up, the release becomes a series of build-ups, but the pay-off remains the same – that change of feeling at the end of the story. There's an episode of *Fawlty Towers* when Sybil goes away for the weekend and leaves Basil to organise some building work. This is the set-up, and it instantly triggers our anticipation of the impending disaster. The more she insists that he uses only her choice of builder, and not the cheap one, because he's incompetent and unreliable, the more obvious it becomes that Basil is going to disregard her instructions. We watch him pretending to agree with her; as soon as she is out of the way, he contacts the cheap one, and cancels the more reliable one. Set-ups are vital. They establish what's going on, and if we don't know where we are, or what's happening, the comedy will start to fall apart. It's a challenge to make the set-up interesting. In *Hamlet*, Shakespeare goes for the appearance of the ghost to raise the stakes and whet our appetite for what's about to come. Basically, set-ups are about giving us information; the great challenge in making the set-up is to do this as quickly as possible and without exposition. If you have to resort to exposition, then dramatise it. That's what happens in this episode of *Fawlty Towers*. Basil lies. He deliberately deceives Sybil. We know he's digging himself deeper 'in the shit' minute by minute, and in doing so, he raises the stakes, and builds our expectation for the impending farce. All conventional narratives fall into these three broad sections; in structuring comedy it's helpful to remember which section you're in.

We wrote an audacious set-up for Told by an Idiot's *On the Verge of Exploding* (1993). We opened the play with a scene about a hugely pregnant bride, obsessively eating bananas as she waited and waited at the altar, but her bridegroom never came. He sent her a banana instead, wrapped in a ribbon for the occasion. The bride was so traumatised and humiliated that she vowed eternal revenge on all men, and decided never to let her own daughter ever see a man. The story then moved on several years to a remote rural settlement. Her daughter was now a little girl of about seven. Whilst she was having her hair combed by her mother on the terrace outside her house, the voice of a man was heard in the far distance.

I remember building up the entrance of the man with the Five Steps to Heaven Game. By the fourth call, the mother was roughly manhandling her daughter and pulling at her hair, this way and that. By the fifth call, she half-chased and half-dragged her daughter across the space, then tied her up in a sack and dumped her in the house. When she came out, the man was there. Mother was trembling; for her there was definitely 'A Bomb in the Room'. In complete contrast, the man, a travelling salesman, was 'Laid Back' and amusing as he took his wares out of his case, trying to sell her mundane things like teabags or scouring pads. For Mum, this little sequence with a travelling salesman trying to make her laugh and jolly her into buying something, was a series of provocations. Mum was playing a build-up right through this scene. Her tension grew with each new object, and when the salesman remarked that the picture in the box of tea looked a bit like her, which in truth it did, she was trembling at the level of 'The Bomb is About to Go Off!' In the end the man produced a banana. By now mother was at a state of 'Rigor Mortis' as he casually peeled it in front of her. Then inexplicably, she relaxed, and smiled psychotically. She wiped her hands on her apron, and went to get her felling axe. Then she attacked the salesman and decapitated him, after which she looked much happier.

The humour of this scene was played against the background of one long build-up. If the mother's tension dropped for a second, the comedy would die instantly. This ascending spiral of intensity was a constant reminder of what had happened to that woman at the start of the play; she was genuinely disturbing to look at, but the salesman was so jolly and enthusiastic, and so persistent. It really mattered to him that he made a sale that day, and the more he tried, the more we liked him for it, and the more he tried to make her laugh, the more catatonic she became. In the end we laughed as much out of fear for the salesman as anything he actually did. The scene worked primarily because of the rhythmic agility of the actors involved. The timing was slightly different every night. In fact the salesman did different things every night, but the mother took us on a rollercoaster ride of emotions from pleasure, to anxiety, to rage, to fury, and finally onto a level of psychosis that's difficult to determine. For the mother there are two cycles of action in this scene; the first cycle started with the idyllic image of her combing her daughter's hair (the anticipation) then chasing the daughter was the release and tying her up in the sack was the pay-off. Then the sight of the man was the anticipation of the second cycle, killing him was the release, and seeing him dead was her pay-off. All those emotions were labelled, and given a context by the set-up. We knew exactly where we were the moment the salesman took the banana out. In terms of the story, that moment was a pay-off for the banana. From then on we knew that the salesman was going to have to die.

Part Three

The Gentle Art
of Idiocy

Life's but a walking shadow, a poor player
That struts and frets his hour upon the stage
And then is heard no more: it is a tale
Told by an idiot, full of sound and fury,
Signifying nothing.

William Shakespeare
(Macbeth, *Act V, Scene v*)

Simple Clown

> **"** *The theatrical clown was invented at the London Hippodrome in 1815, on Saturday, the fifteenth of February, at two thirty in the afternoon. It was raining. The London Hippodrome was an equestrian theatre in those days.*
>
> *Two stablehands, one very tall, and the other very small and very fat, were employed to shovel up the horse shit after each act. On the day in question, both men were very hungover, and they both arrived late for work. The tall one arrived first and in a blind panic scrambled into the first uniform that came to hand, then grabbed his brush and shovel, and ran into the ring.*
>
> *The crowd roared with laughter as soon as they saw him, his thin hairy legs sticking out of his ill-fitting trousers.*
>
> *The short fat one arrived some minutes later. He was furious to find that his partner had run on stage wearing his uniform. The only one that he could find didn't remotely fit him, but he stuffed himself into it, grabbed his brush and shovel, and ran on stage to confront his partner.*
>
> *The crowd laughed even louder. As soon as the short fat one saw the tall thin one in his uniform, he lost his temper, ran at him, and tripped over his far-too-long trousers. Undeterred, he crawled towards his adversary, determined to teach him a lesson. The crowd laughed even more. The tall thin one ran away, and his trousers fell down, and he fell over. The crowd were shrieking with laughter now.*
>
> *Eventually, the fight was broken up and they were both dragged off. The crowd loved it so much that the boss of the show insisted that they did the same thing at the beginning of every show, and so the first theatrical clowns were born.* **"**

Philippe Gaulier told us this story, with a wicked glint in his eye, at the beginning of his workshop, 'Le Clown', in the early eighties. Of course clowning didn't start then – that's a preposterous idea. We all know it happened on a Monday, and it wasn't raining at all. It was a perfect day.

Clowning is another of those great universals of performance. In fact, clowning is pretty universal, full stop. When the conditions are right, most of us enjoy the occasional brief foray into the bizarre and the ridiculous, and in the right circumstances, any one of us could easily find ourselves clowning about and deliberately being silly. In life, clowning is the only socially acceptable expression of stupidity, but for an actor, clowning is the epitome of unbridled theatrical play. It's the only mode of performance that doesn't require you to know why you're doing something. Clowning turns idiocy into an art form. It's an open invitation for you to do what you like, how you like, but only for as long as we like it. Our pleasure as an audience is your only control factor in playing a clown. Being reactive to the audience is the discipline of the theatrical clown.

We all recognise the painted face, red nose, big shoes and baggy trousers of the traditional circus clown, but clowns of one sort or another crop up in all cultures; they're anarchic spirits, madmen, fools, scapegoats, or just popular entertainers adept at being stupid in public. Jacques Copeau was the first theatre teacher to consider the relationship between clowning and acting. But it was Jacques Lecoq who first investigated the physicality of clowning and explored clowning at a theatrical level of play.

Lecoq's Levels of Play

Lecoq was unique in his approach to teaching theatrical form, in that historical accuracy and literary genre were of secondary importance to him. He was preoccupied with trying to recreate the elemental physical gesture behind the most popular ways of representing life on stage that constitute our understanding of performance today. In other words, it wasn't enough for him to be able to say, 'This is how Pantalone walked, this is what Pantalone was wearing, and this is why he was wearing it.' Lecoq wanted to find the physical impulse that inspired Pantalone's walk so that we find that impulse for ourselves, and find our own way of playing Pantalone. Asking 'How do clowns walk?' or 'What do clowns wear?' are inane questions. But to ask 'How do clowns make us laugh?' and, more importantly, 'What physical impulses inspire that comedy?' will take you to a place where you can find a personal ownership of 'clown' as a level of play. Empirical investigations like these take us to the heart of performance, and comic performance is a very pragmatic affair. If what you're doing doesn't work, you've got to change it, or you'll drive the audience mad. But if your knowledge-base is derived from the personal understanding that if you do *this* I'll feel like *that*, and that my feeling will make you play like *this*, then a wrinkled old seed squeezed out of some long-discarded ancient theatrical form can become a fresh inspiration, and develop into a personal level of play that's just as fruitful for you today as it was for another actor hundreds of years ago.

Lecoq taught six levels of play at his school. Were he alive now, I'm sure his list would have grown considerably because tastes change and, with the emergence of the new media, the means of performance is also changing. But in comedy, although the material will change considerably from decade to decade, how we make each other laugh is more enduring and more universal. Lecoq saw each level of play as being a particular key to releasing the imagination of an actor. The idea was that, out of these six different approaches to play, each student would be able to find at least one level that would enable them to experience the most fun, the most confidence, and to find the greatest freedom on stage, in front of an audience. He maintained that very few people, if any, are capable of finding this freedom with all six, but that we can all find at least one level that we feel at home with. Here are the six levels of play, in no particular order:

1. *Tragedy*

2. *Melodrama*

3. *Psychological Realism*

4. *Commedia dell'Arte*

5. *Buffoon*

6. *Clown*

What we have here are six different relationships with the audience. They're not historical or literary reference points; they're different ways of orchestrating an effect on the audience.

TRAGEDY is the level of play concerned with ideals, with the theatrical representation of awe, and ultimate life and death confrontations. Tragedy is distinctly better than life; it's a way of theatrically representing high ideals or encounters with gods and the divine. Considering how little tragedy is used by the average theatre-maker today, it's probably the most exotic for our popular taste and to my mind, it is the least developed popular form today.

MELODRAMA is also better than life in its orientation, and this is a level of play that has evolved as a means of engaging our emotions. Popular taste in film and television drama indicates that melodrama is as engaging today as it ever was. Disaster movies and films like *Pearl Harbor*, and TV soaps like *Coronation Street* or *Casualty* are dripping with melodrama, and you'll find lashings of it in musicals and opera.

PSYCHOLOGICAL REALISM is decidedly lifelike in its orientation. We're all more familiar with this level of play than we are with any other. In fact, we're surrounded by it all the time as nearly all drama we see is played at the level of psychological realism. Most of our writing for film and television, and most of our new writing for the theatre is conceived at this level of play.

COMMEDIA DELL'ARTE is the prototype for farce and physical comedy. *Commedia*, like most comic levels of play, is 'worse' than life. *Commedia* is theatre's answer to the comic cartoon. Most of our rhythmic physical comedy and our knockabout slapstick routines, and in fact most of the work in the previous section of this book has its origins in *Commedia*.

BUFFOON is a level of play that is so much worse than life that it becomes grotesque. Buffoon is the theatrical equivalent of the eighties satirical television series *Spitting Image*. Buffoon is the darkest level of comedy we can work in; it's sardonic and it's parodic. Lecoq once told me that he would never impose a level of play on his students. But he would propose something, and if his students had a taste for it, he would pursue that topic with more vigour, rather than insisting that everybody tried everything.

CLOWN was introduced at his school in the sixties and by the late eighties, it evolved as the most popular of all Lecoq's levels of play. Why this should be the case is an interesting question. Perhaps it was the lack of traditional restrictions that made it so popular, or perhaps it was the postmodern urge to dispense with genre entirely that gave clown its particular potency at that time. From the mid-eighties onwards there was a trend for students emerging from Lecoq's school, and that of Philippe Gaulier, to form small-scale touring companies and enthusiastically produce clown shows where they could put their new-found skills into practice. Companies like Brew Ha-Ha, Commotion, and even early work of The Right Size, Peepolykus, and even Théâtre de Complicité (now just Complicite) were all originally inspired by clown. *On theVerge of Exploding*, our first production as Told by an Idiot, was also made with close reference to clown. A multitude of individual performers also calling themselves clowns have emerged in recent years with varying degrees of ability. Copeau, Lecoq and Gaulier opened up the notion of the theatre clown not in order to train a new generation of children's entertainers or to indulge in mawkish displays of naivety, but rather to confront us with a radical level of play that's capable of subverting everything we hold most dear in established theatre practice. This is why clown is such a seminal level of comedy, and why so many of us have evolved some of our most challenging theatre-making from this starting point.

Unlike *Commedia* and buffoon, clown is like life, which seems a startling observation at first, but clowns come alive at a level that is quintessentially *you*. It's life on stage, without the fancy wrapping. The clown's job is to make the audience laugh by any means possible. To do this you have to 'plug into the audience' at the expense of everything else. The Clapping Game is an excellent starting point for clown. It's the best game I know for developing an easy relationship with the audience without being tempted to act, and without trying to be funny. This is the sort of game that only starts to get interesting when you're 'in the shit'. If you can be 'in the shit', and still manage to keep our interest in the game – just by being you – then you're in an ideal position to play clown. Sometimes I combine this game with the Hands-Up Game. If you start to look too comfortable up there, if your rhythm is getting too predictable or if you're starting to run out of steam, then the Hands-Up Game, especially with the three-lives rule, will give you a shot of adrenalin that might lift the action to new heights of stupidity.

Clowns love the audience and will go to any length to keep that audience laughing. So respecting the integrity of the text, the dramatic situation, the restrictions of genre, and even the most basic theatre conventions like staying on the stage and not wandering into the auditorium, mean very little to the clown. Lecoq thought that clowning could give his students a refreshing view of the world that would provoke them to greater levels of invention, and confront them with the stark realities of presentational acting. He was right. Clowning takes us back to basics. It's not about character, it's not about routines, or structured material of any kind. Clowning is no more than a credible idiot playing for an audience – it's theatre's first base. If playfulness is at the heart of our creativity, then for some of us at least, clowning is the key to that playfulness. Clowns play all the time. Everything's a game; everything is for the audience, and as long as the audience are laughing, then anything is possible. All the work outlined in the first two parts of this book is essential for clown. We're all clowns really, but we've all spent most of our lives trying to hide this embarrassing reality under layers of intelligence, sensibility, sophistication, and social nicety. If you're an actor who plays with openness and vulnerability then there will always be a bit of the clown poking through somewhere. If you successfully encounter clown in the early stages of your career, you'll be able to elevate your natural stupidity into an art form, and you'll be more likely to trust your instincts, and keep a freshness in your work.

The Compliments Game

A is the provocateur and B is the clown. A says to B: 'They tell me that you know all the movements', or words to that effect.

'Yes,' says B, and proceeds to demonstrate one or two movements. As soon as A starts to lose interest, A says something like: 'That's excellent. I've never seen such delicate physicality.'

Of course the compliments aren't real. I find that it's always better to lie when it comes to criticism than it is to tell the truth; it's far less painful. What A is really saying here is that he's starting to get bored, so you'd better do something about it. Because the compliment is so completely ridiculous, the game is declared and B is painlessly rescued from the flop.

It's important that B accepts the compliment, whilst A continues to praise B, making the compliments as credible and as sincere as possible, until B looks genuinely flattered.

'Oh, thank you very much,' B might say. 'That's very nice of you. It just came to me in a flash really.'

The more credibly the compliment is given, and the more credibly the compliment is received, the more the game develops an interesting emotional level.

Then A asks 'Is there more?'

'Yes,' says B, and the cycle continues.

'Is there more?' is not an invitation to make the movement bigger or more athletic. It's just an invitation to do something else.

Once again, there's a very simple structure to this game. Some people fall into the trap of trying to be good – they really try to move well. A can propose anything for B to play with: 'They tell me that you're an excellent singer' or 'You're an excellent acrobat.' The fact that B might be an appalling singer, or a hopeless acrobat is a gift for playing clown. Whatever A proposes is a pretext to play, not a direction that has to be followed to the letter – a clown is happy just to be asked. Whether B can actually do what's been asked of him is immaterial. This is a great release for A as much as it is for B. 'They tell me you do poetic movement', or 'religious movement', or 'mathematical movement'. B will say 'Yes' to anything. It isn't necessary for A to have anything in mind, but having said that this movement is religious, poetic or mathematical, it's astonishing how we immediately will attach that description to what B's doing.

The object of the game is for B to try to avoid getting a compliment. This is the only thing that's going to keep the game alive. B's game is to try to keep A entertained, and if A's eyes are dead with incipient boredom, B must try something else. If B watches A's eyes and tries to change the rhythm or drop the game entirely, then it will soon become apparent how much can be made out of so little.

A useful variation is to play the game in twos. With two people accepting the compliments, and two people copying each other's movement, the game becomes easier to sustain. Provided both clowns accept the compliments, and don't let themselves become too interested in their own interaction so that they forget to watch the eyes of the provocateurs, this version of the game can produce some excellent clowning.

It's more difficult to play the Compliments Game to one person than it is to play it to an audience. An individual has only his or her personal taste, and his or her individual sense of humour. With a whole audience to play to, there'll invariably be someone who'll be chuckling away at what

B is doing, and providing other people can see the joke, that original laugh will be quite contagious. When you're playing the Compliments Game, you're trying to discover what the audience finds funny. During the game, you probably won't have a clue what people are going to like. We're not dealing with wit or reason here; your material is inane, and we're primarily laughing at what you look like. Providing your movement is light – in other words, providing you're not trying too hard or deliberately trying to be funny or, worst of all, playing a 'funny little character' – then somebody is going to laugh at you; not with you or at what you've just said but directly at what you've just done. As soon as they do, you do it again. That's the clown's job: to get us laughing, and to keep us laughing for as long as possible. As soon as we stop laughing – get off.

The Provocateur

This eternal quest to keep us laughing takes us right into the world of the bizarre and the anarchic. It also takes us to a level of simplicity and incredulity that strips us down to our bare humanity. It's this humanity that keeps clown at a level of play that's distinctly like life, as opposed to being worse than life. It certainly isn't better than life. The clown does everything for real. It sounds painful, and a tradition has developed in training that makes it just that. Lecoq used to teach from the principle of via negativa (Latin for 'negative way'). This is a method of teaching that suppresses explanation, example and instruction. He simply told his students, 'No. That's not it,' forcing everyone to dig really deep to find out what 'it' might be. But Lecoq could skilfully navigate his charges to a point where they were compelled to draw their own conclusions, and to find their own way in the work. He used via negativa to avoid theorising and intellectualising about a process that was primarily empirical and spontaneous. Ultimately, via negativa is the deepest mode of learning, but Lecoq used to approach clown with students during their second year at his school. He knew them very well by then, so he had time to develop deeper relationships with them. Unfortunately, most teachers aren't as good as Lecoq used to be, and few teachers have the time to develop lengthy relationships with their students so that via negativa can become a viable option. Certainly I've never been able to bring it off. In the wrong hands, via negativa has more in common with bullying than teaching, with the result that clown is often seen as an ordeal to put yourself through, in the vague notion that it's going to be good for you in the end. It's not. To play clown you have to love being on stage in front of that audience more than anything else in the world, and you can't find that openness and that degree of pleasure if you're terrified. Oh, it's good to be nervous, and it's excellent to be put under pressure occasionally, but if you're on stage in front of your peers, it's the easiest thing in the world for me to raise the stakes, and put you 'in the shit'. If you're up there, alone with your own stupidity, trying to keep our attention with nothing of any substance to play, it's easier for both of us if I'm part of the game with you.

When I teach clown, I become a provocateur. In other words, I assume a role, a sort of 'boss-clown', and my job is to help you keep the games alive and funny. It doesn't work if I try to set myself up as an expert or a critic and try to tell you where you're going wrong. If I start to theorise, or try to give detailed instructions, or if I try to direct you in a more conventional way, you'll start to think and to analyse what you're doing, and then all your playfulness and comedy will quite simply evaporate. Of course there'll be times when we'll talk about the work, but I never let those discussions happen during a game. My job is to keep you playing. Being the boss-clown enables me to be completely unreasonable. I can be as rude, cantankerous, illogical, tyrannical and as stupid as I like. It's the same relationship that's played out in the Compliments Game: A provokes B by giving a compliment, by entering the game, and by saying something that makes B react. If A doesn't like B's reaction then A has to try a different tack:

❝ *You know — that movement was so beautiful that I don't think I'll ever forget it. It was so sensitive, and so uncannily accurate. It was magnificent. Look — I know you don't believe me, but I promise you that I'm not bullshitting you when I say that you're very talented. You are — and you're just going to have to live with it.* **❞**

You know it's a joke, and I know it's a joke, and we both know that it's a criticism at the same time. If my compliments raise a laugh, this will give you more energy to try the game again. As a provocateur, my job is as much to rescue as it is to provoke, but I'm also trying to work you and make you come up with more ideas. If my first attempt at a compliment doesn't make you look as if you believe it, then I try harder and harder, until I get the reaction I'm looking for. In this case, I want to see humility, and a bashful pleasure in my comments. The more genuine these feelings are, the more incongruous they look in the context of what B has just done. Your reaction is heartfelt and real, and when that reaction clashes with the situation, in our eyes you go to a level of unsurpassed stupidity.

The Running and Stopping Game

A few people at a time run about the space as fast as they can, and on my command they stop and face the audience, looking as if they haven't been running at all: as if they've just got out of bed.

The huge physical engagement of your run makes a ludicrous contrast with the apparent ease and lack of tension in the way you stop. That's what makes it look so funny. We don't know why, but the action is clearly imperative to you. It's as if you've been told off so many times in the past that you do everything 'at the double', because you think that'll keep you out of trouble. In reality, of course, you don't know why you were running in the first place. The contrast between your urgent run and your abrupt stop will reveal your habitual holding patterns in the way you stand in repose, and in your personal attitude to being on stage and in front of an audience at that moment. It's this attitude that the game is concerned with.

Every time you stop I ask you to 'do less'. I'm being deliberately obscure as to exactly what I mean by this and to emphasise the point I might say: 'What does he mean: "Do less?" Come on – do nothing. Who's doing the most?' I ask the audience: 'Come on, point – all point! Yes, you know who you are. That's appalling!' I might say to some hapless individual who hasn't a clue to what's going on: 'How dare you do that? I bet he's a Freemason.' The point of the game is to provoke the group into negotiating their physical tension, and to drop their habitual holding patterns as much as possible and to question how they stand and hold themselves.

'We all know who's doing the most – don't we?' I assure them. Instantly, everybody on stage adjusts his or her attitudes. It's obvious to all of us who is doing the most: it's the person with the most story behind their movement. If we find ourselves thinking that he looks aggressive, or she looks depressed, or he looks brainless, then there's clearly a story going on there – which is not so much wrong, as unnecessary. The less you do, the lighter and less tense your body becomes and, ultimately, the more scope we have to place our own meaning and our own interpretation of your attitude.

It's more difficult to run across the stage as if your life depended on it, and then to stop as if you've just got up, than you might think. Basically you're playing a drop here, and in this context, the drop debunks the run; it makes the run look stupid and unnecessary, and we're led to the conclusion that only an idiot would behave like that. In clown you can play enormous drops. The faster you run, the bigger the drop will be on the stop. 'I'm sick to death of you!' I might bellow, like an enraged sergeant major. 'That's not running!' The group look at me with a mixture of surprise and perplexity. 'That's a morning stroll. Now run!! Stop! Run! Stop!'

It's astonishing how much story behind the movement we bring on stage with us, just in the way we stand in the space. 'Are you religious?' I might say sarcastically to someone standing in an attitude of hopeful optimism. 'Run! – Stop! . . . Where's your brain?' I might ask somebody who looks as if they're playing at being stupid, then: 'Run! – Stop! . . . Don't you dare stand like that!' I might say to somebody, looking particularly confident. 'You're sex mad – you can't think of anything else, can you? It's outrageous! Where do you think you are: Amsterdam?'

Again, you know it's a joke, but you also know it's a criticism as well, and the interesting thing is that my sarcastic comments make you adjust the way you stand. Every time I ask you to stop, the attitudes become less pronounced and less extreme. People often look younger and almost childlike, and the less they do, the more vulnerable they appear to be. They often look as if their bodies are like figures cut out from a photograph and pasted on the space. They look as if they have just been plonked there out of context.

This abrupt inertia thrown into stark relief by the grim determination of that desperate run brings us back to rhythm again. The rhythm of clown is unique; it's constantly at odds with the rhythms of everyday life. We're accustomed to seeing people stand on stage for a specific reason, and we're accustomed to seeing people preoccupied in thought, or with a clear objective to play. It's intriguing to see somebody just standing there for no apparent reason, with nothing to achieve and nothing to prove.

We have a tendency when we start clown to look for a formula: 'He must be looking for something particularly funny,' you think, and the temptation to try to look for a 'character' is stronger than you can imagine. Even if, intellectually, you know it's a futile thing to do, it's hard to stand there, just as yourself – you feel naked. We're not dealing with character here – we're dealing with you, and you're not required to assume a persona or a mask or a role of any kind.

Stupidity takes many forms. Not all clowns are innocent. Some are grumpy, others are mischievous, some are terrified, and others look deeply hurt for most of the time. There are as many different clown qualities as there are people, because we all respond to being put 'in the shit' in our different ways. The clown is *you*, as you are now – warts and all. The moment you find yourself assuming a particular way of moving, then you're missing the point completely. Clown isn't fixed; it changes and develops just as you change and develop.

I remember introducing this work to staff at a university trying to develop a postgraduate degree programme in the Performing Arts. To mark the occasion, I invented the following game:

The 'I'm Very Stupid' Game

Everyone stood in a circle and took turns to introduce themselves to each other, by looking each other in the eye, and saying: 'Hello, I'm . . .' You say your full name – rather like children do in primary school – and then add: 'And I'm very stupid.'

The object of the game was to convince the entire group, without the slightest trace of irony or the slightest hint of acting, that you really are very stupid; that it's no big deal, and that you've always been stupid. In fact, you actually like being stupid, and even admire the condition.

At the university seminar, the first person was persuasive. She was candid, funny and endearingly ridiculous. The second person in the group was very hesitant.

'Just say your name and tell us that you're very stupid,' I said, imperiously.

'But I'm not stupid,' she replied. Embarrassed titters from the rest of the group.

'I know,' I said. 'It's a game. Just say it, as if you think you are.'

'But I'm not,' she said.

'Of course you're not stupid,' I said, 'but the game is to convince us that you are.'

'I'm a highly intelligent woman with a doctorate,' she said. The group were spluttering with laughter now.

'Yes. I don't doubt that for a moment,' I said. 'But the game is to say that you're stupid in such a way that we believe you.'

'But I'm not stupid!'

She was getting really annoyed this time, and the rest of the group were convulsed with laughter, as her self-importance became pompous. Her anger was compounded by the fact that everyone was laughing at her expense, and the incident was becoming painful, so I stopped the game. She wasn't a performer, and had no desire to be one, but she had demonstrated the biggest hurdle in playing clown, namely: How do you negotiate your ego in a situation where you've clearly lost your dignity? It was her literal frame of mind, and her insistence that gave her such a successful moment of clowning. The group were hurting with laughter by the end. Unfortunately, she didn't see the joke and she certainly didn't recognise her success. She felt as if she'd made a fool of herself, and of course she had. This is where clowning starts.

We laughed because she'd clearly missed the point of the game, but we laughed even more because she took herself so seriously. The more earnest she became, and the more she insisted that she wasn't stupid, the more stupid she appeared to be. This apparent stupidity was made even more tangible by the fact that she looked round at everybody in an attempt to enlist their support. This only had the effect of making her look ridiculous. She genuinely didn't understand what was happening, so in our eyes she became an entirely credible idiot, and I spent the rest of the session trying to explain what had happened to her. The group assured her that she had made an astonishing contribution to the session, and I think most people left with an intellectual understanding of the work; but it's difficult to approach clown from cold, especially if you've no ambitions to be a performer. Our doctor wasn't a performer. Had she done more playful work before attempting clown, I doubt that she would have reacted so strongly to the game. In the end, I think she felt better about the experience, but I can't emphasise enough that clown is difficult to teach, because it's about *you*, the individual performer.

Clown is one of the richest and the most fascinating introductions into physical comedy, but we can all make a mess of it. I remember Lecoq teaching clown. A young Australian got up wearing a wide- brimmed hat with corks dangling round the rim. He found a particularly unfunny game of swinging the corks about. Lecoq said 'Au revoir' sarcastically, but the man stayed on stage, and carried on swinging. Lecoq thanked him – with even greater sarcasm – and again told him to go. Again the man stayed on, swinging his silly hat. Then Lecoq lost his temper and ordered him to sit down immediately. That person never got up again for the rest of the course. Cruel, you might think? No, I don't think so. The man with the hat wanted to perform; he wasn't an academic; he'd chosen to play the game, and he was ignoring the rule: if you're boring – get off. It's often more difficult to teach clowning to actors – especially actors with 'good technique'.

I remember working with an actor who proudly boasted that she'd done a workshop with Philippe Gaulier. As soon as we started, she assumed a carefully studied facial expression. It was a sort of half-smile with the lips slightly parted. Everything she did from then on looked imposed, and breathtakingly unfunny. I've never worked with an actor with such an interestingly boring face. 'What's the matter with your face?' I asked her, like a schoolteacher reprimanding her for wearing make-up. 'Nothing,' she replied, and a look of alarm flashed in her eyes. Instantly, her face was alive; she was 'in the shit', and delightful to watch. She'd thought she'd found the formula; she'd probably seen somebody being really effective with a facial expression like that, and she'd decided to copy it. Teaching clown to people who have no experience in this kind of work is a bit of a risk, but it's a risk I'd rather take than not. Clown is always on the edge of real pain. It's a game of brinkmanship. The most exciting way to encounter clown is as a complete novice. Our earnest doctor couldn't make the connection between play and performance, and she felt humiliated.

Clowns always work in the 'here and now'. Everything they do on stage is actually happening. Everything is declared, and there's no artifice and no pretence. It was the actuality of the occasion that was so profoundly funny in the doctor incident. There wasn't the slightest trace of acting, nothing was imposed or premeditated. Everything that woman did was for real. The situation laid her bare. The studied facial expression on the actor who'd worked with Gaulier, however, was formulaic and wholly incredible. It's excruciating to see acting in clown. We feel patronised and cheated. I know that it's all acting but, as I've said many times before, if we can see the acting – it's crap. You can't reduce clown to an ambiguous facial expression or a funny walk. We're dealing with a level of comedy here that emanates from moments of complete transparency. 'How can she be so painfully insensitive?' I remember thinking about our learned doctor, my next thought being: 'What a beautiful moment of clowning.' The moment clown turns you into a little character, your work becomes phoney. We want to see a real human being up there without any masks. We all want to see you 'in the shit'.

Anybody talking about you finding your clown character is hopelessly missing the point. Clown has nothing to do with character. A clown is a credibly stupid version of *you*, and we want to see you caught up in a situation that's actually happening before our very eyes. The doctor in my 'I'm Very Stupid' Game was genuinely confused, genuinely outraged and genuinely angered by everybody's reaction to what she did. She believed that she had more in common with a Martian than she did with a clown and against her better judgement, and in spite of herself, she became a perfect clown. Some actors will also claim a greater affinity with Martians than they do with clowns. To train yourself to hide your skill, so that you can make a joke of yourself, is abhorrent to most of us. But for those of us who like to go there, it's the ultimate liberation. After a lifetime of trying to be as good as you possibly can be, the invitation to be like you are, without having to rise to an occasion, is a captivating prospect.

The 'Don't Rise to It' Game

I always play this game if I have a musician in the group, but if I haven't, I ask the group to sing 'The Stripper'.

The game is to make an entrance in two contrasting ways:

1. In the way an actor might use that music to enter in character.

2. As if you're somebody who just happens to amble on whilst that music is playing.

The contrast between the first and the second entrances marks the difference between the élan of an actor making an entrance on stage, and the élan of a clown doing the same. An actor will have made a conscious choice inspired by the music, and will come on stage using the music intelligently, to make an effective entrance. A clown will come on more like somebody who's just strolled in to borrow a cup of sugar. The entrance will look inept and unconsidered, and will have nothing to do with the music. If you change the music, the clown will remain exactly the same. The clown doesn't 'make an entrance'. By refusing to 'rise to the occasion', you do things in your way; you become unpredictable, inappropriate; immediately you don't seem to fit.

It's this inappropriateness that makes a clown so interesting to watch: 'How dare you behave like that?' we think to ourselves. 'That's so inept, so unconsidered, so crude. Don't you know where you are?' The answer is, of course, that you don't; you didn't bother to ask. In clown, you tend to treat everybody, and everything with the same benign incredulity. You're perplexed – as if life has overtaken you. You're not brainless, so much as baffled; and ironically this bafflement is the one thing that clowns have in common with some of our finest actors; in fact, bafflement is a universal human condition. We're all baffled some of the time – for more times than most of us would like to admit. The main difference between clowning and acting is that clowns tend to start from a state of bafflement, whereas actors tend to arrive at this state in the context of the drama.

Bafflement

In one of his acts, Tommy Cooper would walk on stage wearing his trademark fez, bow tie, tuxedo and tails, on the top half of his body, and enormous bright yellow chicken legs, complete with big clawed feet, on the lower half. His act was to walk on, look at the audience, and they would laugh, then he'd say: 'What? – What?' This was his point of bafflement. The great French clown, Grock, would punctuate his work with the constant question: 'Pourquoi?' That was his point of bafflement. Simon McBurne, of Complicite, would use his normal slight stutter: 'I – I – I – er . . .' Angela de Castro will look at us as if to say, 'Oh dear', and then adjust her trousers. For some people, it's an embarrassed little laugh; for others, it's a look of deep disapproval. Some people even look as if they're about to burst into tears. These various points of bafflement are unique to each of us. All they really mean, of course, is 'Oh shit', because they come from occasions when we're flummoxed, caught out, or taken by surprise, but a point of bafflement is also capable of accruing other meanings, depending on the context. A point of bafflement is an instinctive reaction, and it's likely to change subtly, as we change; so don't try to define 'your point of bafflement' and don't try to practise it in the mirror. It's something you've got to find for yourself, or you'll end up like the actor with the boringly interesting face.

There are many ways to provoke bafflement. Lecoq made us run on stage and take a flamboyant bow, expecting rapturous applause, only to realise that the audience were completely quiet, and indifferent to us. We were perplexed; it was a disaster, and we didn't know why! Lecoq called this moment 'Le Flop'. Gaulier made us, one by one, sweep the stage, and turn round to see that the audience were in their seats and watching us. Again it was a disaster. He called it 'the big flop'. I've heard it described as 'the void' and as 'the moment of perplexity'. Basically you're 'in the shit'. All the little provocations in the Running and Stopping Game are there to reveal your point of bafflement. The combination of doing as little as possible, when you haven't the slightest idea why you're doing it, is funny and heart-warming at the same time. We laugh every time I catch you off your guard, and it's your point of bafflement that we're laughing at; it's the point when your confusion is at its most palpable. It's the point when we know, for sure, that you're not acting and that you don't know what to do, and you've got nothing in your head, but it's still OK. You seem quite happy to be in this position, and you can do what you like from here. In fact, anything you do from now on will only develop your perplexity. Even if we're all convulsed with laughter, you'll still won't know why we're like that; it's OK, insofar as you haven't been sent off yet, and everybody seems to be having a good time – so you can do something else. Anything!

The Bafflement Game

Two clowns make a plan about what they're going to do. A might say, 'I'll throw myself on the floor, whilst you kick me to death.' But when they spring into action, they both do entirely different things: A might dance round the room, whilst B might start to clean the windows. It wasn't much of a plan to start with, but now it's a flop, and neither of them knows why.

The game is to share with us your surprise at your failure to do what you've planned to do: to find the point of bafflement, then to come up with another plan, and the cycle starts all over again.

Once again, the challenge here is *not* to act. Don't act bafflement. Throw yourself completely into the action, so that when you both eventually realise that it's a disaster, you're both taken by surprise and you can't hide what you feel. The key is to be totally engaged in the action. In other words, if you decide to jump up and down, really go for it. Enjoy it – give yourself a good time, then when you realise that you shouldn't have been doing that at all, you can play a drop, or a slow change of rhythm, and silently admit to us that what you've been doing is completely inappropriate. If your disastrous plan genuinely catches you unawares, then your point of bafflement will happen naturally, whether you like it or not. Don't decide how you're going to play it beforehand. Admit you're 'in the shit' and see what comes naturally. All you'll have to do is to look to the audience, as soon as you realise that all is lost. We'll do the rest. If your admission is credible, your stupidity will be transparent, and we'll admire your honesty. But if you play the failure of the game, you'll become sentimental and mawkish, and we'll loathe you for it. Be completely honest but completely hopeful as well. You're 'in the shit' at the moment, but it's going to be all right. If you're going to catch yourself out genuinely, the stakes have to be kept as high as possible.

Our eminent university doctor played her point of bafflement magnificently. She declared it by looking at the group, and her incredulous outrage filled the room, but she was unaware that she had touched a quality so uniquely her own. We empathised with her confusion, but had she been aware of her discovery, had she known what she was doing, we could have laughed at her uninhibitedly, rather than feeling embarrassed for her because we were laughing in spite of ourselves. Some people invest enormous time and effort into finding their clown, just as others do in finding their character, but it's a waste of time. You are more interesting, more unique, and more multifaceted than anything you're going to make up. There's nothing to be found. It's all there. Clown is the most uncompromising invitation you're going to have to be you. We're all stupid. Admit it.

I'm often asked if Lee Evans is a clown. Or Norman Wisdom. Or Ken Dodd, or Tommy Cooper. Or Eric Morecambe and Ernie Wise. For me, a clown is somebody who plays from a point of bafflement. If, from the moment the person comes on stage, I get the feeling that they don't know why they're there, then I know I'm watching a clown, as opposed to an actor playing comedy. A performer who declares his or her vulnerability, who can hold our attention and inspire our empathy, simply by being themselves, with no apparent script, and no set routine to play with, is a clown. For me, clowning is acting in its most elemental form. There are many 'actors' that I'd call clowns who'd probably take offence to be described as such, and there are many so-called 'clowns' who're really actors. Some actors go instinctively to clown to generate material, even to the extent of rehearsing in red noses, but they'd never dream of describing themselves as clowns in public. That would be going too far. They might be stupid, but they're not that stupid. Many of our most accomplished 'serious actors' have that tissue-thin vulnerability, and when they declare it to an audience their point of bafflement is perfectly clear. I remember teaching half-mask work to Antony Sher. His physical command of an idea was extraordinary. He played each mask with an engagement that was quite uncompromising, but the moment he didn't understand something or I managed deliberately to catch him out, he would declare it immediately; a bit like a child admitting he was in the wrong. His vulnerability was astonishing. At that moment he was an extraordinary clown, but I doubt he'd ever describe himself as such.

The 'I'm Very Stupid' Game is a useful provocation to bafflement. It worked in this case because it caught the doctor out. This is what you're always trying to do in provoking clown. You're trying to catch somebody off their guard so that they find themselves genuinely 'in the shit', and genuinely perplexed by circumstance. The trouble is that we all want to act. In a workshop you might see someone completely baffled, everybody laughs and you think, 'Oh, that's what he wants.' Then when your turn comes up, you act stupid or confused, yet it's so palpably imposed, we all know you're not remotely 'in the shit'. But old habits die hard.

The Entrance Game

This is my version of a game I learnt from Gaulier. I play it just to provoke you to continually return to your point of bafflement.

Two people stand in the wings. 'On my third beat, you must burst on stage like an atomic bomb,' I tell them, trying to sound as pompous as possible, and I sit in the audience with a drum.

My game is to catch them out. I might give the three beats far too fast for them to catch them, or I might give them one beat, have a conversation with the person next to me, and then give them the other two in quick succession. Every time they miss the beat, I'll tell them off. This part of the game can be littered with points of bafflement if the provocation is strong enough.

Your game is to do everything you can not to be caught out. You've got to be straining at the leash on every beat. The more deadly serious you are, and the more determined you are to get on to do your atom bomb, the more effective your entrance is likely to be.

If I play my game well, you'll be so preoccupied with trying to hit the third beat that the idea of the atom bomb will have slipped from your mind, so your entrance will be not so much a bang as a whimper. Once you've managed to make your entrance, on the third beat, and having done your atomic bomb, or even your atomic whimper, I'll probably provoke you further with something like: 'They tell me that you have an act for us.' Again, if we both get this right, there'll be an excellent point of bafflement here. Now we're into the more familiar territory of the Compliments Game; we're at the stage of 'They tell me that you know all the movements.' Now you can play. Now you've got to keep the curtain up by doing anything you like. What is it that we, as an audience, find funny?

You can play the Entrance Game as a routine way of getting started. It's a good preparation for both of us for what is to come. What you do, once you're eventually on stage, is completely open, but the pressure of finding something to do to engage our attention will invariably make you forget to look at us, and if you do that, the scene will flop. I use the term 'flop', not as an indication of bafflement, but in a much more literal sense: to indicate when the action has died, and it's time for you to go or to do something else.

The Flop

Gaulier described the flop as 'the angel of death sitting in the wings, just waiting to swoop down and take the stage'. If you ignore her, she'll not only take the stage, but she'll move her entire family in as well. The skill is to recognise and to deal with every flop; you've got to teach yourself to keep the curtain up, or to 'save the furniture', as Gaulier would say. Once you've experienced the flop, you'll never forget it, so the best way forward is to become competent with the rescue strategies.

The point of bafflement is a rescue strategy, but you can't use it too often, or you won't do anything. The most effective method of keeping the angel of death at bay is to do something else, but in the heat of the moment that's invariably a very difficult thing to do if you find yourself 'in the shit'. The next few games contain various survival strategies that push you into doing something else, and help to keep your games fresh.

There are no completely reliable formulas for keeping the angel of death at bay. It helps if you declare it and acknowledge, to the audience, that you're dying. Drops can be helpful here: just abandon what you're doing for a moment, and either do something else, or continue with another version of what you were doing before. Remember you don't need a big idea. All we want is a tiny change of rhythm to excite our interest in you again. Flops happen when you become too involved in what you're doing, and you forget the audience.

The Bafflement Game was devised to help you recognise your point of bafflement, but it's worth noting that if you play bafflement too much, it soon becomes irritating because it stops the action, and if you keep doing that, we'll soon get bored. Bafflement is something to play when you're really 'in the shit', and the only way out is to reveal your humanity. If you do this too many times, you'll appear sentimental. Bafflement can easily be read as a plea for pity or approval. Bafflement might be the hallmark of a clown but it's not a fail-safe approach; it's a rescue strategy for emergency use only. The clown's job is to get us laughing, and to keep us laughing, and to do this you've got be able to play fluently because this is the only thing that's going to stimulate our thoughts and feelings and keep you interesting to watch. This is a game to give you a bit more to play.

The Secret Weapon Game

Somebody gives you a secret compliment like: 'You've got beautiful lips', or 'You've got lovely teeth', or 'nice hair'. It doesn't have to be a real compliment. The idea is that some idiot in a pub told you this, and said that as long as you remember that compliment you'll always be all right.

It's important that the audience don't know what your compliment is. The game is to come on stage and subtly play your compliment. Don't think that we've got to guess what your compliment is. That will kill the game completely, so you haven't got to illustrate it. It's your secret weapon, something for you to play with, to have an effect on the audience. Just come on, look at us, and think: 'I've got lovely teeth – have you noticed my teeth? I can do what I like now, because my teeth are lovely. Look, I can run about with lovely teeth. I can sit on the floor with lovely teeth, and roll about with lovely teeth. I can be very angry – with lovely teeth. I can be sexy – with lovely teeth. I can do anything I like because I've got lovely teeth.'

It's a sort of naive preoccupation game. It just gives you something inconsequential to play, that's all. Like a small child with a pair of sunglasses, you feel slightly different, and you like the feeling, so you show everybody else that you like the feeling. The game is to declare your pleasure in having the compliment, and to find the game of being empowered by it. If you get too involved with your secret weapon we'll get bored with you. Our interest lies in the fact that you're playing *something*. We don't necessarily need to know what that something is.

The Preposterous Acting Game

This game gives you even more to do. Now you have a theme to play with. Remember that the theme is only a provocation.

It's a pretext to be on stage. Play the theme as best you can at first, but if we like it when you fall over, or when you hit yourself on the head, then forget the theme, and follow the laugh.

'They tell me that you're all very good actors, and that you can act anything,' I say to a small group of people in the space. 'Yes,' they reply. The more seriously they take this situation – the better the eventual comedy. 'Cockatoos,' I might say. 'Show me a cockatoo. Good.'

Do the first thing that comes into your head. An intricate mime of a cockatoo won't be particularly interesting. We want to see a credible idiot playing a cockatoo. The question is, 'What do we like?' If we all burst out laughing when you poke your head forward and run about, then that's perfectly adequate. If we don't laugh when you do that, do something else.

'Now show me a cockatoo on a skateboard,' I might say.

This last instruction can be taken in a number of ways; it could be met with bafflement but that might be a bit too soon, or it could provoke some ludicrous action. Just put the two ideas together in some way. The more stupid it is, the better. As long as you get a laugh – it doesn't matter what you do.

'Good. Domestic appliances,' I might say. 'A washing machine: a washing machine on fast spin. Excellent. Now show me a Japanese washing machine on fast spin. Now a pregnant washing machine with a full load.'

Once you've started to get us laughing, I can suggest anything I like to keep you going. Birds, domestic appliances, nationalities, monsters and fish are all fruitful starting points, but anything that might inspire either big physical attitude, or a preposterous idea is an effective theme to play with.

Separations

There's a big trap in playing the Preposterous Acting Game. It can seduce you into becoming so engrossed in your 'character' that you forget the audience, and forget to play clown, so I use it to teach separations. A drop is an abrupt and clear separation, a clock is the smallest separation of all, but if you break off from playing your cockatoo, for example, run to the other side of the stage, and join us in a laugh at what you've just done, and give yourself a break from 'acting' for a moment, and look back to the other side of the stage – to the place where you were acting, and then return to playing your cockatoo, you'd be playing a separation.

A separation occurs when you leave your 'role' on one side of the stage, and run to the other side of the stage to comment on it. It's an outrageous debunking of your own work; you can hardly declare the game any more overtly than that. Separations enable you to keep yourself at a comfortable distance from what you're playing. You can even comment on what you've just done. You might join us in admiring what you did with your legs, for example – then run back and do it again. Separations enable you to have a really good look at whether we like it or not, and to share that appreciation with us. Of course, separations are another survival strategy; they make it easier for you to abandon something, or to change your mind, and do something else. However, their main function is to keep the game in the forefront of our minds. Separations leave us in no doubt that you're only playing and that what's happening in front of us is quite spontaneous and 'in the moment'. You're also reminding us all that you can debunk what's happening at any time; that you don't care enough about 'your character' to want to give it more status than you. Separations focus our attention on your clowning rather than on the role you're playing.

In the Preposterous Acting Game, I might ask 'What do policemen do?' or 'What do doctors do? What do psychiatrists do? What do taxi drivers do?' These are all invitations to play the first thing that comes into your head about being a policeman or whoever. Your idea needs to be short and accurate. It's the crude recognition of the action that's most likely to get us laughing. If saying ''Allo, 'allo, 'allo' and bending your knees gets a laugh, then you can sell that stupid cliché to us, and do that action again. If the laugh grows with repetition, then you've probably got enough rapport with us to take the policeman further. You might develop your idea by elaborating the cliché a little by saying 'You're nicked' and looking aggressive. Or you could run to the other side of the stage and deconstruct your policeman if you like, or you might choose to abandon him altogether, and find more games with your legs. You might find the game of being aggressive, so much so that you break something. You might intimidate the audience and have to tie yourself up to keep yourself in control. You might go on to intimidate *yourself*. In the end, you might refuse to play policemen ever again, and refuse even to venture onto that side of the stage again. But then your knees might start to bend, and that aggressive demon starts to take over, and soon you're wrecking anything around that's wreckable, and chasing members of the audience about the auditorium. Eventually, you might separate yourself from the stage completely, and sit down next to a member of the audience for a moment of comfort.

Clowns don't act; they play the audience. As long as the audience recognise your initial theme, you can do what you like with it. It's not about playing a story, or even developing a situation – that might come later, if you have a taste for it. At the beginning, clowning is about staying alive, and trying to keep the curtain up, and maintaining your freedom as a clown. Clowning is the only level of play that enables you to do what you like, when you like and for no better reason than the audience liking it. Separations, drops and clocks, are all devices that develop your contact, and your relationship with us, but they're also devices that give you the ability to debunk not only your chosen theme and your own work, but also yourself, the act of performance, and even the audience sitting there watching you. Clowning puts you on a steep trajectory towards anarchy and chaos, and in studying clown we're actually learning how to use these destructive techniques to make you a volatile and powerful presence in any authoritative structure. You're being invited to rediscover how to misbehave, and being encouraged to reject the key principles of education and society. Reason, logic, responsibility, respect, and even empathy, pity and love are all thrown out of the window when you play clown at this level.

Ultimately, clowning is subversive, but it's too mindless an activity in itself to be political with anything like a capital 'P', because there is no rationale, and no ideology behind the actions of a clown. Clowning in its most simple form is triggered by nothing more than the desire to have a comic effect on the audience and to keep us laughing. Clowning teaches us that there is immense pleasure to be found in mindless disobedience and ignorant naivety. This is the dark side that stops it from becoming twee and sentimental. This is the confrontational side of clowning that takes us to a world that values laughter above anything else, but has no other values beyond laughter. This is clowning in its most basic form: simple clown. Simple clown is fun-loving, childlike, amoral, irresponsible, mercurial, bizarre, destructive, chaotic and anarchic. To play clown to your full potential you have to accept all these aspects of yourself, and all these aspects of your imagination.

The Marx Brothers were the greatest exponents of anarchic clowning during the twentieth century. They had scripts, and they rehearsed, but the problems of getting them to keep to what was written are legendary. If you look at them next to the manicured physicality of Charlie Chaplin, they're like three bulls in a china shop. Born of the great depression, the Marx Brothers have been described as 'unhinged maniacs'. They were as rootless and irreverent in their lives as they were in their art. Harpo and Chico were consummate musical clowns with a point of bafflement that had grown into a predatory sense of mischief. Between them they took an infantile delight in mindless destruction. When they came into a room, nothing was safe. Groucho was more of a half-mask than a clown, with his big round glasses, ridiculous false moustache, and his ubiquitous cigar. He'd stride over all the havoc and destruction created by his two brothers and make wisecracks: 'I've got to stay here,' he said to the audience on one occasion, 'but there's no reason why you folks shouldn't go out into the lobby till this thing blows over.'

Nothing was sacred to the Marx Brothers, and when they swaggered into Hollywood in the thirties, MGM didn't know what had hit them. Scripts, plots and shooting schedules were an anathema to them. They busked their way through everything they did. *Animal Crackers* (1930) and *Monkey Business* (1931) are both shamelessly self-indulgent, yet delightfully chaotic films. Even what's generally considered their best work, *Duck Soup* (1933), with Groucho leading his country into an unnecessary war – a theme as prescient today as it was then – is really little more than a few brilliant clown numbers loosely strung together in a makeshift plot. They must have been a bit of a handful to work with. It's rumoured that some directors would lock them in at night during filming, in case they wandered off somewhere. Their clowning created a world of boundless possibility where there were no rules, but their audiences came from a very real, authoritarian world, where possibilities were steadily closing down for everybody. The Marx Brothers' total disregard for form and convention won them the respect of the great surrealists of the period. Salvador Dali wrote a script for them (*The Marx Brothers on Horseback Salad*), and their fans included Antonin

Artaud and Eugène Ionesco. It's been argued that their work paved the way for *The Goon Show* and for *Monty Python's Flying Circus*. This might be the case. But neither of these shows has the genuine anarchy of a group of uncompromising artists whose imaginations could never be brought to heel by anybody.

By discarding conventional rules, clowning will enable you to rediscover your taste for disobedience, and ignorant naivety. In accepting the potential for chaos and anarchy in your work, clowning gives our imaginations their full range. At its best, clown is the key to a world with no boundaries, and if you develop a persistent zest for play, you'll become a force to be reckoned with, both on stage and in the rehearsal room. Only by accepting these darker sides of the work, and stopping yourself from trying to be either 'clever', or 'good', will you be capable of making audacious choices, and taking the immense risks of a courageous and truly creative performer. Authority will always be there to rein you in, but clown teaches us that authority is to be respected only when it's absolutely necessary. Authority is the essential conflict in playing clown. Clowning comes into its own the moment the stakes are raised and you're in danger of getting into trouble, or of suffering the worst fate imaginable in being ordered off the stage. Like an unruly child needing the restraining influence of a responsible adult, or an eager puppy straining on a leash, clown has a predilection towards anarchy. This is the energy of pure unbridled playfulness. Clown is an invitation to play in a world where there are no barriers other than the transient pleasure of the audience.

But unbridled playfulness is a scary prospect to some of us. If I say, 'Look, there's the stage; you can do whatever you like on it,' a sort of imaginative agoraphobia sets in, and most people freeze like a rabbit in the headlights as soon as the constraints are removed.

The Amnesiac Game

This is an excellent game for exploring bafflement, providing you don't end up thinking that clowns are amnesiacs.

The game is to come on stage like an amnesiac – as if you remember nothing about the world around you: even who you are, or why you're there. In this state of mind, a door, a wall, the clothes you're wearing, in fact anything to enter your field of vision, is going to be a complete mystery to you, and everything is an adventure in a world where you know nothing. The only thing that has seeped into your consciousness is that the people watching you appear to like you – so everything must be OK.

The Amnesiac Game is an invitation to find the game in anything. It's a device to inspire play in a state of mind beyond conventional logic, where you no longer need a reason to do something. In this state, nothing is what it seems, and anything is possible. You might know nothing, but there isn't a trace of sadness or unhappiness about you. Basically, you're just getting on with things as best you can. My only reservation with this game is the fact that by introducing this amnesiac idea, we end up focusing most of our attention on the point of bafflement, to the extent that the audience start to laugh every time they see it. Once this happens you start to drift towards bathos and sentimentality. The biggest trap in playing clown is thinking that you've got to look cute, or that you have to fish for our sympathy: 'Oh, he doesn't know what he's doing – Bless!' Ultimately, this response is wholly destructive. Clown isn't sweet or cute; clown is more robust than that. Bafflement isn't a device to enlist our sympathy; it's a means of liberating you from your natural intelligence, and your innate sense of causality.

This is becoming a litany, but I'm going to say it again: you can only do something – just for the sake of it – in clown. This is the great freedom that clown offers to all of us. In any other level of play, you've got to have to find a very good reason for what you do. If you begin to rely on cutesy ignorance to get your laughs, the audience will grow to hate you. But the great strength of the Amnesiac Game is the fact that you're not trying to be funny, so much as trying to follow your own logic. You're never sorry for yourself; you're much tougher than that. We laugh at you, and we empathise with you when we see you 'in the shit', or when we see that your reaction to something is transparently honest. Sometimes you'll be too irritating and too exasperating to watch, and sometimes you'll be too painful, but in the end we'll love your resilience, and your openness. It's fascinating to see you desperately trying to cope when it really matters to you that you stay on stage, but we like it best of all when we see you genuinely enjoying yourself. There's no pretence in clown. This is why the stakes are so high. Everything you do on stage happens in the 'here and now'. The Amnesiac Game is an attempt to play Stanislavski's 'Magic If': the 'What would I do if I was an amnesiac in this situation?' It's only a starting point, and if you try to use it as a recipe, you'll become a cute little character, and eventually we'll all want to take you out and kill you.

The Wrong Person in the Wrong Place Game

A clown is sent out of the room whilst I set up a situation where somebody is waiting for a specialist service provider, a plumber, or a doctor, or a prostitute, or a professional hit man, to arrive – and a clown walks in. Like the amnesiac of the previous game, the clown doesn't know anything about what's going on, and doesn't know if he or she has ever been a plumber, or a doctor, or a prostitute, or a hit man, or even what any of these things might be. The people waiting for the specialist play as themselves.

It's useful to mix up the levels of play like this because it enables the person on stage with you, as the clown, to provoke you within a logical situation. They become the authority figures for you to play against. You're going to be continually in trouble if everyone around you is rational, logical and determined to follow things through. Putting a clown in this semblance of real life throws everything you do into sharp relief, and it reveals how you react, and exactly how you play in clown.

I remember setting this game up where the situation was a woman in the advanced stages of labour desperately waiting the arrival of the midwife. The clown came in to find a hugely pregnant woman, screaming and breathing frantically, and a tense, but outwardly calm husband, explaining to the clown how her waters had broken, and that he thought that the head might be just visible, but that he wasn't sure. The clown had a look, more out of curiosity than anything else, but as soon as the clown touched the pregnant woman, she screamed. The clown touched the woman again, and the woman screamed again, only higher in pitch than before. The clown ran over to the piano, and played a note, then ran back to the woman, and by touching her and playing the piano, the clown managed to make her scream in tune. Eventually, the woman screamed the tune of 'Happy Birthday', and the baby was born.

This game worked because the clown was able to make that analogical leap between screaming and singing. In its own terms, this leap was completely logical, and the choice of song was a satisfying conclusion to the scene, and it also managed to turn the narrative with some audacity.

Playing clown is very different from playing in the more conventional dramatic play. When you're playing in a written drama, or even in a dramatic impro, the convention is that you respect who is in major, and who is in minor, and that you facilitate an easy exchange from one to the other. It's the equivalent of A throwing a ball to B, and B catching it, and throwing the ball back. If, for example, A is giving a lecture in a conventional dramatic impro, as soon as he or she starts to run out of ideas, B will pick up the cue and carry on with the theme. That doesn't necessarily happen in clown. Here, A might pass the ball to B, but B might refuse to take it, so that A is left high and dry and 'in the shit'. If the audience are enjoying this, B might keep A 'in the shit', and only take the ball when the action is starting to flop.

Provocation is at the root of successful clowning. The provocateur becomes an authority figure. The clown inevitably gets it wrong, and invariably misunderstands the simplest instruction. It's like having a very strict teacher at school. In my experience, whenever we had a strict teacher, the slightest indiscretion or misdemeanour could start gales of suppressed laughter, not because what was happening was particularly funny in itself, but because the stakes were so high – because the teacher was so strict. We were laughing because we were terrified.

Boss-clowns

Some people make excellent boss-clowns. They're like somebody with a very menial job who has a modicum of authority, and it's gone right to their head. They might only be a car-park attendant or a caretaker, but they behave as if they have the power of a Roman Emperor.

Finding the Boss-clown

It's easy to find boss-clowns: I start by asking the group if all the intelligent members could please put their hands up. Then, working in groups of two or three, I put the intelligent ones in charge, and I tell them that they have to teach the others how to stack the chairs, or tidy the bags. Anything clear and practical will do, and I insist that they have to be sure that they do it 'properly' – with no messing about.

I'm always astonished how pompous and self-important some clowns become. Boss-clowns usually emerge as soon as I ask them to brief their team and to demonstrate to us how they do their jobs. Once they begin to take pride in their authority, and show us how they wield that power – how they reprimand people, drill them, punish them – we have an effective boss-clown.

It's important to remember that the boss-clown isn't a role: that would be too limiting, and too predictable. In the anarchic world of the clown, anybody can become the boss at any time. Playing the boss-clown is really no more than another provocation game: it's to give you something else to play. The function of the boss-clown is just to make something happen. If A is the boss in a scene, and the scene starts to flop, then B will probably take over. If the scene flops again, then C might take over, or they might all try to be the boss at the same time. Being the boss-clown is only a catalyst for everyone else in the scene.

The idea of the boss-clown is useful because it introduces dramatic conflict into the work, which gives us more potential for building situations, and nudging clown towards narrative, which is clearly more useful in the long run. During the eighties and nineties, the National Theatre of Brent created a number of excellent clown pieces where a magnificent boss-clown, played by Patrick Barlow and his helper, played originally by Jim Broadbent, would stage preposterous and hopelessly overambitious themes like the Zulu Wars, the Bible, or the history of the world. Patrick Barlow was a beautifully pretentious boss-clown, who was continually undermined by his stupid associate. They developed a style where they would play the scene whilst sustaining continual conflicts between the two of them. For example, the boss might announce the scene, and his idiot would come on, then stop and question why he was coming on at that point, or he might suddenly refuse to continue. Occasionally the idiot would go on strike, or resign, and the hopelessly pretentious boss-clown would be humiliated, and have to carry on alone, whilst his associate would eat his sandwiches in a corner. The challenges to authority, the shifts in authority, the breakdown of authority, and the sharing or abandoning of authority became a continual backdrop to whatever theme they were playing with, opening up a rich vein of clowning and creating some outstanding and resonant comedy.

The Forbidding Game

A is the boss-clown, and A gives B a simple instruction. The game is for B to immediately and quite inadvertently do the very thing that he is not supposed to do. For example:

A. *Keep still.*

B moves towards A, as if B isn't sure what has been said.

B. *Sorry.*

A. *I said, keep still.*

B. *(Looking round) I am keeping still.*

A. *No you're not. You're still moving.*

B. *(Looking round) I'm completely still.*

A. *You're still moving.*

B. *(Looking round for support) But I wasn't moving.*

The effect of doing the thing that's just been forbidden is to instantly make the situation worse. B can make A become apoplectic with rage. A development is for the boss-clown to leave a group of clowns in charge of something very valuable, like an antique chair, for example. So he will go off, leaving the others with strict instructions not to touch the chair and certainly not to let anybody else touch it, or, even worse, to sit on it, because it's so fragile and valuable. The moment that A exits, the forbidding game can come into its own:

B. *I wouldn't touch it.*

C. *No, that would be really irresponsible.*

D. *It would be stupid, wouldn't it? I mean, if I were to do that, for example . . . (D touches the chair with a fingertip) it would leave a mark. Look.*

B. *Oh yes, it's left a greasy mark.*

C. *If I were to do that . . . (C puts both hands on the chair) it makes an even bigger mark.*

You can see where it's going. Our interest in the scene is in the logic of how they end up completely wrecking the chair. When the boss-clown returns, the chair should be in pieces on the floor and they should all be jumping up and down on them, and if we've followed the clowns logically, step by step, towards this lamentable conclusion, then the scene will be more satisfying.

In clown, your partners in the scene are a provocation, your costume is a provocation, and the theme you're playing and the reactions of the audience are also equally valuable provocations. Provocations are the most effective way of generating spontaneity, finding more games, and keeping each other on the edge. You don't need a good idea to start playing in clown. Just walking on is an idea in itself. If nothing happens when you walk on, that's a provocation to do something.

The Three-Hander Game

'They tell me that you know the entire Shakespearian canon,' I might say. 'Yes,' comes the reply, and some of the group might even start to do their 'actor preparations'. 'Good. Excellent. I want you to play the cliff scene in *Lear*.'

That's the provocation, and it's a simple enough idea, but if you're going to play that provocation, and if you're going to be able to sustain it, you're going to need a basic structure to work with. The one that I prefer is the one that offers the most flexibility, and that is a three-hander. It works like this:

A announces the scene – 'The cliff scene in Lear' – then runs into the wings. A's job is to provoke the action from the outside. B and C then come on, and play the scene. As soon as their action dies, A can run on and say: 'Later that night', 'On another hill', 'In Lear's bedroom'. A can say anything, and can even do sound effects, or commercials, if they like. The idea isn't to logically develop the story but to rescue the other two. Once they know they're dying, they can change the scene, do something else, and move on.

The controlling idea in this structure is that there should only be two people playing the scene at any time, except of course when A intervenes. You don't have to always keep to the same roles. If A gets involved in a scene, one of the others can run off and stand in the wings. You don't even have to invent a reason. When playing in clown, there's little to be gained by hiding the game.

It'll help enormously if nobody has ever read Shakespeare's *King Lear* because clown isn't about making meaning, or developing linear narrative. As we saw with the Object Game and with the Wrong Person at the Wrong Time Game, it's easier to work with a logical narrative than it is to be bizarre, but the pressure of playing in clown takes you straight into the bizarre. Find the easiest way of generating material, embrace the freedoms of clown, and eventually you'll find yourself in a narrative because, in the end, a narrative is much easier to handle. The first thing to learn is to keep the action alive, and the best way of doing that is to keep provoking each other. Of course you won't be doing Shakespeare, or anything like it, that's not the point, you'll be playing clown, and you can clown with anything.

The Three-Lives Game

This is the best game I know for keeping the stakes as high as possible and making sure that you negotiate the flops and learn to read the audience's reactions. It's really a development of the Hands-Up Game.

Set up the Hands-Up Game, but restrict the length of the action to three lives. In other words, as soon as you start to flop and the hands start to go up to indicate you're being boring, you must do something. If hands are raised in the audience, then we take that as 'one life'.

It can also help to sell what you're doing to us. For example, I bob up and down, and somebody laughs. If I see who it is that's laughing, I can bob up and down again, and I might get a bigger laugh. I can then look round to see who isn't laughing, and bob up and down for them. Laugher is infectious. If you sell what you're doing, moment by moment, rather than looking at your action as if it were a conventional scene or an impro, then you're going to be more adept in dealing with the angel of death.

The Red Nose Versus the Neutral Mask

The only reason for using the traditional red nose is to amplify your expression of bafflement. There's no magic about this. Putting a red nose on is like having a giant pimple on the end of your own nose. It makes you look conspicuous, and we can't help looking at it, but then we can't resist peeking beyond the nose to look at the rest of your face, and into your eyes – just to see how you feel about it. Unlike a pimple, a red nose is such a ridiculous fake that it fails completely to inspire our empathy. In fact, it's so fake that it encourages our ridicule. We don't care that you look stupid. We know it's deliberate so we feel free to laugh directly at you, but we still can't help looking at your eyes to see what's really going on, and as we examine your feelings more acutely, your point of bafflement becomes more pronounced.

It isn't essential that you wear a red nose to play clown. In the circus the red nose has become a public licence for comedy, rather like the fool's motley was in the middle ages, but it's become a hackneyed convention today. An event like Red Nose Day has made the red nose more of an irritation than a help. It's become synonymous in my mind with naff physical comedy. It's only when I see somebody like Angela de Castro playing in a red nose that I start to become interested in it again. The red nose is an excellent training device, and as I'm always working towards the theatre clown rather than the circus clown, my attachment to the nose is entirely practical.

Lecoq described the red nose as 'the smallest mask in the world', and as 'a little neutral mask for the clown'. The red nose is indeed a mask; initially, it works in the same way as any other mask. Masks engage our imaginations by exciting our innate ability to read other people's faces. We're all born with the ability to read the human face, almost as soon as we can see. It's a survival reflex. We grow up with the ability to read faces faster than we can think thoughts. When we see a mask, we know instantly that it isn't real; we know it's a false face, so we immediately redirect our attention to the rest of the body, and start to read the body language instead.

With a red nose, we know from the outset that it's only a blob of plastic strapped on your face, and it's preposterous to the point of ridicule because there's so little to it. Unlike most other masks, the red nose is not in any way a face with recognisable features. This 'mask' gives us nothing; it's more a painful affliction than a facial feature. You couldn't say, 'Oh, it looks happy, angry, frail or clever', but you might say, 'Oh, *you* look happy, angry, frail or clever.' The red nose is a revealing mask, and in this respect, the red nose is 'a little neutral mask for the clown'.

The neutral mask was a teaching device developed by Lecoq and Amleto Sartori in the fifties, in order to explore issues like power and economy in action. It's a stylised representation of a face in repose. If you put on a neutral mask and stand in a space, with no story behind your movement and then wear a red nose, and stand in the space, again with no story behind your movement, we'll see no discernible difference in your physicality. But our relationship with you will change dramatically.

The neutral mask covers the whole face, and projects an image of an entire face. But it isn't your face; it's an idealised face; it's the face of a person without the usual conflicts that we all have in life. Because we're looking at a 'full face', there's a lot of information to assimilate at a brief glance, but the more we assemble this information into a readable image, the more we start to build up an elaborate illusion in our minds. We forget the person behind the mask and start to believe that you've become a different person. Full masks give us a lot to take in, and so if you move too much, the features of the mask will start to blur. It's more satisfying for us if you keep very still, and focus on something, like the horizon, for example. Once you're still and focused, we get the overwhelming feeling that you're just about to do something. But your presence isn't like life; it's grander than that, more important than we're used to, more assured, and more competent. The neutral mask is 'better' than life.

When we look at you in a red nose, we'll see you at ease, certainly, but you'll look ridiculous. We won't have the idealised face of the neutral mask; instead, we'll have the slightly perplexed face of 'somebody who doesn't know'. If I were to ask you to look at the horizon, it wouldn't make any difference, no one would believe that you knew what it was, and your stillness would only invite us to look deeper into your face. There's no illusion here, and there's nothing grand or assured at all. Instead of being about to do something, we'll be expecting you to move at any moment.

Both the nose and the mask are indeterminate in their attitude to the world. In other words, they're neither happy nor sad. In the red nose, you're not a simpleton; you're just baffled. Both the mask and the nose could be about to eat, or about to kiss, about to pray, or about to swear, but are doing none of these things. The main difference between them is that one of them knows why and the other doesn't. We're not drawn towards the neutral mask. We like to keep our distance, because we want to sustain the illusion of you being this other person, but the lack of comprehension in the face behind the red nose tends to draw us closer. We feel more inclined to help; we feel that it's more appropriate for us to react in some way.

You don't assume a character with either the neutral mask or the red nose. Both these masks are designed to reveal aspects of the way you are. They teach us that we can all be a powerful presence in a room, or we can just as easily be completely baffled. All other masks, apart from these two, if they're any good, present us with an instantly recognisable face of a person that we want to play. A red nose doesn't give us anything in particular. You don't play a red nose so much as wear it, and it has a greater effect on the audience than it does on you.

Costumes

Costumes are another exciting provocation for clown, particularly if you wear your costume with a red nose. No matter what costume you wear, that uncompromising bit of red plastic will be a stubborn reminder that everything's a silly game. Philippe Gaulier has an excellent eye for costume in clown. He'll dress you up as a policeman, a priest, a doctor, a housewife, a spaceman, a boxer, a teacher, a deep-sea diver, an angel, a city gent, a hiker, a soldier in combat fatigues, a decaying corpse, or a mad psychopath with an axe, and as always, that little bit of plastic will tell us that it's all a joke, and that we're invited to laugh at you even more.

If you try dressing up like this wearing a neutral mask, the mask will always be more interesting than the costume. Costume doesn't make a character. It's only an indication of the sort of person you might be, or of what you'd like to be. In the context of playing a clown, costume has nothing to do with who you are. You're not attempting a transformation of any kind. In clown, you're just playing the game of dressing up. To Gaulier, the costume is just another means of provoking you. Sometimes it can become a deliberate physical restriction that might make you even more ridiculous. For example, if you're a bit loquacious, or like to run about a lot, he might give you a deep-sea-diver outfit with tanks, snorkel tube, and flippers. This is a fantastic restriction, particularly if you're asked to recite poetry with the snorkel in your mouth, or to dance in your flippers. Costumes give you things to play with: doctors have stethoscopes, teachers have canes, and housewives have Hoovers. It's astonishing how liberating a good costume can be. If you're the sort of person who doesn't seem to move about with much energy, and if you're rather miserable, Gaulier would probably suggest a costume that you can enjoy playing against like a Christmas fairy or Superman.

Just imagine doing the cliff scene from *Lear* with a nun, a housewife – complete with Hoover – and a deep-sea diver in all the gear. The imagery is fantastic. I haven't a clue what it means, and it's got nothing to do with Shakespeare, but that's beside the point. The most effective costumes in clown are those that give you something that's completely recognisable to us, whilst at the same time giving you something deliciously inappropriate to play. Then the stage is littered with juxtapositions between what you look like and what you're doing. We're in the hinterland of the bizarre now, and there's no turning back. Suddenly everything is a pretext to play. Now you can't be drawn in to trying to do the play or playing the character. Now you can only provoke each other.

The Principles of Simple Clown

The key principles in simple clown are:

- Identify and learn to trust your personal point of bafflement.
- Train yourself to find the game in anything, and to value and respect your spontaneity.
- Develop your skills of complicity with both yourself, and the audience.
- Don't act.

Put these factors together and you'll create a dynamic and volatile level of play that will enable you to make action from next to nothing, and to distil the most complex situation down to a simple moment of humanity. Clowning is profoundly liberating. It will lead you to a healthy disrespect for illusionary acting of any kind. In place of these things, clown will emphasise the volatility of the moment and cultivate a healthy respect for the clarity of a simple choice. Clown is the archetypal performer. In clown there is nothing between you and the audience. The situation is no more than a pretext for you to mess about; something for you to play with. Clown comes from a pre-literary tradition where meaning is of secondary importance and where what happens in the 'here and now' takes precedence over everything else.

Clown transcends genre and elements of clown are evident in the work of some of our most influential postmodernist theatre-makers. Groups like Hesitate and Demonstrate, Ralf Ralf and Ridiculusmus, whether consciously or not, have freely drawn from clown because it's radical, subversive, and will take meaning, chew it up and spit it out. Now that's really defiling a sacred cow.

When Copeau and Lecoq started to take clown out of the circus and variety, and into drama, poetry and tragedy, they were provoking us to start again in our approach to theatre-making. Clown takes us to the lowest common denominator of comedy: to the world of the bizarre, where laughter is always on the edge of pain and discomfort. David Brent in *The Office* doesn't do clever one-liners. He sees everything in his world as a game that he believes he plays with great skill, when in reality his only skill is playing his games in the most inappropriate circumstances. We watch him dig himself into a hole time and again. He's a force of destruction that we love to hate.

Never have the puerile and the profound been so close than in clown, because clown is not intrinsically about meaning. Serious issues, reason, logic, cleverness and wit simply don't count for much here. Clowning is about how you play for that audience at that moment. It's about playing to have an effect on the audience, and having fun for the audience, rather than serving a text. These are the skills of simple clown. There is nothing more to simple clown than this. What you manage to create with these skills is up to you, and any claims beyond these skills are probably no more than a sentimental attachment to the notion of innocence.

Between Clowning and Acting

Most actors are suspicious of clown. They either see it as something quite unrelated to acting, or they seek to disassociate themselves from it. Clown debunks everything, everything's a joke, and there are no real values in a world where nothing is taken seriously. To them, playing clown is the equivalent of somebody whitewashing over a priceless fresco, and to a certain extent, they're right. So far I've been talking about simple clown: this is the lowest common denominator of physical comedy. In simple clown, everything is debunked. In the world where the most precious thing is a laugh, you can remain unscathed by life's hurts and torments, and any pain you suffer will be trivial. But there are different levels of play within clown. After simple clown, there's pathetic clown, and after that, tragic clown. These levels of play in clown take us right to the heart of any drama, and eventually find a point where clowning and acting become indistinguishable.

The point of bafflement doesn't only belong to the clown. It touches us all: shocks, surprises and profound events like love, death, and bereavement take all of us to the same state of bafflement that we see in clown. We all know this feeling: when events are so momentous, and so personally overwhelming that we're momentarily stranded at a point beyond our comprehension. We've all been there, and we can all recognise it as a common state of humanity. But unlike the clown, the vast majority of us don't put laughter quite so high on our list of life's priorities. When we see somebody brought to a state of bafflement over trivial things like taking a coat off, or opening a door, it's ridiculous, childlike, preposterously naive, banal and deeply irritating if it goes on too long. When we see somebody in a state of bafflement through their own crass insensitivity, or their inability to handle other people, like Basil Fawlty or David Brent, this is more painful to most of us, because it's nearer to home. When we see this same ineptitude in a parent trying to look after his child in a Nazi concentration camp, as in the film *Life is Beautiful* (1997), it's almost unbearable. It touches a nerve because it reduces us all to the same state as the clown.

Life might be a vale of tears, but hey – you've got to laugh! Anarchy is electrifying in short bursts, but ultimately, we want to see somebody we can relate to and identify with. We want to see somebody who can go to the edge of the precipice for us, look down into the abyss, and ask the questions we don't have the courage to ask ourselves. At its best, clown is a walking testament to our common humanity. At worst, it's a pain in the arse. Clown reminds us that, deep down, we're all in exactly the same bemused state. Clown makes the bizarre commonplace, and comes from the same place as tragedy: from the actuality of the event. Like any tragic event in life, clowning brings us to a point of witness, where illusion and reality are momentarily indistinguishable, and we think that the situation before us is happening for real, and that there is no illusion here.

Pathetic Clown

There was a mime artist working in the sixties at what is now the Royal Exchange Theatre in Manchester called Julian Chagrin. He made a piece entitled *The Egg and I* about a man making a cake: an activity that involved breaking an inordinately large number of eggs, and a lot of whisking. He broke one egg, and a chick came out. He winded that chick like a baby, taught it to stand up, to walk, and to jump, and eventually to fly and to do tricks. The chick grew strong and healthy. It dive-bombed about the room, and eventually flew out of the window – never to return. Suddenly the piece was about growing up, leaving home and parental loss. We all felt for that ridiculous man as he struggled in helping his fledgling fly the nest. We watched him cheer it on and bellow his encouragement, until it became a tiny speck on the horizon. His face was a glorious mixture of pride and pain. Suddenly, all sense of loss evaporated as his eyes lit on the huge bowl of eggs in front of him, and he started methodically breaking them, one after another, in the merest of chance that there might be another chick inside.

Those transient feelings of sadness and pity, as he cheered that bird on, are what I mean by 'pathos'. It's a word that's been debased, over the past decade or so, to such an extent that it's synonymous with sentimentality to most people today. Those Charlie Chapin films like *Limelight* (1952) and *The Kid* (1921) or the vast majority of Disney's cartoon films have done little to foster our confidence in pathos. The colloquial meaning of the word 'pathetic' now refers to something hopelessly inadequate, and has lost all connection to feelings of sadness or pity. We've grown to suspect these sentiments, and most theatre- makers of my acquaintance will go to great lengths to distance themselves from anything that could be described as being remotely 'sentimental'. Even the word 'sentiment' has evolved pejorative overtones. Perhaps years of Hollywood schmaltz have put paid to the idea that fleeting moments of passive emotion are not necessarily the same as superficial mawkishness.

Pathos is not to be confused with 'bathos', which means, according to the Shorter Oxford English Dictionary, 'a ludicrous descent from the elevated to the commonplace'. The *Monty Python* team made a sketch about the death of Genghis Khan. It started with a long panning shot of the camp of Genghis Khan revealing all his Mongol hordes, with their slaves, elephants, horses, and numerous unfortunate individuals being stretched, flogged and disembowelled. Then, the camera came to rest on an elaborate tent made of animal skins. The flap was thrown back, and there stood Genghis Khan; huge, bearded and ferocious in his fur cloak, and horned helmet. He stretched sensuously, and yawned in the morning sunlight – then dropped down dead. That was the end of the sketch, and that's bathos: it's a comic anti-climax which brings our feelings and expectations down to earth with a bump.

The bathos in this example was deliberate, and executed with considerable skill, and deliberate bathos is second nature to a clown. But bathos is at its most insidious and most destructive when accidental. I remember seeing a film called *Soldier Blue* (1970) that featured a sequence in which the US Cavalry massacred an Indian village. The director had clearly decided to confront us with the gruesome detail of the massacre, but the sight of artificial dismembered limbs, human torsos dangling in trees, and blood-stained cavalry men riding about brandishing human legs and heads, that all clearly had the weight of polystyrene, made his intentions ridiculous. The entire cinema burst out laughing as the film descended into bathos. We expected the gruesome and got the bizarre instead. If I genuinely try to shock you, but my attempts are so inept that you burst out laughing, then we have bathos. Ironically, the more credible I am in my intention to shock you, the stronger the bathos will be when I fail, and the more likely you are to laugh.

Any attempt at pathos will immediately descend into bathos if it fails to reach a credible pay-off. We'll go along with you quite happily through every stage of the anticipation, and the release of whatever emotion you are consumed with at that moment. But if we've spent most of our time laughing at you, and if you've been inviting that laughter, the simple credibility of a moment of sadness will inevitably create tension in the audience. Now we're no longer obliged to laugh. Now we're obliged to watch and to wait in silence, and if you don't reach a credible change of feeling by the end, we'll be laughing at you for the wrong reasons. Your attempts at pathos will have turned into bathos instead. To play pathos successfully you have to be prepared to take us to the 'hot spot' of that feeling – that's the peak of the moment of release – and then we want to see that feeling undergo a change. In Julian Chagrin's piece, *The Egg and I*, I have no memory of him ever playing sadness. The pathos worked because we, the audience, had developed an emotional attachment to that chick: he was too busy playing with it; we were doing all the emoting. Even as it flew away, he was always positive, still cheering it on. Even when he went very still, to watch that little speck disappear from the horizon, he wasn't remotely sad. He was stupidly hoping that the chick might have seen his gestures of encouragement and celebration. This was the hot spot of the scene – for all of us – and this was also our moment of release. It's the release that is always the bit that hurts the most in pathos. The pay-off came when he saw the huge pile of eggs. At that moment, all those feelings, so beautifully developed in our imaginations, became transient. Now we were laughing to break the tension. Now we were laughing to reassure ourselves that everything was OK, and, as we watched him breaking egg after egg, we laughed at his hopeless optimism. 'What an idiot,' we all thought, 'but aren't we all just as bad as him?'

Perhaps the concept of pathos as a transient glow of feeling is a casualty of our contact with American culture. The first thing that struck me when working in the United States was the enthusiasm that everyone had for talking about their feelings in public. It was perfectly acceptable to tell everybody how sad or how hurt they were by a particular occasion, and they could talk the entire room into tears. Alternatively, they'd explain how great they felt, and how marvellous everybody had been, and we'd all be jumping about in delight with each other. It was also perfectly acceptable, and even encouraged, to celebrate intense emotional moments with each other in a way that invariably left me feeling deeply embarrassed. I'm more accustomed to the idea that you have to just 'get on with it', because in the end, 'life goes on'. It's a realisation that puts transient feelings of pathos into a much broader context. The fact that Julian Chagrin played down the loss of the chick as much as he did, and threw himself so energetically into finding another one is testament to the same idea. Life might be bitter, or it might be sweet, but it doesn't end because a bird flies out of a window, no matter how much you loved it. Had he played sadness, had he shed a tear or sung a sad song, the scene would have plummeted into sentimentality. Then feelings would have been indulged purely for their own sake, and the scene would have been more about him than about us. Like my colleagues in the United States, he would have been inviting us to share our emotions together. For all its poignancy, pathos teaches us that everything passes. In this case, the pathos was sufficiently intense to transform a silly bit of physical comedy into an enduring metaphor about education, growing up and leaving home. Remove the pathos, and the scene would be reduced to an amusing bit of nonsense. The fact that it finished on such an upbeat note put that brief moment of emotional intensity into a larger-than-life context that gave us a chance to laugh at ourselves for being moved by such an absurd story in the first place. Ultimately, the emotional content gave the piece its credibility. It was emotionally true to life even though the action was ridiculous.

The Unfaithful Lover Game

A is in bed with B, and they are making passionate love to each other, playing at the level of psychological realism. C, playing at the level of clown, comes home early, and discovers them in bed together. To raise the stakes even more, it's A's birthday and C has come home early with a stupid present intended to be a joke.

If C is playing at the level of simple clown, the game is for C to see the extent that he or she can make it impossible for A and B to continue to play the scene with any degree of tolerance and sensitivity.

To what extent can C wreck the atmosphere and trash the rejected lover theme and turn the situation into something else?

I remember an actor playing this game and completely ignoring what A and B were doing, and just chatting to them as if this sort of thing happened every day, whilst A and B became increasingly embarrassed. C asked them if they found the bed a bit too hot and offered to take some of the covers off the bed to cool them down a bit. A and B were horrified. 'Can't you see what's going on here?' they demanded in disbelief. C just gave a mischievous smile, and jumped into bed with them.

This sent the other two scurrying across the room, ridiculously trying to keep their dignity behind the duvet, whilst C writhed about on the bed going from one lurid pose to another.

This is a typical simple-clown attempt to debunk a painful situation, and on this occasion it was extremely funny. It was robust and outrageous comedy that seemed to turn the tables on A and B, and make them look the more upset.

The more anarchic C became, the more A and B had to raise the stakes and to push the harsh reality of the situation in an attempt to control C. In the end, A and B became very angry with C. A slapped her across the face, twisted her arm round her back, marched her out of the room, then locked the door. B was appalled. Meanwhile, behind the locked door, C apologised as calmly as she could, explaining that she didn't think she'd gone too far in the circumstances, but could she just get a few things together before leaving. C's entreaties had the measured calm of somebody doing their utmost to control their feelings. There wasn't a trace of sentimentality here. In fact, she was almost optimistic saying that, in retrospect, she could see it coming – all those long phone calls, and so many late nights, but now she could see that parting was for the best, and that all she wanted was her purse, her travelcard, her umbrella, and her waterproofs, because it was raining outside. Then she'd go. This was the hot spot of the scene; this was pathetic clown: positive, practical, and although we were almost drowning in empathy for her, all the emotion was implied by the situation. There was no sadness in her playing.

When she was eventually let in, she kept her dignity and wouldn't let anybody help her gather her things. Finally, having put her coat on, she walked up to A, and slapped him across the face. Now the worm had turned and the audience loved it. Meanwhile, she said to B that she was welcome to him, and put her umbrella up with a defiant flourish. She looked proud and dignified and ridiculous standing under a large umbrella, and wearing an anorak that was far too big for her. Had she kicked A in the balls, clocked the audience and run off, she would have debunked the scene again. As it was, she managed to sustain the pathos to the end of the scene.

To play at the level of pathetic clown, the drive to find the action and to have a laugh must be just as strong as it is in simple clown, only now,

C is required to respect the situation, and not to debunk it. In pathetic clown, the human values in the scene, and the feelings of A and B have to be accommodated. In this game, the clown becomes the provocateur. If C takes the upper hand, A and B have to react and insist that C takes the situation seriously. At this level of play, C can no longer ignore the feelings of the other two.

This is the restriction of pathetic clown: you have to balance the desire to have a laugh with the respect for the feelings of the others in the scene. Anarchy is inspiring and liberating in short bursts, but human relationships are a continual fascination to us all. We can watch a skilled clown break a thousand plates for us, and laugh time and time again, but if we see this idiot really getting into trouble, and really having to negotiate a relationship, to the point where we see the clown becoming emotionally engaged, then the human values in the scene will be much richer.

We can watch relationships being negotiated for hours because they're about *people*. Since people are ultimately about us, they engage our imagination and our empathy more than anything else. To any conventional theatre practitioner these remarks are self-evident. But to the simple clown, having to accept the circumstances of the scene, respect each other's dramatic intentions and react to each other, rather than making action at somebody else's expense, are all disturbingly new ideas. Simple clown is refreshing at first because it disregards the conventional rules of theatre-making, and there's a vital freedom here. Pathetic clown requires you to take these skills closer to life.

In *On the Verge of Exploding* (Told by an Idiot, 1993) there was a sequence when Meme, a lonely little young girl of about nine, was playing with her toy rocking horse. Her mother was playing the piano accordion quietly to herself in the background. It was a quiet domestic scene. We saw a child at play: fully engaged one minute, but totally distracted the next. She cantered, trotted, jumped, and galloped about on her imaginary horse in her imaginary landscape, but then the rhythm started to change. It became slower, and more preoccupied, and – with an expression of astonishment more than anything else – she started to orgasm. Her movements became more rhythmic, her breathing more sensual, and her actions as uncontrollable as a sneeze, only interspersed with little giggles of sheer astonishment and delight. Mother had heard it all.

She stopped playing, ran up the steps, and with her eyes blazing with fury, she poured a bucket of water over Meme. The orgasm stopped. Meme froze in shock – dripping with water. Mother also froze – in horror, holding the bucket. Meme was the first to move. She looked at her mother, not in fear, shame or embarrassment, but in sheer perplexity and confusion. She didn't know what she'd done wrong, but she looked more concerned about her mother than herself because her mother was rigid with emotion. Then, as if she'd eventually worked it all out, Meme turned her attention to the rocking horse. She shouted at it, she hit it, and eventually she put it away, with a cloth over its head, in disgrace. Then she played at being speechless with shock and indignation at what the horse had done.

The moment of pathos, the hot spot of the scene, the moment that we most wanted to see, was when Meme confronted her mother. This silent exchange was electric. We expected outrage and even violence, but what happened took us all by surprise. Meme was innocent. She didn't play at being innocent; she simply wasn't aware that she had done anything wrong. We'd all seen what happened, and when she looked into her mother's face, it was more out of a desire to understand, than out of a sense of duty, or because she was afraid. But her mother didn't react. She just stared into space, lost in her own thoughts. It was stalemate. Then Meme's innate playfulness took over again, and to break the tension she started to shout at the horse. The anger we were all anticipating was beautifully sublimated into a harmless parody of exactly what might have happen to her. The hot spot had been played, and nothing had been debunked. We were able to pity her, and to empathise with her completely because her orgasm was so gleeful, and as much a surprise to her as it was to us. Like the incident in the Unfaithful Lover Game, this scene was replete with powerful emotion, but it was far too robust to be sentimental, and all those feelings grew directly out of the situation. Meme punishing the horse had the same function as Julian Chagrin cracking all those eggs looking for another chick. In punishing the toy rocking horse, the scene finished on a moment of hope. No matter how appalling the world might be, that little glimpse of sunlight kept us watching.

The Principles of Pathetic Clown

The key principles in pathetic clown are:

- Play the comedy hard, but without debunking the situation.
- Find the games from the way you react to the other people in the scene, and put their feelings before your own.
- Don't play the obvious. If the scene is a sad scene then sadness is the last thing you should be playing. Go for clashes. Provoke us. Do the things that we wouldn't dare to do in that situation.

To play pathetic clown you have to be able to balance the playful spontaneity of clown with a credible emotional engagement with the dramatic situation in hand. You have to be able to sustain that engagement long enough to engage our empathy, and take us to a point where it hurts. At the same time, you have to continually appear to be unaffected by these intense feelings yourself. It's a tall order; particularly if you're using your taste for clown as a device to mask your discomfort in engaging emotionally in a dramatic situation. Having just discovered the freedom of debunking everything, now you're confronted with a harsh reality: if you're intending to represent the more painful aspects of life, rather than simply mastering the art of falling over, you need to be engaged with life just as much as everybody else is. If your bafflement has become a mask, then your comedy will be a cop-out, and you'll miss the point. The best comedy is a key to some of the darkest areas of human experience, but to use that key you have to engage with life in the first place – in all its aspects.

I started work on the idea of pathetic clown by accident. I had a student who was a very accomplished clown but who was incapable of doing anything else. He debunked everything. One day he turned up to an acting workshop. I was working on a suicide scene where the main protagonist had to die, in agony, having taken cyanide. He did his best, but couldn't contain himself. He'd start by being quite credible at first, and we were just beginning to empathise with him as he desperately tried to control his agonising convulsions. Then he'd suddenly break off, and smile at us, as if to say 'Only kidding.' The more he repeated this, the funnier it became. It was pointless persuading him to take it more seriously, because we were all rolling about the room in gales of laughter. Then I made the observation that he would be even funnier if we actually believed in the situation, and that if that was the case, we could empathise with the pain he was in. The more he repeated the exercise, the more disquieting and moving his little comments became. Although he played the comedy right to the end of the scene, right up to the point of death, by the end, none of us was laughing any more. His frivolous little quips had started to acquire a distinctly unfunny subtext: they'd become a sham. We knew he was deceiving himself. He wasn't OK at all. He was dying, and dying horribly, and we'd grown to like him, and now we missed his jokes, and even admired him for having made them in the first place.

The Death by Poisoning Game

The main thing you need to play this game is a wall. Start the scene by standing close to the wall, and during the course of the action you get closer and closer to the floor. The wall is important because it gives you something to lean against, enabling you to find clear moments of stillness and to slow you down on your agonising journey to the floor.

The game is to die as credibly as you can whilst never losing your optimism. No matter how badly it hurts, and regardless of how close you might be towards death – it's still going to be all right.

It's worth noting that when I say 'whilst never losing your optimism', I don't mean that you assume a fixed smile. If you do that, the work will be dead in the water. In fact, you don't have to smile at all. You can be in deadly earnest, or even passionate in your optimism. Just convince us, in your way, that there's nothing to worry about, and that you know you're going to be perfectly well, once you've got your breath back.

Start the game in exactly the same way as before, only this time find a number of fixed points on your journey to the floor.

It's too technical to ask you to go to a fixed point for no reason, but if you find a fixed point every time you want to speak to us, then these little 'full stops' will start to accrue more meaning for you, and you'll find them easier to play. In *The Egg and I*, Julian Chagrin found a fixed point as he looked at the speck on the horizon. That moment of stillness facilitated huge emotional changes. We only go to a fixed point in life for a very good reason,

> and in that stillness you'll invite the audience to read every detail, and root out every visual clue as to what you're thinking and feeling. When you reach a fixed point, use the wall to keep yourself really still, and look at us, and try to reassure us. Remember that the slightest wobble on your part will take our attention from your face, and make it more difficult for us to read the expression in your eyes.
>
> As the agony increases, and you get closer to death, let the fixed points become more frequent, and let the sentences become increasingly fractured so that, by the end, you can't say anything, but you're still trying to reassure us that all is well.

Fractured sentences are a useful device for maintaining a vocal reference whist leaving you free to play the action. If you're the sort of person who can verbally extemporise for hours on end then you might find fracturing your sentences more of a hindrance than a help. But if you are that sort of person, be wary of trying to develop the action and the text at the same time. It's always easier to make action than it is to make text. You're most likely going to stop the flow of the action, and get drawn in to either telling the story, or trying to make things up that we simply don't need to know, rather than keeping everything as simple as you can. In life, language tends to fail us all in moments of mortality. Imagine someone dying in agony against a wall and trying to keep up the pretence that all is well: it's so much easier to do if you don't complete your sentences and say something like:

" *Oh, it's nice . . . you know . . . in the sunshine . . . maybe take a little walk . . . you know . . . Soon . . . I'm . . . Oh yes, that's . . . Did I tell you about my . . . Well . . . he's not going now . . . to . . . you know . . . Oh, every cloud's got a . . . hasn't it . . . I . . . I've got silver . . . but the catch won't work . . . I think . . . somewhere . . . must have . . . Oh well.* **"**

You can go on for ages like that without hindering the action, or getting bogged down in details. You can also slip easily from subject to subject because there's no requirement to be logical or to make sense. Fractured sentences are an excellent device for sustaining anything that's preoccupying your thoughts.

Clashing realities is another characteristic of working with pathos. In *The Egg and I*, the encouragement for the chick to fly clashed with the departure. You can clash anything with anything. In the past I've success-fully used themes like:

The Fractured Sentence Game

Two clowns talking in fractured sentences about how they're going to decorate their flat, whilst being trapped in a cave with the waters rising further and further up their faces, and eventually over their heads. Or two clowns eating a hearty meal, whilst sobbing over the death of a friend.

Your text will be interesting as long as it's not telling us the same things that the action is telling us, so go for clashes between what you're saying and what you're doing. To what extent can you keep being positive right up to the point of death? As we've seen, this is a major characteristic of pathos in general, but in pathetic clown you can take these clashes as far as you like. I re-member one person in the Death by Poisoning Game attempt-ing to lead the audience in a chorus of 'Happy talk – keep talking – happy talk' from *South Pacific* whilst dying in agony. On another occasion, somebody was demonstrating a tap dance with one foot whilst lying on the floor, very close to death. We're not so much interested in what you say, and we're certainly not inter-ested in how you feel. Our interest lies in the meaning behind what you say, and we deduce that meaning from what you do.

In pathetic clown, we laugh at your hopeless optimism, whilst empath-ising with your predicament at the same time. You can flip at will from the harsh reality of the drama to trying to make us laugh deliberately, and then you can flip back to your agonising journey towards the floor. If you play both realities with the same commitment, engagement and credibility as the moments of forced good humour, eventually we'll stop laughing at you. We'll hear the comedy, and there might even be a few uneasy nervous giggles in the audience, but most of us won't believe your jokes any more. Even if you do something very funny, if the dramatic context is equally balanced with the humour, the effect in the end will make us feel for you far more than we're likely to laugh at you. There's a lot of space for subtext and empathy in pathetic clown, and the emotional shift from laughing heartily to not being able to laugh at all is potentially very moving.

The technique is to play the switch between these clashing feelings as if you were switching the television from channel to channel. There are no transitions here. Sharp and abrupt clashes are by far the most effective, because they take us by surprise, and amplify the incongruity of it all. Each clash will read like a moment of bafflement, and this is what we're really interested in. You have an emotional life in pathetic clown and bafflement at this level of play is astonishingly ambiguous.

The Angry St Peter Game

Moving on from the point of death, let's imagine that our suicidal clown is dead and has gone up to the Gates of Heaven. St Peter, an angry boss-clown, is waiting at the gates.

'What happened?' he demands, and the clown tells the entire story, right from the start. As he's talking, St Peter keeps slapping him with a rolled-up newspaper.

This is another version of the Slapping Game. The boss-clown can hit anywhere on the body, apart from the head. The rolled-up newspaper is a modern version of the slapstick (a padded stick designed for hitting people on stage – used widely in the *Commedia dell'Arte,* but popular in physical comedy since ancient times). If you roll the paper into an elongated cone shape, you'll find that you can hit somebody about the body quite hard, and it doesn't hurt, although it makes a loud thwacking sound, which is most effective. The object of the Angry St Peter Game is to inspire fractured sentences, as well as using the slaps to keep the tension up between you, and keep our hapless suicide on tenterhooks.

The Good Angel/Bad Angel Game

St Peter interrogates the clown about why he took his own life, slapping him with his rolled-up newspaper, and insisting that the story makes complete sense, and that there are no contradictions. Meanwhile, the good Angel Gabriel comes by, and starts complimenting the clown on how well he or she has handled everything, how intelligent and thoughtful the clown had been in those appalling last few hours of life, and how it would have been very difficult for the clown to have done anything else in the circumstances.

The Angel Gabriel's job is to make you genuinely accept the compli-
ments whilst St Peter's job is to make you face the realities of what's
happened without pulling any punches. To be effective you have to
play the game hard. Both the good Angel Gabriel and St Peter have
to provoke the clown to a credible reaction. The clown's job is to
react to each of them in turn, and to switch as fast as possible from
being intimidated by St Peter one minute to being flattered by the
good Angel Gabriel the next.

This is a reaction game of the kind that we've seen many times before. It's designed to make you respond to the world around you without debunking anything that happens to you. If somebody hits you and intimidates you one minute, and then somebody else flatters you the next, without giving you time to draw breath, and insists that you listen to them, you have no choice but to react, and to take their feelings into account.

The point of bafflement is sustained in pathetic clown, and develops into an expression of your vulnerability. You end up looking very like one of Lecoq's neutral masks: as if you're about to eat or to kiss or to swear, but actually doing none of these things. It's a fragile and ambiguous quality: optimistic yet deeply troubled, determined to carry on, yet profoundly uncertain about the outcome. The Good Angel/Bad Angel Game is an amplified version of the 'Yes/No' Game but working with a good angel and a bad angel, you have to learn to 'turn on a sixpence'. The two angels have to push you so hard that it becomes impossible for you to play any changes of feeling and gives you no opportunity to debunk anything or to try to find a game. You've simply got to react credibly to the angels, but they're going too fast for you to know exactly how you're supposed to react. The more rigorous the angels are, the quicker you have to flick from the defensive to the bashful. In the end, you're oscillating somewhere in the middle of these two extremes looking vulnerable, like someone who thinks that they haven't done anything wrong but isn't completely sure.

There's a beautiful French film called *The Lacemaker* (1977). It traces the mental breakdown of a young girl who follows her boyfriend to university, but doesn't fit in with his new friends. Gradually he blocks her out. They hardly speak to each other throughout the film. He ignores her in company, and at mealtimes. He crosses the street, through the traffic, and fails to notice if she is keeping up with him or not. Alone in their bedroom, in a final attempt at contact, she takes all her clothes off, and smiles at him, but he turnes away to read a book. In the final scene of the film he visits her in a psychiatric hospital, where she's undergoing treatment. For the first time she looks happy, and reasonably animated. 'What do you plan to do when you leave here?' he asks. There's a pause, and she replies, 'I'm going to Spain – on holiday.' He looks genuinely pleased for her, and they appear to part well – then the camera pulls back to reveal a poster on the wall, behind where he was sitting, advertising holidays in Spain. Is she making it up, or is she cured? That's the unsettling ambiguity that the film leaves us with. But the film is full of ambiguities, not least in her bafflement and her vulnerability. She wasn't playing clown, far from it, but she was a hair's breadth away from pathetic clown. She had the same quality that's generated by the Good Angel/Bad Angel Game: a sustained look of 'Yes/No', of not really knowing but trying desperately to carry on anyway.

The actor Javier Marzan once told me how his younger brother, when he was about three years old, was playing with a baby chick. His games became so rough that he killed the chick. He was so puzzled that he ran to his father to tell him that the chick was 'broken'. This incident gave me the idea for a useful theme for pathetic clown.

The Pet Owner Game

The game starts with you playing with an object, like a sweater, for example, as if it were a pet dog. It helps to start to play the game at the level of simple clown because there's a satisfying transition to play from one level to the other. 'How do people play with their pet dogs?' The game starts credibly enough, but gradually it gets rougher and rougher as you try to work the audience with it, until by the end, you're swinging this little dog round your head, and throwing it with immense enthusiasm against the wall. Eventually, you realise that the dog is inert, and lifeless on the floor. Now you're caught on the cusp between your enthusiasm to continue the game, and your realisation that the dog is dead.

The game is to maintain this 'Yes/No' quality, this bafflement, and to talk to your dog, focusing on all the benefits of not being alive. The idea is to stay completely positive, and to convince yourself that being

*dead is the best possible option, that nothing will change, that in the
end you're very pleased at what has happened, and that you
wouldn't have it any other way.*

I'm interested in the vocal quality that an improvised monologue like
this can inspire. It's important that there isn't a trace of sadness, and it's
equally important that your love for the dog is clear and entirely
credible.

Pathetic clown has much in common with melodrama in that it works
directly on our emotions. This is always a risky thing to do because you're
dangerously close to bathos on the one hand, and sentimentality on the
other. The idea in pathetic clown is not to play a specific emotion at all
– at least only by implication. By sustaining your perplexity, you sustain
the ambiguity. That's the theory. If you apply it as a formula, you'll end
up like the girl with the fascinatingly boring face who'd worked with
Gaulier, and so catastrophically missed the point of his teaching. In
pathetic clown, you keep yourself 'in the shit' by not even trying to
clarify your feelings. You don't know how you feel at the end of the
Good Angel/Bad Angel Game. You're confused – and that's an excellent
place to start from. Your confusion is our ambiguity, and this ambiguity
keeps us clear of sentimentality and bathos by keeping those powerfully
clashing feelings in all our minds. Confusion isn't the same as being too
generalised when negotiating what you want to play in a scene. The girl
in *The Lacemaker* was confused all the time. She didn't know what to do
because she was undergoing a mental breakdown. The story gave us that
information. Had she tried to play being mentally ill it would have been
a disaster. Being confused is a concrete choice, and it's a powerful choice.

This sustains the ambiguity of the scene with the pet dog, giving us
enough space to interpret the situation for ourselves. In letting the pain
of the drama affect us in the way we see fit, rather than in the way you
tell us to accept it, the emotions end up affecting us more than you. The
more you exploit the idea of finding clashes, the more effective and
compelling the scene will be to watch.

Playing the Pet Owner Game with a group of drama students in
Madrid, one actor created a powerful monologue about how her dog
would always bark and get in the way whenever she started to dance,
but now they could both dance together as much as they liked. As she

said this, she started to dance a flamenco, but she danced so badly that the audience were cringing and laughing at her efforts, which made the scene all the more poignant and disturbing.

A Minute Too Late was one of Théâtre de Complicité's early shows, made in the mid-eighties. It was largely set in a chapel of rest, and Simon McBurney played a clown visiting a funeral. The entrance of this awkward man who stuttered his way from seat to seat, talking to one mourner after another, and apparently trying to join in with their grief, disrupted the solemn dignity of the occasion. He was a walking personification of the 'Yes/No' Game and almost all his sentences were fractured. He was always courteous and apologetic, and full of sympathy, but he was obviously out of place. He was a stranger, gate-crashing somebody else's funeral. He knew nobody there, and his only connection to the bereaved was the fact that he was hopelessly grieving himself, over the death of his wife. From his first entrance, his awkward hesitancy, as opposed to the dignified stillness of the other mourners, set him apart. He was irredeemably the outsider. In the course of the show we saw him in the graveyard, in the chapel, and, after having been given a terrifying lift home in a madly driven hearse, we saw him sitting in his flat, on his own, ineptly cutting up a photograph of his dead wife. He was trying to put it in a frame that was clearly far too small for it.

The pathos of *A Minute Too Late* was at times almost unbearable, but it was too disturbing to be sentimental, and too close to bad taste to be mawkish. It was at times very funny, and at other times very sad indeed, but never purely sad, and never purely funny either. At the end, the little face of his dead wife peered out at us from a mutilated photograph, whilst he proclaimed satisfaction at his handiwork. A child in primary school would have made a better job of it. In tones more matter-of-fact than sad, he told us how he'd not been able to say goodbye to her. This was what I call pathetic clown.

Simon McBurney's eccentric rhythm as he fumbled and stuttered his way through the play was as incongruous as a clown making an entrance to 'The Stripper'. If we were on a tube train and somebody were to enter the carriage with a similar rhythm to the one that Simon was playing, we would all assume that someone with learning difficulties had just got on. We'd probably become more vigilant or start to move away. Put this quality on stage and it becomes an alarming metaphor of our own perplexity and confusion in life. The clown in *A Minute Too Late* might have been inept, but right to the end, he was never sad. He just got on with it, like Julian Chagrin in *The Egg and I*, or Meme in *On the Verge of Exploding*. All these creations give us a heady mixture of playfulness and gravitas that's surprising in its candour, and alarming in its logic. To see any of these idiots in action makes us question our values. For the clown's nonsense is *our* nonsense, and the clown's bafflement is also our own.

Tragic Clown

In the late seventies I was renting a house with a group of friends, when our lives were disrupted by a catastrophe that happened to our landlord and his family. Their home had burnt down, killing their two children. The incident is etched in my mind because of the occasion a couple of days later when our landlord and his wife came to see us to tell us why they wanted us to move out. The husband talked and talked, but my attention was focused on his wife. She was continually lost in thought, and set apart from everything that was happening around her. Clearly she was traumatised. She was there, but not there. She smiled politely when I offered her a cup of tea and a choice of biscuits, and I watched her holding her teacup, and staring into the middle distance, whilst her husband, who clearly hadn't slept for days, talked incessantly. I remember feeling embarrassed by the frivolity and incongruity of our polite hospitality in this context. Then, without warning, she slowly got to her feet to go.

The conversation was hurriedly cut short, and we all stood up. We all escorted them out: opening doors for them, and ushering them down the hallway. Nobody cried. Our attempts at compassion felt like empty gestures in the face of the appalling realities that had overtaken these people. We led them to the front door, down the path, and into their car as if they were royalty, and we stood in silence, at the side of the road, as they drove away. We were a chorus in their tragedy. Their appalling circumstances, and the presence of the bereaved mother in particular, with her quiet dignity and polite distancing, gave us a glimpse into a hurt that was too awful to contemplate, and thankfully beyond the experience of most of us.

Tragedy is one of the most misunderstood levels of play. The popular understanding of tragedy is that it emerges when situations are taken to unbelievable extremes of human suffering, but this is only part of the picture. To play at the level of tragedy you have to create a credible world that enables the protagonist to go to the furthest extremes of human misery. We're not talking about extreme sadness here. Tragedy doesn't make you want to cry – that's more the province of melodrama. Tragedy takes you to a level of dignified pity that demands as much respect as it does empathy. It's a place where life goes on in spite of everything, and where the weight of misfortune gives gravitas to the most mundane actions. The paradox of tragedy is that profound misery inspires admiration.

In his book *The Moving Body*, Lecoq describes how he started his work on clown at his school, in the sixties:

> ❝ *One day I suggested that the students should arrange themselves in a circle – recalling the circus ring – and make us laugh. One after another, they tumbled, fooled around, tried in vain! The result was catastrophic. Our thoughts dried up, our stomachs tensed. It was becoming tragic. When they realised what a failure it was, they stopped improvising and went back to their seats feeling frustrated, confused and embarrassed. It was at this point that they saw their weakness, that everybody burst out laughing not at the characters that they'd been trying to show us, but at the person underneath, stripped bare for all to see.* ❞

The clown fails in some stupid enterprise: we see the flop, the void, the moment of bafflement – call it what you will – and we burst out laughing on recognising this spark of humanity. At that moment the clown is rescued from the flop. The fascination of simple clown lies in us seeing the separation between the pretence of the game and the naked reality of the person behind the game. In pathetic clown we see something very similar. At this level, you realise that something terrible has happened – but now it isn't the game that's gone wrong but life itself. Now it's a huge emotional flop for you personally, and again it's 'becoming tragic'. You must do something else to rescue yourself, and we become interested in the resilience of your clowning. In pathetic clown, the drop, the moment of separation, becomes an emotional transition, and this change of feeling re-launches your clowning, so you start another game to rescue yourself from the flop of the first. In tragic clown, there is no rescue. You don't start another game. The emotional impact of the drop is so great, and the dramatic circumstances so overwhelming that games of any kind are out of the question. Now the separation becomes the moment of realisation.

This is where tragic clown starts – when it's impossible to continue clowning, when games are unacceptable, and you're trapped in real life. In pathetic clown, you rescue yourself from the tragedy of the situation by your ridiculous optimism. Here, your naivety and your insatiable sense of fun becomes a buffer from the slings and arrows of life. In pathetic clown, we can watch you grieve, for example, and with ironic smiles and half-laughs, we'll empathise with you to the point of tears, safe in the knowledge that your resilient naivety will rescue you in the end. In this respect, pathetic clown has more in common with melodrama than tragedy. In tragic clown, there is no buffer, no optimism. Life hits you hard and knocks you over. You might get up and dust yourself down, but now you're determined to do something, rather than being vaguely optimistic that something might happen. There's no laughter to break the tension and get us all off the hook. Now bafflement looks more like trauma. You might be weak and helpless, but your only redemption lies in your resolve to do what has to be done. In tragic clown, our interest lies in your fortitude and your determination.

There isn't much of a change in pathetic clown: you're naive at the beginning, and you're still naive at the end. But in tragic clown, there's the potential of a huge transcendent arc – from the hapless idiot, deserving little but our ridicule, to the focused, dignified and determined protagonist, whom we've all grown to admire and respect.

The Stone-Throwing Game

Throw an imaginary stone in a vertical line high above your head, hold the image of the stone magically hovering up there in your mind's eye, and look round the room.

Clearly this isn't a mime of a real situation. The stone doesn't come crashing down again – it's what Lecoq in *The Moving Body* calls a mimo-dynamic image. In other words, it's an image made more vivid and more real for us by being played out in mime. By playing the action of throwing the stone as credibly as you can, you engage the body in an appropriate physicality that will enable you to find an effective level of energy to work with. Actions give us bigger, tangible and more manageable impulses than more subtle physicality.

The action of throwing the stone gives you the added advantage that the audience can immediately see when the image is starting to fade because your alignment and your physical engagement will also fade at the same time. Mimo-dynamic images are easier to work with because they stop you from waffling. Every time you find the image starting to fade or your alignment slipping, you can always repeat the stone-throwing, and you'll soon teach yourself how to maintain an appropriate level of physical engagement to keep the game going.

Once you've trained yourself to walk round the room and do simple actions whilst holding the image of the hovering stone in your head then you'll be ready to engage somebody in conversation.

Like the woman who'd just lost her children in a fire, the Stone-Throwing Game will make you look deeply preoccupied. But the action of throwing the stone and thinking about it will also change your alignment. In other words, you'll find yourself walking, standing and sitting with a longer back. You'll also find yourself only moving when you have to, and when you do move, you'll probably move slower than you would normally. Your speech will also be slightly slower, and you'll become more aware of having finished your sentences.

The Stone-Throwing Game is my way of finding the tragic élan: the physical impulse in playing tragedy. It enables you to translate the movement quality instinctively into an emotional sensation, a state of mind, and an entirely different way of looking at the world. All you're doing here is putting one of Michael Chekhov's imaginary centres several feet above our head, and the effect is extraordinary. You'll look peaceful and serene, yet deeply preoccupied to the point of appearing mentally disturbed. Feelings of joy or anger become amplified and distorted when you work from this centre. It generates a physicality that could hardly be described as normal behaviour: laughter sounds unnatural, and even enthusiasm looks manic. Perhaps the most alarm-ing quality to be inspired by this centre some feet above your head is the feeling of being disengaged. This is an excellent starting point if you're going to tackle Medea or Creon, because the protagonist in a Greek tragedy is living life on the edge of sanity. In classical tragedy, we see man in conflict with the gods. The stakes could hardly get much higher. In both Shakespearian and modern tragedy, we see one human being in conflict with another.

A strong characteristic of the Stone-Throwing Game is that you begin to feel that you're playing at a very high status level. Which is great if you're a king or a warrior planning to take on the gods, or even if you're an ordinary person planning to confront some guy next door who's recruiting a personal army of thugs. When using the term 'high status', I'm referring to how economical you are with your movement, and how sustained your eye contact can be. In this context, high status has nothing to do with your social standing, or how much money you've got. High status is a study of the theatrical representation of power and economy. A military officer with a peaked cap pulled down low over the eyes is using the physical restriction of that low peak to sustain a stillness in the head, and a prolonged eye contact, and this naturally induces high status. It makes you feel strong, powerful and in control. If you combine those feelings of strength and power with those more alarming feelings of being disengaged, and of being on the margins of your sanity, then you're probably in an excellent mental state to murder your children like Medea, or to stab King Duncan like Macbeth.

Madness has fascinated theatre-makers for centuries because it's a superb device for taking us to the wildest extremes of human behaviour: to the bizarre and the irrational. The representation of madness enables us to go into the heart of the nightmare. Tragedy is a level of play that takes us to the limits of our understanding, and the furthest extremes of empathy. The bizarre and the irrational are second nature to a clown, and madness is only a short hop away from the intuitive associations of wild comedy and unstructured play. Comedy and madness are ancient bedfellows. Up to the eighteenth century, for example, it was perfectly acceptable for the general public to visit Bedlam to laugh at the lunatics. But few clowns go easily to high status. Some do, and John Cleese is an obvious example of one who naturally plays from a position of power and superiority. The vast majority of clowns play from a lower status than this. They tend to be either gleefully anarchic like Harpo Marx, or naively stupid like Angela de Castro, utterly bemused like Grock, or eccentric and burlesque like Max Wall. Of course, there are as many different types of clown as there are people, and I'm not proposing typography of clowns here. These are the crude extremities of clowning, and most clowns can find a place somewhere in between these broad parameters. Tragic clown and pathetic clown aren't clown types but levels of engagement in the drama. If you can learn to juggle your emotions in pathetic clown, and find the confidence to mess about in the darkest, most extreme dramatic circumstances in tragic clown, then the barriers between clowning and acting will dissolve, and you'll be able to play anything.

The Slap on the Head Game

A tells his or her life story to the rest of the group. B stands to the side of A, and with the fingers of one hand taps A lightly on the back of the head whilst A is speaking. (I must emphasise that the idea isn't to knock your partner senseless. If you keep your hand relaxed and give a firm tap with your fingers, you might hear a sharp slapping sound, but it won't hurt.) The game is to surprise A with the slaps sufficiently to interrupt the logical flow of A's speech.

Each slap is like a short burst of interference on a television screen. If we look into A's eyes just after a slap, we'll see an expression of surprise and perplexity in them. When the game is finished, A will be able to feel a slight tingling at the back of the head, and if they were to walk round and look at other people whilst focusing on this imaginary centre, he or she will start to look perplexed and preoccupied at the same time. A will also feel distanced from the 'here and now', and look as if there's something hugely important that has to be done.

Like the Stone-Throwing Game, this is an excellent imaginary centre for tragic clown; but when you work from this centre you feel slightly softer, less intense than when you work from the space above your head. There isn't the same feeling of high status here. With an imaginary centre at the back of your head, you'll probably take on an expression of mild surprise, or innocent astonishment. You'll be looking out, but not necessarily seeing anything. You'll appear more confused than manic; you'll seem more approachable, and less disturbing to encounter, but you'll still be far from 'normal'. Again, it's an attitude very reminiscent of the grieving mother who'd lost her children in a fire. It was her stillness, and her deep preoccupation that gave her that compelling presence.

Of course it's the dramatic context that carries our emotional investment, and defines what we mean by a tragic situation, but games like these induce sensations and attitudes of mind that make it much easier to enter the nightmare that's the substance of tragedy. Both the Stone-Throwing Game and the Slap on the Head Game will empower you to be stiller, more direct, and to block out any distraction that might hinder you in pursuit of your objective. Either of these games can be used as the driving force behind a tragic protagonist who is compelled to do what he or she has to do, against impossible odds. All we're dealing with here is a physical impulse that's capable of generating the physical symptoms of somebody in a traumatised state.

Pathetic clown is more passive than tragic clown. Life tends to overtake you in pathetic clown, you tend to react to things that are generally beyond your control. Pathetic clown is invariably in the position of the victim. In tragic clown, circumstances drive you to act for yourself and to take responsibility. Tragic clown puts you in a state of mind where you realise that 'it has to be done'. Circumstances are ranged against you in such a way that you've got to be assertive. This could be logical, courageous and genuinely heroic, or it could be stupid and ill-advised. In either case, you know it has to be done.

The Trigger-Line Game

Take the phrase 'It has to be done' and say it to yourself in such a way that you mean it. Then keep saying it under your breath, every now and then, to remind yourself of it. Then give yourself a simple objective such as you want to walk across the room, or you want to stand on the chair, read the newspaper, put on your shoes and your coat, or go and sit next to somebody.

The idea is to let the trigger-line inform the action. In other words, move across the room in the manner indicated by the trigger-line: 'It has to be done.'

Gradually your movements will become more determined, and your objective more imperative. We'll read a huge personal conflict in your body language. The smallest movement will look like an enormous personal challenge for you. This simple phrase has the ability to put you in the frame of mind of somebody who is about to do something momentous. It's the attitude of somebody who is about to become a hero but they haven't got there yet. They're determined but deeply uncertain of the outcome.

Trigger-lines are an excellent device for giving you a clear and simple imaginative impulse: something that you can keep at the back of your mind as a constant reference. They're remarkably accurate in inspiring movement qualities, and if the previous two centring games leave you cold, you can use trigger-lines in exactly the same way – but remember to keep it simple. Don't use a centring game and a trigger-line at the same time – they'll cancel each other out. Trigger-lines, like imaginary centres, give us movement qualities that we read as emotional subtext. On the inside, you're focusing on the imaginary stone above your head, or telling yourself that 'It has to be done', but on the outside, we're seeing somebody desperately trying to hold themselves together in the most disturbing circumstances.

Trigger-lines enable you to clown with a preoccupation. To try this, play anything you like at the level of simple clown: a morris dancer, or a window cleaner, or anything that you've explored already and have enough vocabulary to be able to keep alive for some time. Then try the same game with the trigger-line, 'It has to be done'. Everything will change when you try to play with a trigger-line like this. Your movements will take on an entirely different meaning than they did before. Don't be at all surprised if you're not remotely funny when you play in this way. This isn't a device to get laughs, but to give your work a gravitas, seriousness and sense of purpose.

One of the characteristics of tragedy is what some writers call 'the spur'. This is an incident that spurs you on to fight for your objective, in spite of the odds that are stacked against you. In Shakespeare's *Henry V*, the king is spurred into battle again after the French knights have massacred the young squires who were left looking after the camp. Hamlet is eventually spurred on to kill Claudius when he hears of the plot against him. You can introduce the Trigger-Line Game to help define the moment when you're being spurred on to bigger things.

When I met the mother who'd just lost both her children in a fire, I was struck by her absolute preoccupation with her own thoughts. In her head she was in another place entirely, and the look in her eyes was frightening. She was uncannily relaxed – she must have been too exhausted to be anything else – so that she'd gone to a point beyond tears. Tragedy is too high on the Richter scale of human emotions for tears. We're kept watching by the gentle dignity of a person who's come to accept the worst. When she slowly got to her feet, she could easily have had 'It has to be done' at the forefront of her mind. We can't take our eyes off somebody who we know has fallen off the edge but somehow is still standing. We scrutinise every detail of that person for the slightest trace of conflict and resistance, and on not finding any of these things, we start to generate these feeling in ourselves. We want to rage at the wind, break down doors, or to tear buildings apart. Then we see humanity, and we're stopped short, and left to watch helplessly as life goes on. What I saw in the face of the woman who'd lost her children was, in clown terminology, the flop or the point of bafflement but then when she got up to leave, she was a dignified woman with a sense of purpose.

In *She'll be Coming Round the Mountain*, a young drunken soldier raped a child. She was traumatised, and when she tried to tell her father what had happened, she couldn't get beyond telling him in fractured sentences that she had lost her wellington boots. Her father put her in a small tin bath – it was more a large bowl than a bath – but there was no water. He ran about with an old plastic bottle, and didn't know whether he should leave her on her own and go and get some water, or stay and try to comfort her. In other circumstances this could have been funny. The timing was much the same as in a conventional clown number: he played exactly the same reversals, exactly the same doubletakes. But the audience sat in perfect silence. In the end he ran to and fro abstractedly, holding the bottle in front of him, as if he couldn't remember what it was for. Squatting in the bath, the girl started to go through the motions of washing. She absent-mindedly splashed imaginary water over her body, tunelessly humming to herself. Again, in other circumstances this game could have been funny. Now we recognised the reference, but the context was too appalling for anybody to laugh. Her father heard her singing, stopped running about, and watched her. He dropped the bottle, and helped her with her imaginary bath. Even pretend bath-time was better than no bath-time at all. Like the woman who'd lost her children in the fire, they were lost in a sustained moment of bafflement. They were there but not there, and apparently relaxed – apart from their eyes, which constantly scanned an empty and distant horizon.

It wasn't necessary for them to play the emotions of the scene because the dramatic context was more than enough to engage our empathy.

Their sustained bafflement and their preoccupations focused our attention on the powerful emotions in the scene. The performers were clowning much the same as they usually did, but now the context stifled any potential comedy, and those vacant looks of incomprehension continued to proclaim their emotional turmoil.

During rehearsal, I remember provoking them by asking, 'Do you think you might be able to make her laugh at this point?' Jason Thorpe, the father, tried playing his 'silly walk game', whilst still maintaining that sustained quality of bafflement. Inevitably it was a half-hearted attempt. Earlier in the play it had made her giggle uncontrollably, but now she was barely looking at him, and it raised little more than a mirthless absent-minded smile. It was more a memory than anything else. It wasn't sentiment that we were dealing with here. Nobody murmured, 'Ah bless,' on a wave of superfluous emotion. We were playing with the symptoms of severe emotional trauma. We were beyond comedy. In the end, the father knew that there was no way out of this situation. That was his spur. So with all his strength, he picked the girl up – as she was – still in the bath, and walked away. They had to move. They had to get away from that place.

The King's Game

The conventional way of playing this game is as follows:

A is the king or queen, and a group of three or four others become a sort of mini chorus, trained to react to every need. If the king or queen puts out a hand, the chorus might put a glass into it, or take a glove off, or give a manicure. If the king or queen goes to sit down, they would instantly fetch a chair, or one of them might even become a chair, and the monarch would sit on them.

It's a basic master-and-servant game but it can be played at many levels. In its most basic form, this is a game about action and reaction, and an inexperienced group will probably play purely at this level. Play this game in simple clown and you'll push this action-and-response mechanism to its limit. I remember one group carrying the king about on their shoulders; with the dismissive wave of the king's hands, they threw him in the air and caught him again. But this is really a game about status; namely, about how much, or how little, you move. The king or queen will probably be very minimal in their movement, and if they're sufficiently relaxed they'll probably look powerful and authoritative. But if the chorus of servants charge about like lunatics, the king or queen will be made to look as stupid as the chorus. On the other hand, the chorus can be very attentive to the king or queen, only maintain a similar status in their movement, and never rush or appear harassed. If the chorus work together efficiently and economically in this way, then the king or queen will look very powerful indeed, because their status will be supported.

When I use this game in the context of exploring tragic clown, I switch the roles around. Instead of the chorus being reactive to the king or queen, I make the king or queen react to the chorus.

If the situation is that you, as the clown protagonist, are going to say goodbye to the body of your dead friend, or you're having to revisit the scene of some appalling atrocity, or you're having to make that final walk to the gallows, or confront the man who's recently murdered a member of your family, then the inverted version of the King's Game is invaluable. In this version of the game, the chorus are used as ushers, they open doors for you, and guide you to your final confrontation – to 'the hot spot' of the scene. The chorus stay with you, and guide you through everything that happens, right through to the bitter end. The role of the chorus in this game is to keep you on your course of action, and to support you along the way. They don't do this by rushing you, or empathising with you, or trying to bolster you up, or even sympathising with you particularly. They imbue you with dignity by patiently waiting for you to move forward. They watch you, and they wait with you uncritically. If you were to fall they might pick you up again, but they'll never try to cheer you up, rush you or hurry you along. The chorus are there to be with you, and to empower you with their dignity in order that you can continue as best you can. It's as if they know exactly what's going to happen but they're unable to stop it. Their job is to be a silent witness to your fate.

If you play this game first with a chorus and then take the chorus away and play the same scene on your own, it's relatively easy to remember their presence. The memory of them waiting with you, for example, gives you courage to take your time, and the memory of them opening the door and showing you the way gives you more space to play each unit of action. The chorus enables you to do less, to be more economical, and to take your time. The presence of the chorus in this context also enables us as the audience to be more objective. The presence, and the sight of them watching and waiting without being solicitous, encourages us to stand back a little. We watch with them.

We're not particularly interested in emotion here, which doesn't mean to say that there aren't rip tides of emotion swirling about all over the place. It's simply that we don't need to play these emotions – they're far too complex and multifaceted. Anyway, they're already established in the writing. This isn't melodrama designed to arouse and channel our feelings – this is a level of play that's more about us seeing how you cope than us feeling what you feel. In its purest form, tragedy deals with the representation of human values at their best, and in tragic clown we want to see how you confront these horrific circumstances in the best possible light. You might be an idiot, but the irony of tragic clown is that we see you transcend this idiocy to the point where you gain our respect, and our admiration as a courageous and dignified human being. At this level of play you'll feel yourself pulled in a number of different directions at once. First there's the desire to make the audience laugh but this is immediately compromised by an overriding preoccupation that blights your sense of humour, and kills comedy stone dead. Nobody is laughing, but you've got to do what has to be done.

Tragic clown is an invitation to play powerful motivations and huge dramatic objectives from a position of stupidity and ineptitude rather than injustice or moral outrage. It's not an invitation to find yet another way of making us laugh, but to continue to play – way beyond the point where it has become impossible for any of us to laugh.

The Principles of Tragic Clown

The key principles in tragic clown are:

- To sustain your point of bafflement as a dramatic preoccupation.
- To continue to find the games beyond the point when we have finished laughing.

- To indentify 'the spur' that drives you on to face up to the natural conclusion of your actions.
- To let the emotions look after themselves.

As I've said before, we don't weep buckets in a tragedy; we're brought to a state of witness. We're invited to watch you reach the moment when you face the worst things that life can offer. As an audience, we're there, with our pity and our respect, to support you and to watch. You can clown with anything, so theoretically any drama could be approached from the level of clown. Any play with an element of madness in it is a gift for the clown. We're only limited by our taste, our sensitivity to the material, and by the courage behind our convictions.

In Ingmar Bergman's film *Sawdust and Tinsel* (1953), there's a sequence where a tired old clown is waiting outside the big top to go on stage. Suddenly he sees his wife being jeered and humiliated by a troop of soldiers lazing on the beach. To his horror he sees that she's doing an impromptu striptease for them, and inviting them to swim in the sea with her. The soldiers roar their approval. Some of them hurriedly strip off their uniforms, ready to join her. As she tosses yet another garment in the air, the clown, in full costume and make-up, dashes headlong towards her, stumbling and falling over in his desperation to stop her. The soldiers are convulsed with laughter at the sight of this. Eventually, he grabs hold of his wife, stops her dance, lifts her into his arms and slowly stumbles all the way back along the beach with her, in front of the jeering soldiers.

There's nothing remotely funny, or remotely sentimental about this sequence. The image that sticks in my mind is that of a dowdy middle-aged circus clown in his threadbare costume, stupid wig, red nose and make-up, slowly making his way across the sand, with as much dignity as he can muster. He's looking straight ahead, gently cradling his wife's scantily clad body in his arms, as he shuffles along to the deafening jeers and catcalls of the soldiers. All he's got left is his dignity, and the more he clings on to it, the more the soldiers laugh.

Part Four

The Gentle Art
of Ridicule

I prefer to be true to myself, even at the hazard
of incurring the ridicule of others, rather than to be false,
and to incur my own abhorrence.

Frederick Douglass

Parody

❝ *She marched back and forth across the space: heels pounding the floor, shoulders hunched, head forward, handbag clamped under one arm and a large cardboard box under the other, stacked to the brim with books and bits of paper. She looked more determined every time she crossed the space, and she stamped her heels even harder. Eventually, we started to laugh; only then did she start to relate to us.*

Oh, there you are, skulking about as normal. Excellent. That's exactly as it should be. Well, SBW215: a disappointing turnout again. Good. That's very encouraging. At least you're doing something right.'

She rummaged about in her cardboard box, flinging books and scraps of paper all over the space. Eventually, she produced an immaculate exercise book and held it up for everyone to see. Her eyes settled on a member of the audience.

'Well. Leroy. What's this?' Her voice was dripping with sarcasm. The audience bellowed with laugher. 'Not only did you hand it in on time but you actually did the work! Why do you think you get bullied, Leroy?' she said, tauntingly. Then suddenly incandescent with rage she shouted, 'Look at this — you've actually backed it in brown paper! Are you gay, Leroy? And look — you're even listening to me now!' She kicked the box across the room and it slammed against the wall. Then she stamped and drummed the floor with her fists, like a two-year-old having a tantrum. 'You're even looking me in the eye, Leroy.' She ran into the audience and started hitting her unsuspecting victim about the head with the book. 'Have you no self-respect? I'm a woman, Leroy! Have some pride! What's the point in coming to a school like this with an attitude like that?' She was in tears now and digging into her bag for a tissue. 'We'll never get you excluded at this rate; I'll never get to be head of department. OFSTED are going to rip me apart. We're a failing school, I'll have to move house, sell the car, take a checkout job . . .'

As she spoke she ripped the pages out of the exercise book, screwed them up and

crammed them into her mouth until her speech became too distorted for us to
understand.

(*A Course for Teachers*, London, 2000) **99**

This wasn't clown, it was parody, or to be more precise: it was caricature. Clown and parody are two very different levels of play. She had
too much to say about being a teacher to play clown. There wasn't a
trace of bafflement, she knew exactly what she was doing, she had a
clear target, and she hit that target time and again – to the delight of
everyone in the room. Her audience of fellow teachers recognised the
situation instantly and reacted to every nuance. They loved her mad
inversion of an all-too-familiar situation. Some of them could barely
stay on their chairs, and were laughing as much out of outrage as
agreement. Others laughed mirthlessly, as if it was very close to the
bone. The teacher on stage was just as concerned with making meaning
as she was with making her audience laugh. She knew exactly what she
wanted to say, and her passionate engagement with her theme was an
indication of her own depth of feeling. To that audience she was the
funniest thing on the planet. I'm not saying that clowns can never be
parodic, or that there weren't elements of clowning in what she did.
Her work was silly, playful and performative, and these are all typical
characteristics of clown, but this was clear, intentional parody, whereas
clown drifts into parody unintentionally.

Max Wall used to do a brilliantly funny clown number when he'd come
on stage, incongruously dressed in tailcoat, tights and a pageboy wig.
Then he'd strut towards an impressive grand piano, like a serious
concert pianist, struggle to adjust the piano stool, elaborately flex his
fingers, summon his inspiration, then slam his hands down with a dull
thud – he'd forgotten to open the lid of the keyboard. When we
laughed, he'd shout at us to be quiet, which made us laugh all the more,
of course. Occasionally, and for no apparent reason, a marching rhythm
would be played on a snare drum, he'd burst into an eccentric march
across the stage, and we'd erupt into laughter all over again. We saw
bafflement in everything that happened to him.

Unlike the teacher with her box of papers and her exercise book, any
parody that Max Wall was playing was completely incidental. He had
nothing to say about classical pianists; that was his theme and not his

target. After the show we came away still laughing at Max Wall rather than at the pretensions of a classical musician. The teacher, on the other hand, played caricature and showed us the absurd nightmare of her situation. Her target was the impossibility of her job of teaching students who despised her sex, didn't want to be there, and didn't want to know anything she had to teach them. It was a feast of parody, but in comparison with Max Wall, we saw nothing of her, because everything she did was exaggerated to the point of ridicule thus obscuring her own personality.

Clowns have nothing to say other than, 'This is me, and this is what I'm doing': that's the vacuous freedom of clown, and to many performers it is an appalling freedom. They might start a game in clown only to discover that they've slipped into parody by the end of the number. In clown, your job is to make us laugh; in parody, your job is to make us think and laugh – at the same time. Meaning is never far away in parody, but it falls apart as soon as we lose sight of what you're really saying. We'll find meaning in the daftest things, but in clown, that's our affair. The power of clown lies in your abject honesty; the power of parody lies in the game of being honest. It's the world of 'only joking': a world of ambiguity, absurdity, nonsense, hyperbole and exaggeration. If clown is on the knife-edge of comedy, then parody is on the knife-edge of meaning. But parody isn't analytical in the way that satire often is, although there are great similarities between the two.

Satire

The word 'satire' originally comes from 'satyr'. Satyrs were mythical figures, characterised in ancient Greek drama as creatures in transition: half-man and half-beast. They were lewd, lustful, unpredictable, violent and destructive. A chorus of satyrs would have performed dances and short 'curtain-raisers' before the main drama. Today, 'satire' covers a wide range of comedy from the gross to the most subtle. Like parody, satire is also concerned with ridicule, mockery, causing offence, and pushing the boundaries of acceptability. A good satire can fillet an idea and lay bare its component parts for all to see, whereas parody is cruder.

Satire erupted into the public consciousness in the UK in recent years with the outstanding success of the Oxbridge revue, *Beyond the Fringe*, which went on to generate TV shows like *That Was The Week That Was*, and *Not Only . . . But Also* with Peter Cook and Dudley Moore. These shows broke away from mainstream comedy with material that was more immediate, more credible, more unpredictable, and more political. *The Frost Report* produced a sketch, now regarded as something of an icon, about the British class system. John Cleese, who is very tall, stood next to Ronnie Barker who was considerably shorter than him. But Ronnie Barker stood head and shoulders over Ronnie Corbett, who stood next to him. All three of them stood in a line, representing the upper, middle and lower classes. The text went something like this:

66 *John Cleese: I look down on him (looking at Ronnie Barker). And I also look down on him (looking at Ronnie Corbett).*

Ronnie Barker: I look down on him (looking at Ronnie Corbett) but I look up to him (looking at John Cleese).

Ronnie Corbett: I know my place.   **99**

This is satire. It's very different from something like French and Saunders doing their version of *The Silence of the Lambs* (1991), which is clearly parody. They're both concerned with exaggeration and distortion, but the main difference between satire and parody is the element of imitation. Satire hits its target by examining detail, but parody relies on its ability to capture a distorted likeness. Our understanding of both these words comes, of course, from literature, but in the context of physical comedy, the element of imitation makes parody more visual and more physical than satire, which today is firmly rooted in writing. Both satire and parody have their ancient roots in the grotesque. Just as the concept of satire grew out of satyrs, so the concept of parody grew out of buffoons. A buffoon is a grotesque misshapen clown; not a creature in transition, like a satyr, but a human being 'gone wrong', one of God's little mistakes. In Roman times, buffoons were bizarre, nonsensical, and occasionally malicious entertainers, who were probably seen as much as bringers of good luck as good cheer. The Roman historian, Pliny, describes a scabrous character called Gryllus, probably the earliest recorded buffoon, as being of 'ridiculous appearance', probably half-man and half-pig, who would take nothing seriously, not even meaning itself. A buffoon is a parody of a human being; too outlandish to be taken seriously and likely to reduce everything to mockery.

All this sounds very distant and arcane today because we're more accustomed to the grotesque being neatly contained in the genre of fantasy, horror, or science fiction in films like *King Kong, Alien* or *Lord of the Rings*. But the grotesque is as potent a force in comedy today as it ever was. Our jokes and comic monologues are peppered with grotesque imagery, while the language we use to talk about comedy – 'He died the death', 'She knocked them in the aisles', 'She blew them away', 'They were doubled up with laughter' – is full of violence and grotesque metaphor. Physical parody soon becomes grotesque because it operates on an ascending scale of exaggeration. It's the logic of: 'Oh, you find that funny, do you? How about this then?' When French and Saunders make a parody of *Silence of the Lambs*, it's the combination of the ridiculous casting and ingenious make-up that makes the resulting parody funny. They're at their best when the intended likeness is least effective because then the results are grotesque. Similarly, when a well-known celebrity is parodied in a show like *Dead Ringers*, it is less funny when the imitation is one hundred per cent accurate than when the likeness is less strong, because a distortion of something recognisable makes for better parody than mere imitation. A grotesque comment is more savage but we feel more able to laugh at a grotesque image that's clearly deliberate and affected than at something that's naturally grotesque. Because we know it isn't real.

Grotesque Comedy

❝ *I was in Dempasar, visiting A.S.T.I., the official academy for training in the traditional Balinese forms of dance, drama and music. I was on a quest to work with Bondress masks. (These are grotesque buffoon-like, half-mask characters unique to Bali.) An enthusiastic young teacher of Bondress, called Wyan, was showing me round the academy. Wyan was eager to practise his English on me so he was keen to talk.*

'I want to study Bondress masks,' I said.

'Ah, Bondress very funny. Bondress have funny faces.' He had already repeated 'funny' several times before in our previous conversation: the word was obviously a new acquisition.

'What do you find funny in England?' he said. I hesitated at the enormity of the question. 'Oh, lots of things,' I said, trying to hide my discomfort.

'What things?' This was a teacher talking. He had no intention of letting me off his hook.

'I think we find surprises funny.'

'Can you show me a surprise?' I was on the spot and there was no getting away from it.

'Well,' I said, 'a man comes casually out of a building . . .' I did the action as I spoke. 'He has a cigarette in his mouth. The wind is blowing straight into his face. He tries to light his cigarette, so he turns to the side. He still can't light it, so he turns with his back to the wind. He lights the cigarette, walks confidently off, and straight into a wall.' He laughed as I sprawled against the wall. 'The surprise is when he hits the wall. That's funny,' I said ironically.

'In Bali, anyone who is different is funny.'

A red light flicked on in the back of my mind.

'What do you mean by different?'

'If I have one leg longer than the other.' He contorted his body and demonstrated a distorted walk. 'This is different from everybody else,' he said, waddling round with the easy grace of a man who had practised this walk many times. 'If I teach you to dance like this it is funny,' he insisted, and began to demonstrate a hobbling version of a Balinese dance, and to give me elaborate instructions in Balinese, as if he were an important dance teacher. He demonstrated the same step over and over again, until he looked so preposterous that I burst out laughing. His eyes sparkled with pleasure.

'He is funny because he is so different. He will never be able to dance properly, and his teaching is all wrong,' he said, convulsed with laughter.

'Yes,' I said. 'Could you do that dance if there was someone in the audience who genuinely had one leg longer than the other?'

'Oh yes. He would laugh because I am a bad dance teacher, and I teach a funny dance.'

'In England we would worry about making fun of him.'

'No!' he nodded in disbelief. 'A dance teacher with one leg longer than the other is very silly to be a dance teacher,' he explained patiently.

'Yes, but don't you think he would be uncomfortable watching you dance like that?'

'No! I show you.'

He led me down the corridor to a small classroom. Out of a cupboard he produced a half-mask wrapped in cloth. He looked at it for a moment, with his back to me, and I watched his back gradually change its shape as he put the mask on. He seemed to become smaller, and I could hear his breathing. He began to mutter in a distorted voice, and move about the room, limping. I recognised the limp from his previous demonstration, only this time it was more defined, and more expansive. Suddenly he spun round, and I was confronted with a face twisted to the side in a hideous grimace of a smile with teeth that stuck out at odd angles. It was as if the whole of one side of his body was longer than the other, not just the leg. Again he demonstrated his dance.

The mask was shocking but fascinating at the same time. I couldn't take my eyes off it. It was more a creature than a human being. He danced with a delicate dignity, and he smiled his twisted smile of pleasure that was as endearing as it was ridiculous. The repetition of the steps, his precise and exaggerated gestures made him look even more ridiculous. Suddenly he stopped, and began giving me a lecture in Balinese. As before, he was gesturing to me to copy the steps, and clearly I wasn't paying attention, or I was just too stupid to understand. His abrupt seriousness, and his outlandish, lop-sided appearance made me laugh out loud. He turned away from me, and took the mask off.

'I liked him,' I said. 'He was so serious.'

'Of course, Bondress are very serious. We are all serious. We are all Bondress, all of us! Not just man with one leg longer than the other. I am Bondress. You are Bondress. If you laugh at Bondress, you sleep better.'

'I'm sure you do,' I said. 'Could you do a Bondress of me?'

'Oh yes: big red Western tourist. Very funny.'

I laughed and went even redder. 'Tourist,' I shuddered, but to him that's exactly what I was.

(Personal Journal, ASTI, Dempasar 1993) **99**

The grotesque is an ancient, and universal comic device. There's one of Richard Dawkin's 'memes' here: the deep-seated belief that human folly is absurd and misshapen. I had felt more comfortable laughing at Wyan when he was playing the mask than when he wasn't. He was too human without the mask, and I wasn't sure whether he was joking or not. But when he put the mask on, I was in no doubt. Those facial deformities were too ludicrous to be taken seriously. That mask had a face that was an anatomical impossibility; it was a parody of a dis-figurement, a silly imitation of ugliness that was horrific insofar as it momentarily caught me out. Wyan's skill in playing the mask made me accept that stupid face as if it were real, and – on realising my mistake – I laughed. I laughed because I was taken in by it, and not because it was intrinsically funny. In the end, I could comfortably accept this persona as a 'creature' with human characteristics, but I suspect that there was more anthropomorphism than empathy going on here. I reacted to Wyan's games in the mask in the same way I might when playing with a large friendly dog.

You don't have to dig deep to find times or places where the grotesque was more acceptable than it is in present-day Britain. As recently as the fifties I remember, as a child, visiting a freak show in Blackpool, and even today in Gujurat in Pakistan, at the Shrine of Shah Dola, it is believed that barren women who worship there can be made fertile. The price they have to pay is to dedicate their first-born to the temple where the child is then deliberately deformed and sold as a street beggar, to become one of 'the rat children'. These are holy beggars with curiously small heads, and grossly deformed bodies, that people are persuaded to 'give generously' to in the belief that by doing so, they are closer to God.

Enid Wellsford in her book, *The Fool, his Social and Literary History*, distinguishes between the 'natural fool' and the 'allowed fool'. The natural fool was a congenital idiot, or a grotesquely deformed indivi-dual kept for amusement or as a lucky mascot, to avert the evil eye, or because it was believed he was clairvoyant or had the ear of God. For 'fool' read 'buffoon' because the two words are interchangeable in this context. The allowed fool, sometimes also knows as the parasite, would gatecrash the world of the rich and famous, and earn his living by trying to entertain the guests. These buffoons were tolerated because of their skill or their wit. They might tell a story, sing a song, juggle, and do acrobatics, and sometimes all of these things at the same time. Out of a patchwork of references taken from ancient Egypt, Greco-Roman times, England, and central Europe, a pattern begins to emerge where the powerful and privileged members of society used the mentally ill and the deformed as scapegoats, in the belief that they will absorb bad luck or that they might have the ability to give them good fortune. In

Russia, buffoons were valued for their 'God talk', because it was believed that the insane spoke the word of God – cryptically, of course.

Some fools were in the enviable position of being both deformed in some way, yet still in possession of their wits, which gave them greater licence to push the boundaries of their work to the extent that they could parody the king to his face, insult or even mock him, and still be rewarded for it. Aesop, although not strictly speaking an allowed fool, was, nonetheless, a black hunchback, who through his fables managed to rise from the status of slave to that of diplomat. We can only speculate as to the part that his appearance played in this meteoric advancement, but in being 'a grotesque' he would have posed no threat to his superiors. His shape was probably seen as a lucky omen, and gave the things he had to say more status, so his presence would have been welcomed at the houses of the rich and the influential.

According to Wellsford, the tradition of the household fool died away at the same time as the idea of the divine right of kings. Before then, when confronted by an all-powerful monarch, you had to be either mad or too ugly for words to be able to speak your mind. To be grotesque at that time was a badge of office in itself. Today, with greater equality, we can say what we like, but the tradition of the eccentric entertainer exploiting their appearance – or their apparent insanity – in pursuit of a laugh is still alive and kicking. It's just that our fools have long lost their divine status, and any element of mental illness is, for the most part, carefully stylised. Spike Milligan suffered mental breakdowns that were not part of his act, and we can only guess the extent to which his state of mind contributed to his groundbreaking comedy. Peter Cook, on the other hand, suffered from a 'terminal boredom' with life that, in retrospect, looks very like a depressive illness. He channelled these feelings into his work and, like Milligan, also made groundbreaking comedy. Ken Dodd still soldiers on with his protruding teeth and his mad hairdo, as does Jo Brand with jokes about her knickers being the size of Buckinghamshire: jokes like that can only be said by a person of uncompromising size. Such material from a person of 'normal' size would be unacceptable and potentially malicious parody, but a woman in a ridiculous fat suit, or someone wearing the mask of a fat person, or even a ridiculously fat puppet would get away with it. But are any of these options as funny and as confrontational as a real fat woman saying something about herself that most of us wouldn't dare to say? We like the actuality here, but if we were to see a group of rat children in Gujrat, we wouldn't find them remotely funny, because the actuality would be too much for us.

Today we take pride in our humanity; we prefer reason to superstition, and honesty to illusion. In our egalitarian society, free from gods and kings to hamper us, we're all buffoons at heart, and we comfort ourselves that we're all grotesque. We admire comics who speak their mind and our laughter signals our personal recognition. 'I think that too,' we say to ourselves, 'but I wouldn't dare talk about it in public.' The more personally exposed we seem to be, the closer we seem to get to the boundaries of acceptability, but effective physical parody is impossible without some element of the grotesque. The grotesque is the most efficient way mankind has found of generating feelings like anger, terror and disgust: feelings that aren't usually associated with comedy. But parody is at its best when it's pushing those boundaries, when it's on the verge of offending us. The grotesque is a device we've always used to personify our horrors and our taboos; it's our way of facing up to 'the Devil' and of visually representing how we 'conquer evil'. But most of us don't believe in bogeymen any more, so there's less mystery in the world and in the theatre. Imaginary terrors soon deteriorate into sensationalism.

Conceptual Parody

Whenever I see a collection of the work of Pablo Picasso, I can't help but marvel at his playfulness and his sense of humour. I love that mischievous way he has of taking a shape, a material or a simple object, then messing about with it, and doing something completely astonishing with it in the end. Picasso could make art out of anything; no conventional form was ever safe in his hands for long. Fur-lined cups and saucers, or an animal head made out of a bicycle seat and a pair of handlebars are some of the more obvious examples of his parodic sense of humour, but his taste for displacement, inversion, abstraction and juxtaposition was taken into every aspect of his art. This is conceptual parody: the ability to make fun of a convention by inverting or by rearranging its various elements in such a way that it could be affectionately ridiculed without debunking the subject. The fur-lined teacup, for example, is a visual parody on the representation of reality. It poses the question, 'Does art have to show reality?' And it leaves us with the answer, 'Yes and no'. The story goes that a young ambitious art critic bought a small Picasso from one of his exhibitions but his friends said it was a fake. Fearful for his investment, the art critic took his painting back to Picasso and asked him if he'd painted the picture or not. 'Yes, of course,' said Picasso. 'Thank God,' said the young man, 'my friends said it was a fake.' 'Oh, it is,' said Picasso, 'I often paint fakes.' This is the game of being honest; he's 'only joking', or is he? Is it possible to fake your own work? Conceptual parody enables us all to work with a similar blank canvas, and with the same disrespect for rules as clown, only without the risk of becoming addicted to laughter. We're dealing with a knowing grin rather than a belly laugh here; with inference and irony, rather than disarming honesty. In theatre, conceptual parody has produced some astonishing and satisfying moments of invention.

Emma Rice's production of *The Bacchae* (Kneehigh Theatre Company, 2004) is a case in point. She created a chorus of men who made their first entrance naked except for old-fashioned women's underwear. They entered, one by one, with a tongue-in-cheek grin on their faces. They made no attempt to play for laughs; they just enjoyed the joke of looking the way they did. Tutus were lowered down from the flies, and the men put them on. It was a funny, grotesque and parodic image that set the tone for the entire evening. Dionysus appeared in pinstripes, gold high-heeled shoes, and a tall conical fez. In trying to intimidate Dionysus with his power, the King strutted in with a newspaper under his arm, which the chorus opened up to reveal a paper cut-out frieze of little men: the sort of thing that might grace the walls of a primary school. Dionysus and the King then made a show of inspecting 'the troops'. When the King threatened Dionysus with incarceration, the King sat on a bale of newspapers, implying that he could summon any number of troops under his command; but we all knew that to Dionysus they'd be nothing but paper cut-outs.

The power of this production lay in its ability to confound our expectations by creating a world that shattered clichés. They were parodying the concept of Greek tragedy. The rulebook was shredded in front of us, and the production led us gently, and with a knowing grin, towards its gruesome and tragic conclusion: to the point when the Queen wrapped her son's decapitated head in a piece of old newspaper. The actors declared their games, and parodied themselves from beginning to end; we were left in no doubt that these were actors dressing up – just for the fun of it. They enchanted us with their audacity, and created a world of surprises where we could accept the action for what it was, and on its own terms. This was highly effective theatre that held its audience from moment to moment. It was an affectionate ridicule of the conventions of Greek tragedy, but in the end their 'target' was misplaced and they fell short of creating that feeling of intense pity so typical of the form. If your 'image system' is going to be as outlandish as men wearing tutus, you need something even bigger for that culminating brutality or you'll be in danger of debunking the subject matter at the heart of the play. It's as if they'd put all their energy into creating the world of the play without exploring the heart of the drama. I couldn't pity the mother wrapping her son's head up in a piece of old newspaper. The image was too small, too understated and mundane to a point verging on bathos; we saw the mother's predicament but couldn't touch her tragedy. In conceptual parody, the idea is to attack the means to the end and not the end itself. Parody isn't a substitute for tragedy unless tragedy is your target; you've got to have a good aim if you want to play with parody. In this case, conceptual parody alone wasn't enough to take us into the nightmare of The Bacchae. To do that, the performers needed to go to a place beyond reason, and beyond human dignity to the grotesque, which is ultimately closer to tragedy. Then the stakes are higher and we're more likely to encounter those feelings of terror, anger, pity and disgust that push at the boundaries of acceptability.

Misplaced ridicule is unsatisfying, but the thought of hitting a recognisable target in an appropriate context is deeply satisfying. The actors in The Bacchae were 'only joking'; their mockery of the form fell well within the barriers of acceptability but in the end they weren't offensive enough. Good parody is inspiring and enables you to say things that can't be said in any other way, but it's a gamble between giving pleasure and causing offence. Parody thrives on the possibility of offending somebody either through devastating observation or a flagrant disregard for propriety and respect. Parody is seeded as much by hate, anger and frustration as it is by fun, affection and love. Just to make things even more difficult, offence is also seeded by hate, anger and frustration. Offence is always politically sensitive and culturally specific. What might be thought of as an innocent quip in Europe could create a major incident in the Middle East. There was a scene in a play I was making in Singapore that consisted of a young woman miming the act of putting on a sari. This involved a lot of complicated draping and folding and making innumerable pleats at the front to accommodate the vast length of the material. Because this pleating was repeated for such a long time, I suggested that she look at the audience and sigh in the middle of it, and then return to the task. On our first showing, a Sikh gentleman in the audience took great exception to this mime. 'All I'm saying is: a sari is very long,' I said, but he saw it as a disrespectful act that was greatly offensive to the women of his culture. He felt too culturally insecure to accept the idea that ridicule can also be affectionate, but there is no tradition of parody in Singapore, and the 'only joking' culture is aggressively discouraged. But 'offence' is the risk and 'offence' is also the provocation in parody. If you never hit your target, we'll think it a cop-out, but crude, inept and misplaced parody is irresponsible and destructive.

I teach parody because it possesses a vibrant creative energy fuelled by a deep-seated desire to misbehave, to send things up, and to trash the rules. In the appropriate circumstances, a little encouragement to 'send it up' is an irresistible invitation to be worse than you are and to enjoy being crap for a change. The constraints fall away, eyes light up, and a genuine pleasure fills the stage. Parody is one of the most powerful motors behind our desire to play. We're drawn into a game by the desire to exhibit our skill, wit or intelligence. Sometimes we're drawn by the thrill of competition; sometimes through a personal delight in being ridiculous and inane; and sometimes by a ravenous appetite for mockery and poking fun. Parody is energising and creative because it respects nothing beyond our essential humanity. In parody, your appearance and your actions compel us to look beyond the text, to see what you're really saying.

To the conventional acting teacher, the notion of bringing parody into your work will probably be seen as a betrayal of your craft. It's generally believed that if you approach acting through parody, and cultivate a taste for mocking the world around you, then you'll end by sending everything up, lose your taste for empathy and humanity, and your work will become cold, superficial, tedious and unwatchable. And of course that's absolutely right: persistent parody is a pain in the arse. But that doesn't mean that in the appropriate circumstances, parody isn't a perfectly reasonable choice to make, or that there isn't considerable skill to be found in mastering effective parody. This disapproval of parody stems from an approach to acting and theatre-making that harks back to the late nineteenth century. It's based on the notion that effective theatre stems from a credible illusion of reality that encourages our 'willing suspension of disbelief'. Like clown, parody is more about building a credible relationship with an audience than trying to sustain a credible illusion of reality. Parody celebrates 'disbelief' rather than suspends it. Parody is just another level of play: another way of empowering you as an actor, another key to your imagination. To study parody isn't to become trapped in it for life; it's just an inspiring way to start.

Parody is the largest and most diverse form of physical comedy and it dominates our popular culture: *Little Britain*, *The Fast Show*, *League of Gentlemen*, *French and Saunders*, *Rory Bremner* and *Dead Ringers* are all parodic sketch shows. Before them, we had the grotesque parody of *Spitting Image*, and before that the bizarre parodies of *Monty Python* and *The Goons*. Conceptual parody is endemic in all aspect of the arts; in our culture it's becoming more the rule than the exception. Historians tell us that parody thrives in times of uncertainty: the cultures of Ancient Rome and Weimar Berlin both sported thriving parodic cultures. Parody becomes the last resort of the creative imagination when artistic values are in meltdown. Today, after twenty years of deconstructionist theory, it's hardly surprising that many of us can't distinguish the parodic from the real any longer. Art is in the melting pot, and there are no more masterpieces. We're living in a time where every aspect of artistic expression is being questioned; our most cherished values are being 'dumbed down'. Everything is in a state of flux. On the one hand it's alarming but on the other, it's profoundly exhilarating. Uncertainty puts us all firmly in the moment. In some hands, to say 'only joking' is just a convenient cop-out. But in others, it's a key to ambiguity: a way of saying something that might be exactly what we think it is, but might

– just as easily – be something else entirely. Ambiguity is a lifeline allowing you to swim out of your depth whilst never losing your contact with the shore. In times of uncertainty, everything is a potential target, and in parody anything can be used to express anything.

A Scale of Parody

The saying goes that to know what is enough, we must know what is more than enough, and this is particularly true in parody. I evolved the next game during my initial investigations into parody, and it gave me the idea of a scale of parody. Exaggeration, hyperbole and excess are the driving forces behind parody, and it soon becomes evident that the greater the exaggeration, the stronger the parody is likely to be.

The Exaggeration Game

The group walks around the room, all following the same person, and all copying the way that person moves: their rhythm and their alignment.

As soon as everyone has found their version of the person they're following, I ask them to exaggerate what they're doing, and to make it their own.

Then I choose the simplest and the most effective exaggeration I can find, and invite the group to abandon their individual exaggerations and to follow that person, and to copy that person's choices as accurately as they can.

Again I ask them to exaggerate and to make it their own, and the same routine is repeated again and again.

The key is to keep your exaggerations as simple as possible. Don't rush. It helps if you restrict yourself to just one change of attitude, or to just one additional movement. We have a tendency to waffle and make everything too broad when asked to exaggerate, but with a skilful group, I can usually repeat the game about five or six times before it becomes too ridiculous for words. If the group are clumsy or too elaborate in their exaggerations I probably won't get more than three or four repetitions before I start to lose interest.

The scale goes through four stages, four levels of exaggeration that reflect an ascending scale of parody:

- *Pastiche*
- *Caricature*
- *Burlesque*
- *Buffoon*

The first exaggeration is generally an affectionate pastiche; namely, a slightly exaggerated version of the person they're following; something only slightly bigger than life. The second exaggeration tends to be more like a caricature, which is a more ridiculous exaggeration that's making a direct comment about the person you're following. By the third exaggeration you'll probably be playing such a ludicrous mockery that it will be too outrageous to be a recognisable caricature. This is burlesque. The final stage is buffoon: this tends to become more hideous, or more mysterious, or almost too disgusting and uncomfortable to watch. This is grotesque, and if you push this exaggeration even further you'll have to 'send it up' a bit. You can't get more ridiculous than this. This is the bizarre level of exaggeration, at the top of the scale, and it's generally too ludicrous for words. It's all parody, but you'll have to play the dressing-up version of the game before the mischievous delight of the buffoon starts to show itself.

The Exaggeration Game – With Dressing Up

This is exactly the same game, only in this version you add a range of clothing: other people's coats and sweaters, hats and scarves are generally enough, plus a few cushions and odd bits of material for padding. All these things are set out along one side of the room.

The idea is to play the game as before, but on each exaggeration you use one or two costume pieces to clarify it.

This is always more tricky than it sounds because we all want to do too much too soon. Be specific and be accurate and keep it simple. This version takes slightly longer than the previous one, so I tend to ask the person we're copying to keep on walking up and down the room while everyone gets ready with their new 'costume' to play the next exaggeration.

Something interesting happens once you start dressing up, covering your face and changing your shape. A simple addition, like a hat, a scarf, or a pair of shoes, will probably make you feel slightly different but this is a subtle feeling and not a cue to start showing off, or demonstrating what you're wearing. Don't let the costume pieces make you forget the game. You're either copying somebody else, or you're exaggerating the characteristics that you've already captured. The costume is a means to this end: you're dressing up to make a point. Be accurate.

As soon as you start padding your tits out or giving yourself knobbly knees, or big feet, you'll probably want to play the joke of your appearance, so you'll probably assume an inane grin, and take much more pleasure in playing the audience. Do this, but keep playing the game at the same time.

Once the padding starts to get even more extreme, and if your face starts to get covered, you probably won't be able to move as much, and you'll probably start giggling. These last two characteristics are very typical of buffoon. By this stage of the game, you'll probably start to feel that the costume is beginning to dominate, and in order to play both the costume and the game, you'll have to play innumerable separations, and drops in order to keep both things going.

Costume is vital in playing parody. It enables you to build a mask for yourself. As we saw in the Shoe Game, costume pieces give imaginative impulses that make you feel different. The more elaborate your costume is, the more hidden you start to feel. Carefully concealed behind your costume, you start to feel safe and mischievous. If your costume is preposterous, so much the better. Safely covered up, you get the feeling that you're not there any more, and that we can't see you. This imaginative release is ideal for playing parody. It gives you the confidence to take the space, to take your time, and to have fun in playing the audience. Effective parody is impossible if you don't feel completely comfortable in yourself.

I like to keep costume pieces constantly available when I'm working with parody, no matter how subtle that work may be because, unlike clown, there is little to be gained in making you feel vulnerable. In playing parody, the idea is to feel empowered.

Pastiche and caricature have dominated our popular culture over the past two decades or so. They both have the immediacy to attract a huge audience with clear and simple targets and have occasionally touched the zeitgeist, and given us catchphrases that pass into the language, like Harry Enfield's 'Loadsamoney' or *Little Britain*'s 'Only gay in the village'. Barry Humphries created such a detailed caricature in his Dame Edna Everage that in some people's eyes she became a celebrity in her own right. *The Royle Family* took pastiche to new heights, and artists like Steve Coogan made us squirm with embarrassment at his beautiful pastiche, the socially inept Alan Partridge. Sketch shows like *The Fast Show, The League of Gentlemen, Little Britain* and *Dead Ringers* aim at beautifully observed targets, and employ running gags that fully exploit the immediacy and snap-shot quality of effective caricature.

The burlesque and the grotesque are more extreme levels of parody that tend to be more physical, more savage, and more metaphorical. They thrive on their ability to shock. *Blue Lips* revived burlesque parody in the eighties, and more recently *The Whoopee Club* and *Cirque du Soleil* have evolved their own take on burlesque. The TV series *Bo' Selecta!* was a superficial burlesque parody that rarely developed its targets beyond an initial reference, and the show drifted into a generalised parody of itself. *Jerry Springer – The Opera* was a splendidly silly burlesque in the theatre, and *The Young Ones, Bottom* and *Spitting Image* found a vast audience on television for their individual styles of grotesque parody.

Buffoon is a form of malevolent clown. There are innumerable literary references for buffoon such as Richard III or Victor Hugo's Quasimodo, but I have few references for buffoon in popular culture. *Little Britain*'s caricatures certainly touch the grotesque but they lack sufficient malevolence and mystery to give their work the sardonic edge of buffoon. The Scottish company, benchtours, toured one or two buffoon pieces in the eighties, and Philippe Gaulier staged *No Son of Mine*, a play he wrote himself, exploring his take on buffoon. Neither of these ventures really took off: they were too esoteric for a popular audience, and appeared to be pursuing a personal aesthetic rather than effective theatre. Lecoq introduced buffoon at his school in Paris in the seventies, as a means of liberating his students to be empowered on stage. It was never his intention to inspire a new theatre form, but generations of students have come out of Lecoq and taken their newly acquired skills in clown or mask work to establish themselves as key practitioners of the form. This is all well and good, but Lecoq's entire curriculum was designed as a series of provocations and proposals to his actors. Buffoon might not have found a popular audience, but parody has. The skills to be found in playing buffoon take us to the heart of parody. If you can play buffoon well, you'll be able to play any of the other forms with considerable ease, so I often start with buffoon and work backwards towards pastiche. Here, however, I will work up the scale of exaggeration, from pastiche to buffoon via caricature and burlesque.

Pastiche

Pastiche crops up everywhere. Virtually every presenter in light entertainment and countless actors base everything they do on a sympathetic pastiche of themselves that occasionally slips into caricature. Anyone who's spent years working under pressure is bound to develop habits and as we get older, these habits become more ingrained and entrenched. It isn't the personal pastiche that's a failing so much as the habit, or rather the lack of awareness of that habit. Habits are unavoidable and in trying to eliminate them, the best we can hope for is another set of habits. Your personal pastiche emerges from an awareness of what's typical about you. How do you move? How do you hold yourself? And what are your personal idiosyncrasies? A pastiche is an affectionately enlarged statement of the truth and 'the truth', in this context, is more important and more valuable than fiction. In asking yourself how you move, you'll soon discover what's funny about you.

The Pastiche Game I

Find a partner who's physically as least like you as possible. If you're a large man, find a small woman, or vice-versa.

The game is in two parts:

A studies B and copies B's rhythm, physical attitude and how they walk. It helps to ask B to do simple tasks like combing their hair, or saying their name and address. At this stage, the game is about A trying to capture B's personal mannerisms.

A's job is to be accurate, and to capture B's personal rhythms and movement qualities. It helps to walk in unison with B, and then to stand back and look. Observe the angle of the head, the movement of the hips, and the shoulders. Watch the breathing and see how B says their name and address. Copy the voice as accurately as you can. Try to capture its rhythm and texture. It's fascinating to observe the movement quality and the level of intensity behind how someone says something as simple as their name and address.

The big problem here is that B knows that he or she is being copied, so B is likely to become slightly self-conscious, and not do what he or she would normally do. To capture those personal unconsidered gestures, and all those quirky little habits, B needs to be preoccupied with something else, so it helps to get B to recite the thirteen times table or anything that's awkward enough to really get B thinking, and to be made to work things out. Now A will be able to capture B's more instinctive gestures because their self-conscious barriers will be down and the real B will start to emerge.

Avoid the temptation to exaggerate. I know it's all parody, but pastiche is the subtlest form of ridicule. If you're not careful, you'll miss it entirely and jump straight to caricature, which is essentially cruder and more restrictive. Pastiche is on the edge of 'only joking'; most people don't trust what they see so they over-compensate because our unconsidered natural movement qualities are invariably subtler, lighter and more delicate than we think they are. So watch and copy.

A plays their version of B, including saying the name and the address, to the rest of the group. When A has finished, B comes on, and demonstrates the genuine article including saying the name and address.

We've all got personal traits – they're a sort of trademark – and they're all potentially ridiculous. The idea is to consciously exploit them for the audience, but as subtly as you can. These personal traits aren't 'wrong' or 'inadvisable': they're part of your personality, and can either be a meal ticket, or a noose to hang yourself with. If you don't like them, you can get rid of them later. At this stage, awareness is all. The question is: what happens if you play them?

If the group know each other pretty well, this stage of the game will have everybody falling about with laughter. All we're doing here is defining what's typical of B. The idea isn't to comment about B at this stage, just to be typical. We'll laugh at anything we recognise, providing it's truthful. We want to see accuracy, not exaggeration. Just seeing a big fat man trying to capture the movement qualities of a small and delicate woman, or a small person capturing the movement of someone much bigger and heavier than they are will be all the exaggeration we need for the pastiche to be effective. The parody is incidental when you play a pastiche — it's revealed in your attention to detail. Pastiche is a gentle and affectionate form of copying somebody.

The Pastiche Game 2

Something interesting happens when you play the game in reverse: A teaches B how to 'make the most of themselves': to exploit the little personal mannerisms, and to be more like themselves than they really are. Then B plays his or her 'new self' for the audience.

Having identified B's personal traits and little habits, the game here is to teach them back to B, so that B can play a caricature of him or her self. This is a satisfying twist in the game. The idea is to give B some useful vocabulary that can be exploited for the audience. When I say 'teach them back to B', I don't mean that A should rehearse B in his own way of moving so much as to make B aware of what she's doing. If you rehearse B, you'll end up exaggerating: the work will get too big too quickly, and we won't be able to recognise B at all in the end. An awareness of your personal traits is exaggeration enough at this stage. If you show B how she pokes her head forward when she walks, for example, or how she twitches her hand slightly when she stops, then when B spots herself doing these things for an audience she'll know exactly what she's playing with and she'll have plenty of scope to develop that little twitch according to the reactions of the audience.

Both parts of this game emphasise the primary decision in playing parody. Basically you've got two choices: you can either work from your own movement qualities or from the movement qualities of somebody or something else. When I was directing *King Ubu* at The Gate,

I remember being concerned with the problem of finding appropriate reference points on which to build caricatures. At one stage I asked the cast, 'How do you think a child might draw you?' and they all produced their version of a child's drawing that could have been an invaluable external reference. As it happens, I didn't pursue it any further because they instinctively started work from their own movement qualities, beginning at the level of pastiche and then developing to caricature and burlesque as the rehearsals developed. External references can be fascinating, and the discipline of capturing somebody else's movement is a vital skill.

In the seventies, the director Mike Leigh evolved a highly effective process for devising with actors based entirely on pastiche. He would ask his cast to study members of their family or close friends, and then use these detailed studies of their personal mannerisms as a basis for the roles they were evolving in the production. Occasionally an actor might use combinations of different people in the same role: a bit of Aunt Doris here, and a bit of Uncle Alf there, for example. The audience of course would be oblivious to these personal references, but because the actors were working from accurately observed external references they brought astonishing detail and subtlety to their work; they had the sort of quirkiness that only real life possesses. The lesson here is to be accurate and to keep it subtle.

Mobility

The Pastiche Game is about developing an awareness of what you do and, with this insight, exploring what's funny about you will ultimately gives you more choices to play with. I remember, as a young actor, being immensely impressed by the actor Francis Matthews who could be chatting to a colleague in the wings then, with barely a pause for breath, amble on stage and play his scene, there being scarcely any distinction to be made between his persona in the wings and the one on stage. But I also noticed how during his performance he might occasionally play a slightly 'bigger version' of himself and then go back to his 'normal size'.

This is what I mean by 'mobility'. Habits have a tendency to become fixed so that if you rely on them, and always do the same things, you can easily end up getting trapped in a personal cliché. In life this doesn't happen because we're continually reacting to things around us. Francis Matthews playing a bigger version of himself then returning to his 'normal size' was a case of just reacting to the dramatic circumstances; his apparent size changes kept him interesting. He was clearly still the same person, but his mobility enabled us to see him from different perspectives.

The Size of Movement Game

Rather than using detailed direction in raising B's awareness of his or her movement qualities, the game here is to give feedback on the 'size' of B's movement by counting. For example, when B moves naturally and without a trace of exaggeration call this 'one', when B moves with a slightly exaggerated quality call this 'two', and so on.

The counting is a useful device because it enables you to negotiate different levels of exaggeration with the minimum explanation, and prevents you getting bogged down in detail. The game forces you to reach an agreement with your partner through trial and error; it encourages you to achieve an empirical understanding of exactly what you mean by each number. If you restrict yourself to just repeating the numbers rather than discussing what you mean, you'll find the physical definition easier to find and easier to remember.

Each number is a command for you to adjust the size of your pastiche and you can use the Size of Movement Game to either increase or reduce that size. Some people have great difficulty in moving without exaggeration, so you might end up demanding 'minus one' or even 'minus two', and it's always interesting to see what happens if you take your partner down to the minus numbers. With some people, you'll get to the state of bafflement round about minus two.

You probably won't need to go any higher than four or five: by the time you hit three, you'll probably be drifting into caricature. Mobility is the real skill in parody. Exaggeration is easy; learning how to control and modulate your exaggeration is more difficult.

The Pastiche Game 3

The final stage of the Pastiche Game is for B to play the audience to see what we like. Just like clown, if the audience laugh – do it again. Try to discover what we find funny about you. Keep it subtle, and once you know what makes us laugh, you'll be able to exploit that knowledge. Once you've identified what we like, exaggeration becomes an enormous temptation. Be subtle, or pastiche will elude you.

It helps to consciously play one thing at a time. Maybe you've discovered that you do something slightly peculiar with your feet when you walk, or that you tend to brush your hair out of your face every time you engage in eye contact with someone. Just choose one thing to work with, or you'll find yourself rushing to an extreme exaggeration too quickly. It helps to play this part of the game in small groups: every time you do something the group likes, they put their hands up. You'll probably think that you're just playing yourself, but you'll be surprised how much tension your body builds up in the apparently simple task of playing the audience.

If you have enough mobility to be able to play a drop in the middle of your personal pastiche, you'll open up a whole new area of possibilities. If you're entertaining us with this new awareness of how you move, and if you then suddenly let it go, we're confronted with the 'real' you, as opposed to the 'assumed' you, and we experience a strong moment of direct contact. Suddenly you'll look sincere and serious, as if something significant is going to happen. If you're playing a text from your personal pastiche, the occasional drop will enable you to interact with more intensity, more subtlety, more sincerity, and with as broad an emotional range as you'll find anywhere. You're at your most credible when you drop your personal pastiche, insofar as we think we're seeing the person behind the mask. When you return to the pastiche, we'll become more aware of the game, but all your subsequent choices will then have the potential for more resonance.

Sometimes parody is at its most effective when it's at its most subtle. There's a medieval mystery play called *The York Crucifixion*, which was originally performed by the Carpenters Guild of York. The action consists of a group of incompetent Roman soldiers trying to build

Christ's cross, nail him to it, and hoist him into the air. Of course, the soldiers botch it. The cross is far too big, so Christ has to be stretched to fit the holes they've made for the nails. Then they have enormous difficulty in raising the cross to a vertical position, with him dangling on it. The cross sways and jolts about in the air and the soldiers go to ludicrous lengths to make it secure. It's a situation that could easily slip into slapstick, but the sheer brilliance of this writing lies in its irony. The most basic mistakes in the construction and the erection of the cross are what cause the most horrible suffering for the 'Saviour of all mankind'.

It's an enduring metaphor but it's a subtle and beautifully placed parody as well. The target here isn't the brutal act of crucifixion, neither is it the incompetent Roman soldiers, as you might think. The soldiers are never demonised or portrayed as stupid foreigners, as might happen today. The real target here is the tradesmen of the day doing an ordinary job – badly. All Christ's suffering is incidental: it's the product of the carpenters' ineptitude. Everything grows directly out of the dramatic situation in this play. The carpenters were ridiculing themselves. The image of somebody dangling, in agony, from a precariously swaying cross is grotesque in the extreme, but this isn't grotesque parody; these images are the focus of our sympathies rather than our ridicule. It's the actions of the carpenters that we find so funny and so appalling. The carpenters who created the play were making a bitter self-parody; they were playing pastiche. I can assure you it takes considerable technical skill to realise the action of *The York Crucifixion*. To medieval carpenters performing the play, the task of securing a vertical wooden structure would have been commonplace. So to entertain us by doing the job badly takes even more skill than doing it well. These tradesmen probably played a pastiche of themselves. I bet if they got their audiences really rocking in the aisles at Christ's expense, some zealous churchman would have taken offence. Pastiche is the delicate side of parody.

Caricature

A caricature is a stylised visual representation of a character. Like most aspects of parody it's a term that is often used pejoratively because it thrives on stereotypical two-dimensional acting. But these limitations stem not from the device itself so much as from how it's used. If you drift towards caricature whilst making an intense psychological drama, you'll inhibit resonance and nuance with the result that your work will become dangerously predictable. But if you're working with masks or puppets, then caricature will be in the foreground of your work. If you're making a complex visual farce to be played in the street, or a sketch show for television with short inter-cutting scenes, or an exuberant and irreverent parody where situations have to be established in seconds, caricature is essential. It's the most effective means we have of creating instantly recognisable characters that are sufficiently larger than life to be spotted from a distance across a crowded town square.

Commedia dell'Arte was a form of theatre based almost entirely on caricature. It developed from street entertainers playing parodies of the country bumpkins that used to turn up at hireling fairs in pre-Renaissance Italy. Like many parodic forms, *Commedia* thrived on the attempts of the authorities to suppress it. Imagine a small group of players satirising a powerful priest in an Italian city-state. Let's say that they were so popular that it would have been more trouble than it was worth for the authorities to ban them completely. But when the company came to the city again, the authorities were wary of them, so they forbade the actors to use speech, in the belief that this would cramp their style. So imagine the actors mimed and grunted and invented a gibberish language that made them even more eloquent and their imagery even more graphic than before. The next time the actors returned, the authorities were so incensed that they forbade the use of mime or speech of any kind, so the resourceful actors sang and danced their feelings about the powerful priest instead. Of course, this is a huge simplification of a trend that emerged over many years in a highly complex political climate; but, as a result of various restrictions in the different city-states, *Commedia* developed as a versatile popular entertainment that could cut across language barriers and cultural differences. *Commedia* companies travelled all over Europe, and even ventured into China and Indonesia.

This success was based, for the most part, on a style of play which was largely improvised and which gave the actors scope to play the audience. They developed a style where gesture and movement worked in conjunction with the spoken word, giving the audience more to see and less to hear in a crowded open-air space. This physicality makes *Commedia* unique in European theatre. Just as the language was simplified, so was the presentation. The same set of masked characters appeared in every production. These stock characters were instantly recognisable types; contemporary parodies portrayed through hugely exaggerated mannerisms and movement motifs. Today, the closest parallel to the physicality of *Commedia* is to be found in knockabout cartoon films like *Bugs Bunny* or *Fritz the Cat*. Here we see the same stylised violence, the same extreme physical reactions where the fear of dropping a single china cup can result in an elaborate juggling sequence with an entire dinner service, or an innocent remark to a passer-by can lead to a complex chase sequence involving the entire neighbourhood. *Commedia* was the prototype for farce, and *Fawlty Towers* is replete with examples of the form. Here we see a similar use of stock characters and heightened physicality.

In *Commedia*, the audience were encouraged to laugh at the characters as much as they were to empathise with them, and to do this they had to balance the recognisable with the abstract. This balancing act is typical of all satire and all parody – and it's at the heart of caricature. When you identify your target and design your exaggerations, you end up with a sort of shorthand; you create a stereotype rather than a person. We're suspicious of caricature because it trades on stereotypes, and we see stereotypes as being simplistic and patronising. We want to see humanity on stage, which we all know is unique. But for all its quirkiness, that humanity must be typical. If we can't recognise the 'type' of person we're dealing with or if that person is so unique that

that we have no references to bring to bear, then we'll be confused and waste precious time trying to work out who or what that person is supposed to be rather than engaging with the action of the scene.

Stereotypes

I remember Monica Pagneux giving an international workshop in the eighties. She divided us into groups according to nationality, so we had groups of French, German, English and Spanish working separately and in their own language on a choreographic task that required a lot of organisation. As an added provocation she gave us a restricted amount of time to work on it. The results were fascinating. Each group instinctively reverted to its national stereotype. The Germans were highly disciplined and well organised. The French talked at lot and didn't finish what they had to do. The Spanish group were very loud and flamboyant. And in the English group we argued so much that we ended up doing something that we hadn't planned to do at all. We all came to the conclusion that national stereotypes, as expressed through movement and behaviour, are inextricably linked to the rhythm of a particular language. Clearly this wasn't in any way a controlled experiment conducted in an academic environment – it was a just an intriguing line of enquiry in a workshop – but the connection between language rhythm and national stereotype became more convincing the more we worked with it.

The Nationalities Game

Working in groups of four, the group improvise in French gibberish. It helps to have something to talk about, like how to make the perfect cup of coffee.

Of course, it could be any language and the less you can speak that language, the better. The idea is to capture typical speech tunes, cadences and rhythms that are typical of the language you're working with. It helps at first to work all together in small groups, because as soon as you see that one person is capturing the quality, you'll be able to copy it and find it for yourself.

Once the game is underway, you can keep calling out different lan-

guages, because we tend to have stronger references for one language compared to another. It's satisfying to find rhythmic contrasts between Russian and Japanese, for example, or Italian and upper-class English. The question is, what do you think is typical? Try to find a consensus in the group and keep referring to each other and copy anything you think is appropriate.

Two people in each group try to explain in French gibberish to the other group how to do something quite complicated. For instance, how to tie your shoelace, or how to start a car, or how a CD player works. It doesn't matter what the procedure is as long as you yourself understand it well enough to go into precise detail.

The pair watching then caricatures what the previous pair has just done. To do this you have to exaggerate the vocal qualities and the movement qualities of what you've just seen. You'll probably find that the gibberish alone will flip you into caricature but the task of 'making it bigger' can often clarify exactly what you're saying in the stereotype.

The Samurai Game

This is my version of a Philippe Gaulier game.

Two people stand opposite each other holding broom handles like two Samurai in combat. The action is as follows:

A strikes B; B then slowly descends to the floor and dies. As soon as B is dead, A celebrates, but B comes alive again, as a ghost, and strikes A in revenge. Now A slowly descends to the floor and dies. The cycle can go on for as long as you like.

Once the action is established and the actors have learnt to control their sticks, and not to send them clattering to the floor, I introduce gibberish, starting with Japanese. It always astonishes me how even mock languages like these can have such a profound effect on physicality.

The game is for the person 'in major' to talk and move at the same time, through each stage of the action. When A squares up to B, it is A who talks all the time – even during the strike itself. As soon as the strike is completed, and B starts to die, B talks through the entire descent to the floor and right up to the point of death.

People tend to rush the Samurai Game at first, but if you relax into it, and extend both the movement and the gibberish at the same time you'll give yourself much more scope to play the audience on the way down to the floor.

Once the game is established, I start to change the nationalities in mid-action. Once again, the contrasting rhythms and the different reactions that these rhythms inspire are fascinating to watch. I remember the actor Alan Riley playing a particularly ferocious Japanese samurai, and making deep nasal grunts with so much tension that his face turned red. It sounded more like a bad case of constipation than a language, but when I switched the game to 'Irish samurai', he suddenly relaxed, and looked quite happy, chattering away to himself in a tripping brogue. When he received his mortal blow, he looked disappointed as he descended towards his death, and complained sadly to himself at his own misfortune. As he came alive again, as a ghost, I demanded 'Italian samurai', and everything changed again. Now he looked assured to the point of arrogance. He relished every gesture, and intimidated his partner with his skill, and then sobbed at the thought of what he was going to do to him, and eventually delivered the fatal blow with such panache that it demanded applause.

How much can you arouse our empathy during the death scenes? This question is particularly pertinent if the audience are laughing heartily. The Japanese samurai would probably have died heroically, but the Irish samurai did it by surprising us with his acceptance. The sight of somebody thinking 'I just can't believe what's happened to me' is both ludicrous and human at the same time.

External References

The Samurai Game will produce any number of caricatures based on national stereotypes, but there's an external reference behind every caricature, an impulse behind the movement: something that shapes and controls that movement to such an extent that you can follow a clear logical line when you start to play it. You can find external references in almost anything: costume pieces, personal mannerisms, photographs, children's drawings, paintings, music, and even literary descriptions. In the Shoe Game, the shoes were an external reference. If those shoes are far too big for you, or so small you can hardly wear them, they'll probably inspire good caricature.

In the *Commedia dell'Arte*, the most obvious external references are the masks, but the mask-maker was also working from an external reference. He would have had an animal in mind when he was making the mask, probably something very ordinary like a bird or a dog or a cat. So it helps to recognise the animal motif the maker was using before attempting to play the mask yourself, because the animal gives you a rhythm, a level of intensity, and a way of looking at the world that you can constantly refer to in bringing the mask to life. It isn't a question of having to go on all fours and mime the animal so much as trying to capture how the animal might breathe, turn its head or move about; it's just a reference, something to give you an idea.

In the early eighties, the director Mike Alfreds, with his company, Shared Experience, developed a style of story theatre where he'd take a novel with strong characters, such as one by Dickens, and he'd train his actors to play both the descriptive passages and the dialogue. The text might read: 'He slowly turned the door handle, then thrust the door open with a sudden jolt. "I knew you were in here," he said.' Using this text, you'd say and play everything at the same time, including all the narrative descriptions. It was a remarkably economical and vivid way of playing prose, and a versatile and effective way of generating atmosphere and exploring situation. The text came alive more or less as it was written, with little to impede it. Mike Alfreds created some vibrant theatre with this technique and evolved a whole body of work including *The Arabian Nights* and *Bleak House*. The following game is my version of one of his exercises.

The Top to Toe Game

Think of someone you know. It could be a friend or a relative, of any age and either sex.

Starting from the top, describe the hair, and illustrate the hair style in gesture, then describe the angle of the head, and illustrate that by holding your own head in the same way. Then do the same with the face, starting with the forehead, the nose, the lips, and the mouth. Hold your mouth in the appropriate configuration but don't attempt to change your voice yet, keep talking as best you can. From there, you go on to the torso, and describe what the person is wearing, and how they wear their clothes, and if there's anything worth noting about their breathing. Now you can illustrate the voice and you go on to describe the hips, legs and what they wear on their feet, and eventually how they walk.

If you can't remember something – make it up. The important thing is to be as clear and as accurate as you can, and that you illustrate everything as far as you can.

The result will be a remarkably detailed caricature of your chosen target that's not only larger than life but imbued with all the information you've given us about this person. Because we've seen the caricature develop in front of us, and followed your logic, every detail will have far more resonance for us than a caricature developed from a cruder external reference. I'm not saying that this is better than other caricatures – it's just different. This is a technique where the caricature is more interesting in the making than it is in the playing. We end up knowing more about the subject with this technique, but it's harder to bring into action than if you were using a dog as an external reference, for example.

The Invisible Caricature Game

It helps to sit down in such a way that you can support your back for this version of the game.

The idea is to play the Top to Toe Game, with all the illustrations, only this time, no movement is allowed.

The game here is to reduce the exaggerations to a minimum, but the exaggerations must still be there. There should be no reduction in the detail, but because you're forbidden to move in this game, your illustrations are more internalised. In other words, you're forced to rely on shifts of intensity and subtle holding patterns, as opposed to elaborate illustrative gestures.

An invisible caricature is impossible because caricature is primarily visual. All that's happening here is a subtle move, back down the scale, to pastiche, but I'm always astonished at how credible a pastiche made in this way can be.

Physical Definitions

External references lead you to discover a series of exaggerated physical traits or typical characteristics that signal who you are at remarkable speed. What starts as an external reference for you becomes a physical definition for the audience. Because all we see is the shape and the movement, we're not interested in how you arrived at what you're doing – just what you look like and what you do in the context of the scene. This is physical definition: a sort of visual shorthand for who you are, which can be either a blessing or a curse, depending on how it's used. Inexperienced actors tend to want to cling on to their definition, as if it were a lifeline. They see it as 'the character' when in reality, nothing could be further from the truth; it's a reminder for the audience, but if you never depart from it, you'll end up looking like a badly operated puppet. Once you've signalled who you are, and by implication what you want to show to the world, you can get on with playing the scene and reacting to everything around you, only returning to your definition at key moments. This way your caricature will transcend our expectations by moving towards a more unique representation of humanity; this preposterous individual will be seen to have credible feelings after all.

The question is, of course, where are these key moments? And when should you return to your physical definition? When is the best time to make a comment about your target; when do you want to remind us who you're supposed to be? Key moments tend to occur either during the anticipation or the pay-off of an action (there's normally too much going on in the release to find time to play anything else). To see a larger-than-life version of Margaret Thatcher trip over a doormat is potentially very funny, but is it more interesting to see her looking powerful and dignified before the trip, or to see her trying to regain her dignity after it? You might think it's more interesting to see the definition on both occasions. I'd try as many permutations as possible, because ultimately we're dealing with visual statements here, and it all comes down to what you look like. These carefully selected physical traits, designed to signal who you are, take on varying levels of significance depending on the action. They're fixed, like a mask, but we want to see behind that mask; we want to see what you really feel; we want to catch a glimpse of those personal moments when the mask slips, and you're forced to abandon the definition.

These glimpses behind the mask give caricature even greater credibility. We know the definition isn't real; we know it's a front, and we delight in being reminded of this and can accept all the ludicrous exaggerations in the manner they were intended. Physical definitions are like key signatures in music. Once you've established that you're playing in the key of C, for example, you can do what you like within that range, and your occasional return to the 'home notes' will be satisfying and reassuring. We're back to mobility again: if you get yourself stuck in a rigid physical definition, you'll no longer be able to react effectively to what's going on around you. It will be like playing the chord of C over and over again without variation. Boring.

The Running About Game

Having found your caricature and established a physical definition, the game is to abandon the definition on command, and run about the space in any way you like, and then again, on command, to return to your definition as comfortably as you can.

You can drop the definition in an instant because the game of running as fast as you can, on command, is too imperative an impulse to do anything else. It's as if the run is more important than the definition and as soon as you drop it and run, you drop the mask and you'll look wholly engaged in the action. But returning to the definition offers you more choices. The run was an instantaneous reaction but the return to your physical definition offers more interesting opportunities and you can play that return in any way you like. It might be as if you're trying to regain your dignity, for example; or it might be to show your irritation, your embarrassment or your contempt. The return is more expressive than the departure because this is where we see you assuming the mask again.

Problems emerge in playing caricature if you think that playing a stylised movement is the same as choreography: something that you've got to sustain and got to get right. These movements aren't choreography; they're reactions to an effective dramatic impulse. That might have come from your reaction to your target or from impulses derived from props and costume pieces. These gestures aren't made in the abstract; they're a reaction to an external impulse and a source of obvious pleasure when you play them. That pleasure is infectious. It's fun to see you having a good time in caricature.

I was once invited to direct a production of Shakespeare's *Richard III* by a small-scale touring company called Third Party. The production was to play huge open-air summer festivals to large family audiences and then various small-scale venues up and down the country. They could only afford six actors so we started by rigorously cutting the text to reduce the number of characters and to clarify the core of the drama. Doubling was unavoidable, and, having decided that the only character not to be doubled should be Richard, it became apparent that some people would have to play as many as three characters.

Our solution to these problems was to think of the play as a sort of grotesque cartoon. By developing bold caricatures, we would leave the audience in no doubt as to which character was being played. We devised a framing device of a travelling Victorian freak show: so Queen Anne became the Fat Lady and was played in a huge fat suit, and the same actor played Queen Elizabeth as the Tattooed Lady; Buckingham was a dwarf or, rather, an actor clearly pretending to be a dwarf; Hastings was the Strong Man; and Queen Margaret, the Bearded Lady.

It was an audacious conceit, but it clarified the drama and opened up an entire image system. Our vivid caricatures helped us evolve a macabre world with mad Queen Margaret vigorously defending the coffin of her dead husband and putting the fear of God into Richard. The colossal Queen Anne accidentally crushed Hastings to death which only exacerbated her guilt over marrying Richard. This was a conceptual parody that was clearly irreverent in the telling of the story whilst never parodying the drama itself. We lost much from the original text. In replacing Richard's ruthless ambition for the throne with a ruthless ambition to be head of the family firm, we clearly lost the original political resonance and the play became smaller and more parochial, but we made an effective drama that caught everyone's imagination.

A major problem was the great battle scene on Bosworth Field at the end of the play. I remembered watching an episode of *The Simpsons* where Homer and Bart played a headbutting game wearing plastic buckets on their heads, so we devised a brutal combat game where the two combatants were joined together by a short length of rope, with metal buckets on their heads. They crouched on all fours and head-butted each other until a winner was declared whilst the audience were encouraged to place their bets, and ghost after ghost conspired to terrify Richard.

Caricature is a natural by-product of cartoon. If you're going to look grotesque and ridiculous, what's to stop you behaving in a manner that's equally preposterous? We loved to hate Richard's infamy and found his contempt for human life and his ruthlessness curiously life-enhancing. We followed his logic and marvelled at his daring. When the cart rolled on, leaving his mangled body in the mud, we all felt he deserved everything he got, but we missed him all the same.

Burlesque

Burlesque came into its own in the late nineteenth and early twentieth centuries and began as an entertainment that 'sent up' some other form of entertainment (typically tragedy or opera) or social organisation (typically army or 'posh' society). Burlesque is a random combination of radically different elements in the same act. Contortionism, acrobatics and magic acts might be freely put together with song, dance and broadly parodic material to create fascinating entertainments that could constitute both grotesque and light-hearted mockery at the same time. Burlesque also featured cross-dressing, animal acts and elements of a freak show. It's a form where anything can go with anything. It's a surreal world where our interest lies in shocking juxtaposition and displacement. There's a joyful exuberance in pulling elements out of their traditional context and mixing them together – just for the fun of it. On one level, it's alarmingly meaningless but on another, these hybrid combinations pose awkward and disturbing questions.

In America, burlesque developed into a risqué erotic entertainment combining acrobatics and circus with song and dance routines, much as you're likely to see in the American productions of Cirque du Soleil today. In Germany, burlesque was taken more seriously and was more akin to the avant-garde. To the Dadaists and the Surrealists in France it became exotic cabaret. The burlesque failed to emerge as a distinct form in England because of the eclectic nature of music hall, vaudeville and variety. An act described as burlesque on the continent, in England would have been called a speciality act. The film *Cabaret* (1972), set in Berlin just before the outbreak of the Second World War, is replete with burlesque images. The band are all men dressed as women and in one number, the Emcee does a song and dance routine with someone in a gorilla suit, which culminates with the line, 'If you could see her through my eyes, she wouldn't look Jewish at all.' Is this mocking anti-

Semitism or promoting it? We could take it either way, but the issue is further confused by the image of a man contemplating a sexual relationship with a gorilla.

More recently, the play within a play (*Springtime for Hitler*) in *The Producers* is a burlesque. So is *A Funny Thing Happened on the Way to the Forum*. In burlesque, you don't so much reference a target as juxtapose it with something completely different. In *Jerry Springer – The Opera*, for example, we experience a clash of two entirely contrasting forms, namely the 'high art' of opera with a sensationalist American chat show that thrives on exhibitionism and social taboo. These two forms clash like cymbals, creating a playful exuberance where anything is possible and nothing is sacred. We're treated to volley after volley of beautifully articulated obscenities which, like the famous Derek and Clive sketches by Peter Cook and Dudley Moore, soon become ridiculous self-parody. For the most part, the actors play at a level of pastiche and caricature, but time and again the clash of the two forms moves the parody up a gear and shifts it into burlesque with images like the tap-dancing Ku Klux Klan, or a sequence were Christ takes some twenty bars of music to tell the Devil to 'Fuck off.' The action reaches its splendid burlesque climax when Christ and the Devil become guests on the *Jerry Springer Show* and the host has to officiate over this archetypal conflict. Eventually, God arrives and asks Jerry to join him in heaven because, 'It Ain't Easy Being Me'.

In spite of all these crude religious references, religion isn't the target here. That dubious privilege is reserved for American moral values portrayed as an irreconcilable mixture of mindless Christian fundamentalism and an equally mindless amoral liberalism. But the prime target of the show is Jerry Springer himself and, like most effective parody, there's ambiguity here. On the one hand, the production makes him wholly culpable for everything that happens because of his lack of moral leadership and his apparent pleasure in watching inarticulate people goad each other and want to tear each other apart. But on the other hand, it seems to be saying that amorality is the only way forward in a so-called liberal society, to the extent that Jerry would be welcome next to God in heaven. It was probably this latter interpretation that persuaded Jerry Springer himself to support the project. Ambiguity is essential. Like all art, parody is at its best when it poses a question rather than giving an answer. We don't want to be told what to think, and if you err on the side of obliqueness and double meaning, that question will have more resonance than what you *appear* to be saying. The result is that we'll watch you for longer and are more likely to tolerate your parody even if it makes us feel uncomfortable. But if you come with all the answers, you'll end up preaching to the converted and alienating everybody else. In parody, there's nothing more compelling than when you're in close proximity to what might be considered to be offensive.

Like clown, burlesque exposes both who you are and what you're doing to mockery, and demands that we accept it on its own terms. If you attempt a song and dance routine with a live animal, the event will have an actuality all of its own. There can be no pretence here. A chorus of hooded Klan members suddenly bursting into a tap dance is equally uncompromising, especially when it's perfectly clear that there are a few black legs under those white gowns with the pointed hoods. All they seem to be saying here is that the Klan are glad to be there, but the dance is funny because tap dancing is the last thing you'd expect the Ku Klux Klan to do. It trivialises their sinister image and the sight of all those pointed hoods bobbing up and down makes them look ridiculous.

I once watched a transvestite strongman entertain the crowd in a street in Amsterdam. This squat, elderly man was about as tall as he was wide: he made an extraordinary woman. Dressed in high-heeled shoes, short skirt, fur wrap and an elegant blond wig, he/she minced round her car, which had apparently broken down. 'Who will help me out?' she said, fluttering her enormous false eyelashes. She looked so extraordinary that nobody came forward. She wept pathetically, hurriedly adjusted her make-up, and occasionally smashed her fist on the roof with such astonishing force that it made everybody laugh. In the end, out of sheer exasperation, she rolled the car over, single-handed, her vast muscles bulging under her flimsy costume. She clearly wasn't a woman, but she wasn't exactly a strongman either.

In *The Firework Maker's Daughter* (Told by an Idiot, 2004), Amanda Lawrence played a fuse. She appeared dressed in a red jumpsuit, wearing red washing-up gloves with strands of glittering tinsel attached to the fingers. When she was 'set alight', she made a 'siss'-ing sound and wiggled her fingers along a stretch of rope laid out across the floor so that it looked as if the fuse was burning. It was quite a long stretch of rope so she would occasionally break off from her 'siss'-ing and sparkly finger-acting, do a little dance and then go back to being a fuse again. When the fuse eventually reached the explosive and nothing happened, she stopped, pulled herself up to her full height and said, 'I feel completely humiliated', and walked off the stage.

This is basically clown. We see each game declared and the clown's preoccupation with playing the audience, but there are subtle moments of burlesque here as well. The clash between the person and the fuse is fully exploited and it reads as a witty solution to the question of how you represent a fuse on stage. This is about as subtle as you get in burlesque. But the clash between the transvestite and the strongman was crude and disturbing. The image of that squat, muscular body straining to lift the weight of the car, that red, distorted, heavily made-up face and those huge shoulders bulging under a frilly blouse wasn't remotely witty or particularly funny. It was a grotesque and uncompromising image. We weren't aware of an actor messing about here so much as two irreconcilable realities clashing together. The fuse and the strongman are examples of the burlesque at its most subtle and at its most crude, respectively. They were both compelling because, in their different ways, they were both entirely truthful.

Playing the clash of opposites like this is immensely liberating and can lead to some compelling theatrical imagery. Like clown, burlesque is a world where anything goes, but unlike clown, is at its best when placed in a dramatic context which is more preconceived and deliberate. It's another level of parody: another means of making mockery.

I'm always fascinated by the unique skills that different people have. For example, you might be able to wiggle your ears, make your eyes move independently, or have more conventional specialities like being able to play a musical instrument, stand on your head, ride a unicycle, or do animal impressions. Genuine skills and personal idiosyncrasies are excellent starting points when approaching burlesque, where any deviation from the norm, either congenital or carefully cultivated, can really come into its own. In a line of dancers at the turn of the last century, the one who was fatter, smaller or taller than average would probably end up playing burlesque. The most enduring burlesque has the same level of actuality as somebody with the strength to roll over a car.

I once worked with an actor who had flat feet. He could also hold his arches up, so that his feet looked completely normal. He could also drop them and stand with no arches, his whole foot flat on the floor, which would make his entire body drop about half an inch and his legs go into a different alignment. He would entertain us for hours with this. Eventually, he found the game of raising his arches every time he had an idea and dropping them again when he changed his mind.

The Speciality Game

Having investigated the personal skills in the group of actors I'm working with, I invite the group to invent clashes where they have to use their skill in an apparently irrelevant or inappropriate context.

Circus, dance and music are excellent points of reference in burlesque because of their indisputable levels of expertise. There was an acrobatic clown called Freddie Frinton, who specialised in playing a drunk. He would execute an elaborate trip and emerge unscathed, except for a broken cigarette dangling from his fingers which he would raise to his lips only to be distracted by something, and fall over again. Drunks and acrobatics are an obvious combination, and there's not much of a clash here. Freddie Frinton was playing physical comedy rather than burlesque, but if an acrobat were to play a brain surgeon doing an intricate operation, or a politician giving a speech, or an expert flower arranger, or an undertaker at a funeral, then more interesting and more unusual clashes will start to emerge and the work will move closer to the burlesque and the parodic. Fractured sentences and simple text work very well at this level of physicality and can easily add another layer of meaning.

The ability that dance, music, acrobatics and circus skills have in absorbing meaning is astonishing. As we've already discussed in Part Two, emotions are established more by the dramatic situation set in place by the writer than anything you might do in the scene, so it's difficult to find clashes by exploring emotions. The key is to find clashes in the action. For example, can your trombone player play a dirty joke? Can your dancer explain why she's leaving, 'speaking' only in dance and without resorting to mime? Answer questions like these and your work will shift closer and closer to the burlesque and you'll cultivate the habit of seeking out clashes and making imagery.

In *Out of the Blue* (Reject's Revenge Theatre Company, 2005), I wanted to find the image of a submariner close to death, seeing the image of his wife in his mind's eye – an image that could inspire him into action. We started with his wife appearing and singing a song he associated with her. Charming, but too sentimental for my taste, so the next time she appeared, she played a passionate version of the same tune on a trombone. The captain's wife was a demure and dignified woman and the sight of her playing a trombone was a complete clash with anything that we'd seen of her before. It was a burlesque image verging on the comic. Every time she played, it looked as if she was goading him to do something, and the music was replete with feeling, so the captain had to play against the image and the music, and become more aggressive in his determination. Burlesque is essentially a visual form of parody that invariably creates strong images through counterpoint.

The Ad Hoc Game

'Ad' is Latin for 'to', and 'hoc' is Latin for 'this', so if you make an ad hoc disguise by holding a plastic cup between your teeth so that it covers your nose and start to grunt like a pig, you're saying: 'Add this meaning to this meaning.' The Ad Hoc Game is a means of finding ridiculous clashes between one thing and another whilst never losing that essential grain of truth. It's an excellent game for cultivating a taste for burlesque.

Choose a theme: birds, dogs, insects or tropical fish, for example. Any simple target will do. Let's say you choose a bird. You're looking for the crudest and the most recognisable bird that you can find, and in this game the 'recognition' is the easy bit. All you need to do to imply a bird is to flap your arms about a bit and go 'tweet, tweet'. We're not interested in what type of bird you are. Just be a bird.

The game is to use what objects, bits of clothing, and odd bits of material you might have to hand to give yourself a beak, a tail, feet, wings, or maybe a headdress of some kind. Keep it simple. These are all possibilities. You don't have to cover them all. Choose the characteristics you like.

Having created your bird, the game is to play the audience with it. The Compliments Game, or the 'And . . . And' Game are good preparations for this.

The cruder and the more inaccurate your costume is, the more we're going to laugh. Once you've established the fact that you're a bird, the last thing we want to see you do is bird-like things, so forget eating worms and fluffing up your feathers. Play the game as if you were playing clown, so repeat whatever we find amusing. The key is to be outrageous.

I remember Paul Hunter pulling the waistband of his trousers up to somewhere near his armpits, sticking a large scarf down the back as a tail, and putting a woman's wig on, the wrong way round. For his beak, he found a microphone with a short cable attached to it which hung down like a long curling bill when he held the mike to his mouth. All he had to do then was to move his elbows up and down to indicate wings, and find a silly chirpy walk, and from then on he could do anything. He tried running about a bit, and then he sang a few snatches of popular songs down the microphone, and did a little dance. Every now and again he'd have a rest, but he could have gone on with that for quite some time. It was all acutely bird-like, without him actually playing a bird. This is the freedom of burlesque. The clashes between the microphone and the beak, and an actor messing about and the image of a bird, add one meaning to another and create something that's recognisable and ridiculous at the same time. You can do what you like, and you can drop what you're doing whenever you like. The more you declare the pretence, the more we believe that you're playing a bird; there's as much actuality as a strongman rolling over a car.

If caricature grows out of the exaggeration of little details, burlesque grows out of juxtaposition. Paul's silly wig and his stupid microphone beak serve a similar function to Max Wall's silly walk. They are both incongruous clashes that take us by surprise. Astonishingly, burlesque can sometimes appear to be more real than the real thing, but these occasions are very rare. Most of the time, people try to do too much, and become heavy-handed with their choices. So limit yourself to playing one thing at a time, and to let the exaggeration emerge out of the way we react to what you're doing, rather than trying to present everything from the very start. There's a visual interaction to be found in playing burlesque. It's a question of saying to yourself, 'Oh, you like that, do you, so how about this?' Or 'Oh, you don't like that – how about this then?' Let us tell you what we like. You're going to feel an impulse from your disguise. No matter how stupid it might be, it's going to make you feel slightly different, and imply that you should move in a different way. But if the objects you're working with don't give you an impulse to move, it doesn't matter. Most of the comedy that Paul Hunter found with his stupid 'microphone bird' came out of the games he found with the objects he was playing with.

Burlesque isn't a parody of big ideas so much as little games to keep us amused. In burlesque, we laugh more at what you look like than what you do. It's more parodic than the pastiche or the caricature because, in burlesque, you're not only commenting on the target but you're commenting on yourself commenting on the target at the same time. The transvestite strongman made himself look ridiculous by dressing as a woman, and he created a grotesque woman at the same time. Paul Hunter make himself look ridiculous with his pulled-up trousers, microphone beak and woman's wig, and he also made a grotesque version of a bird at the same time. We need to see both elements for the burlesque to work.

The Demonstration Game

This is a useful application of the Ad Hoc Game.

Two ad-hoc birds stand in the space. A makes a derogatory comment to the audience about B, such as, 'Have you seen her arse?' and follows that comment with an exaggerated demonstration of B's sagging arse. A then continues with: 'Have you? Have you seen it?' followed by an even bigger demonstration. 'Her buttocks trail behind her on the floor as she walks along.' This is followed by an even more grotesque demonstration for the audience.

It's a classic Billy Connolly technique. The game is to make an exaggerated observation then to share the joke with the audience, as if to say 'You know what I mean?' Watch the audience, and if they like what you're doing, don't do it again. Just make it bigger. This is the maxim behind any parodic play beyond the level of pastiche. It's very satisfying to see a pair of outlandish ad-hoc individuals being rude about each other's anatomy. Keep your remarks personal. Remember that you're talking about each other's bodies, not taste in clothes, so be specific, and don't make anything up. It's a great freedom when you realise that you can be as rude, insulting and personal as you like in this game because you look so preposterous yourself. But there must always be that little grain of truth, or we won't believe you. If we see the evidence and follow your logic, we'll accept your hyperbole all the more.

Once your parody starts to get personal, and once it's developed into a contest in trading insults, a clear separation between you and your target starts to emerge, very much like the separation in clown. I've seen an audience erupt into laughter as soon A or B walks on stage in disguise. They are laughing in anticipation of what is going to happen, which only feeds your desire to make even bolder choices at the dressing-up stage. But if you look hurt or resentful in any way, the game will cease to be amusing, and the parody will soon become mawkish. Be robust. It's as much a lesson in self-acceptance as it is in mockery. Parody can be vicious. You can point the finger at anybody and hold anybody up to ridicule, but as a ludicrous burlesque, you're immune to the worst of it. So you can go as far as you like as long as you take the audience with you. Your remarks are validated if we share the joke. On the other hand, if you're on the receiving end of all this, keep your dignity rather than trying to play for our sympathy. It's generally much funnier to get angry and pompous when you're dressed as a stupid bird than it is to try to play pathos. Go for it one hundred per cent: this game is not for the faint-hearted.

The Acceptance Game

If A targets your 'sagging arse', for example, now you retaliate by admitting the observation and going on to demonstrate how it trails along the ground, or how it makes it impossible for you to sit down. Your legs become so weak that you have to drag yourself around on your knees, which many mistake as a sexual invitation so you're constantly getting into trouble. The game here is to beat your partner at their own game by making even more ridiculous personal observations about your own anatomy.

You can generally go much further when you're making admissions about yourself than you can if you are insulting someone else. You have the added advantage in the Acceptance Game of being able to arouse our sympathies because self-parody tends to be more acceptable than confrontational insults, even when you're dressed up as a silly bird.

The 'Don't Say the Obvious' Game

This is a slightly more sophisticated version of all these games.

Rather than making confrontational demonstrations or self-parodying illustrations, in this game the idea is to be oblique with your comment. For example, A might say to B: 'Maybe we shouldn't talk about . . .' (A mimes the shape of B's tail.) 'Oh, don't get me wrong, I like the . . .' (A develops the mime, exaggerating its size and the way it moves.) 'I know most people think otherwise, but I don't. I think it's . . .' And A exaggerates the mime of B's tail even more, playing the audience all the way.) 'You're very brave and you bear it very . . . . (A mimes how B must be feeling about his tail.)

It's the game of damning through faint praise but pushing the physical comments as far as possible. The mimetic elements in this game enable you to be far more eloquent than you might think. These visual illustrations enable you to play the audience more freely because you're not reliant on the audience being quiet. You can keep on going though the laughter and through anything your partner might say.

Buffoon

" *There were once two hunchbacks begging in the same village. The pickings were so meagre that one of them decided that enough was enough, so he moved away to find a better life. Travelling through the forest he felt safer sleeping in the treetops. One night he found a splendid old tree, climbed up it and fell asleep. In the middle of the night he was woken up by what he thought was a gentle breeze on his cheek, but when he opened his eyes, he saw three witches flying round his tree. One by one he watched them land, and start walking round and round the tree chanting over and over again: 'Saturday, Sunday, Saturday, Sunday, Saturday, Sunday.' The chant went on and on, and the hunchback became so irritated by its monotony that he couldn't help himself calling out 'Monday!' The women paused for a moment, then started a new chant: 'Saturday, Sunday, Monday. Saturday, Sunday, Monday.' They liked it. They liked it so much that they burst into a jubilant dance, screeching their chant hysterically into the night sky. They invited the hunchback to come down and join them, and as soon as they saw him, they promised to give him his heart's desire.*

'I want to lose my hump,' he said. Instantly, the hump disappeared, his back straightened and the old women whirled off, chanting into the forest. He ran all the way back to his village. He was a new man now, but when he got home, nobody recognised him except the other hunchback, and he was less than pleased to see him. 'How did you lose your hump?' he demanded. 'Tell me, or I'll kill you!' So the man told his story.

That night, the other hunchback ran deep into the forest and climbed the same old tree. He waited, and he waited, and was just about to drop off to sleep when he heard the happy chanting of the old women getting louder and louder as they whirled round and round the tree, faster and faster beneath him: 'Saturday, Sunday, Monday. Saturday, Sunday, Monday,' they chanted. The hunchback couldn't control himself. 'Tuesday!' he bellowed.

The women paused for a moment and then started a new chant: 'Saturday, Sunday, Monday, Tuesday. Saturday, Sunday, Monday, Tuesday.' They tried it, and they didn't like it.

'*Come down here!' they commanded. As soon as they saw him, they produced the hump of the first hunchback and, giggling uncontrollably, they stuck it on his front to make him a big belly. Now he had two humps: one at the back and one at the front. He snarled at them, and in his rage he tore up the old tree by its roots, cursing everyone and everything around him. The old women danced round and round him, then whirled off into the night sky — their chant getting fainter and fainter, until it was no more than a gentle breeze through the trees. Punchinello just smiled, and the birds sang their dawn chorus.*   **"**

This is Punchinello's story, and it's probably almost as old as him. There's nothing charming, lovable or optimistic about this tale. There's no idealism here, just a hard-nosed pragmatism that tells us not to expect life to deal us anything other than a bad hand, and that ultimately, we're on our own. God's got a hangover, so we'd better get used to it, and remember to keep our wits about us. If we try to respond to this story from our complacent, liberal, twenty-first century values of equal opportunity and inclusion then we won't get very far. Punchinello's story comes from a culture of absolutism. In his day, Punchinello was a scream of triumph for those with nothing, or for those who lived in perpetual fear that nothing was always just round the corner. Far too ugly for conventional society, the story tells us why Punchinello just doesn't fit in. He's a nasty individual to start with, and he just keeps on getting nastier, until he's become his own person setting his own values. When he smiles at the end of the story, it's a smile of revenge on all of us. Punchinello is a pugnacious iconoclast. He's the Alf Garnett of his time: someone we love to hate, yet we marvel at his audacity. He's more politically obscene than politically incorrect; he'll say the unsayable and do things that only he can get away with. He comes down to us today in the children's puppet show Punch and Judy, where he throws the baby out of the window, murders the policeman, hangs the judge, goes to hell, and kills the Devil.

There is something of Punchinello in Shakespeare's *Richard III*, or Alfred Jarry's *Ubu Roi*. There's also something of him in Caliban, Cyrano de Bergerac, Quasimodo, or even the Elephant Man. Punchinello is the archetype, and there are countless variations of him in every civilization. On the one hand, he's the product of a tough, independent, peasant culture, deeply mistrustful of authority of any kind, and other people of any kind. On the other hand, he's a personification of the grotesque, a universal expression of our fears, of our loathing, and of the unknown. Punchinello captured the popular imagination in the *Commedia dell'Arte* of southern Italy during the fifteenth and sixteenth centuries, but his origins are primeval and deeply embedded in the human psyche. Punchinello is the embodiment of the 'meme' that beauty is good and ugliness is evil.

Punchinello is a buffoon. If the clown loves the audience and is driven by an insatiable appetite for play, the buffoon hates the audience and is driven by an insatiable appetite for parody. A buffoon is a grotesque parody of a human being. Like Punchinello with his extra hump, a buffoon is marked and set apart from society: never to get the beautiful girl, and never to share the social achievements of those of us who don't have two humps. If you're set apart like this, it's perfectly under-standable to feel bitter and resentful, but those humps also give you a licence to say more, do more, and to speak the truth – or rather your version of the truth. A buffoon believes in nothing and laughs at every-thing. If you've got one hump at the front and one at the back, your career as a dancer, a model, a sportsman, an acrobat or even a normal member of society is going to be very limited. We'd laugh at the sight of Punchinello dancing, or strutting up and down a catwalk. If we saw him fall in love, we'd raise an eyebrow. If we heard him speak beautiful and exciting poetry, we'd be constantly asking ourselves: 'Is it really him saying that?' or 'Does he really mean it? Surely not.' Punchinello's ludicrous shape turns anything he does into a parody of the real thing – except, of course, an act of violence or defilement – we'd probably expect that. 'No one,' we think, 'can go around with one hump at the front and one at the back without feeling a little bit pissed off about it.'

A buffoon is a grotesque clown who holds his or herself up to ridicule by performing the sort of comic antics that are generally considered to be below skill, or wit, or competence of any kind. The Shorter Oxford Dictionary defines buffoon as 'a low jester – implying ridicule, contempt or disgust.' We're dealing with the lowest denominator of physical comedy here that, on the face of it, is socially unacceptable today because we pride ourselves on knowing better, and because we aspire to a diverse society. We demonise prejudice and intolerance, and so we should; but archetypes are stronger and more deep-rooted than education and legislation. In every adult, there's still something of the three-year-old in there: we might be big enough to name the Devil with impunity, but the 'unknown' and the 'different' are still a bit scary. The opportunities to be conspicuously naff, tasteless, irrational, disgusting and puerile make buffoon as delectable to play today as it ever was.

Grotesque Realism

Pastiche, caricature and burlesque are endemic in popular culture but the ultimate development in the quest of 'making it worse' is buffoon. Once you hit buffoon, you encounter grotesque realism. This is an idea developed by Mikhail Bakhtin (1895-1975), a Russian scholar of literature and linguistics who specialised in the works of Rabelais. Bakhtin maintained that medieval popular culture, as expressed in the 'carnivalesque events of fairs and markets', was defined as much by physical deformity as physical skill. He was talking about a time when the medieval year was punctuated with festivals of distinctly ambiguous religious origin, like the Feast of Fools, where boots were baptised in the font, and the local simpleton was made king for a day. It was a time when madmen were amusing, physical deformity was a form of physical comedy, fools were the comics of the day and parody was endemic.

Bakhtin maintained that these popular folk traditions designated a way of looking at the world that was distinctly earthbound; a worldview that was anti-hierarchical, anti-individualistic and anti-spiritual. He believed that this prevailing attitude confronted the elite with values like equality and community, and that it spawned a pragmatic materialism based more on a healthy working body than the acquisition of wealth. I'm sure Marx would have been proud of him. According to Bakhtin, these 'carnivalesque events' and secular celebrations were a temporary relief from the rigid structure of the established order. They marked the suspension of rank, privileges and prohibitions. But he felt that the 'carnival nucleus' of this culture wasn't an artistic form and that mock coronations and mock baptisms weren't art, but occupied a more liminal place: somewhere on 'the borderline between life and art'. He concluded that in reality what they were calibrating in medieval popular culture was life itself, or rather, life shaped by 'a certain pattern of play'.

Trinidadian carnival is a useful point of reference here. When slavery was finally abolished, the newly freed slaves were understandably bitter. They danced in chains in the streets and parodied their former masters. They took the French tradition of Mardi Gras and made it African. The plantation owners called them 'black devils', so they thought to themselves, 'You want devils – we'll give you devils.' Some covered their bodies in molasses and danced up close to anybody watching them and rubbed themselves against them, leaving sticky black stains all over their clothes. It was part aggressive parody and part practical joke at the same time. To the victim, it was mischievous and unpleasant, but to the newly freed slave it was liberating and self-affirming. It was a pattern of play where life and art were indistinguishable.

Bakhtin was writing in the 1940s; today that borderline between life and art is fainter. We're more aware of liminality, the no-man's-land where we can no longer identify the difference. In theatre, grotesque realism is at its most powerful when we can't be sure if it's real or not. If you confront us wearing a phoney 'disguise' that's hideous to the point of ridicule and we don't know whether to laugh at you or look away, you'll be taking the 'only joking' concept as far as it can go. Bakhtin maintained that this popular medieval mindset spawned numerous forms of grotesque realism, whose fundamental attributes were our old friends exaggeration and excess. These characteristics corresponded to a recurring image system involving copulation, pregnancy, birth, growth, old age, disintegration, madness and dismemberment; the direct antitheses of the classical aesthetics of youth, beauty and proportion. This same image system is still at the heart of parodic imagery today. Look at the mildest of parodies like *Shrek 2* or *Team America: World Police* (both 2004) and you'll find they freely exploit much of the same image system. It's worth noting that both these examples favour cartoon and puppetry to facilitate greatest flexibility in portraying 'growth', 'disintegration' and 'dismemberment'.

Deviations from the Norm

We live in a more equal society with more social mobility than in medieval times. But it's just as conformist as it ever was, particularly as far as physical appearance is concerned. Anthropologists contend that, where other species recognise their own by means of smell, human beings use facial recognition. It follows that the decisions that determine what we regard as 'beautiful' or 'ugly' are made at an instinctive level. On a continuum of faces ranging from 'the beautiful' to 'the ugly', the majority of us occupy the middle ground, by having largely acceptable faces, and we view the extremes at either end of the continuum with great ambivalence.

Most of us in our heart of hearts secretly resent the 'beautiful people' for what we haven't got, yet at the same time admire them for showing us attractive aspects of ourselves, and for giving us something to aspire to. A lifetime of television commercials has taught us that beautiful people are the embodiment of health and goodness, but we secretly suspect them of being superficial or unintelligent, and resent them even more for their apparent superiority.

We also resent the 'ugly people', not that anybody would ever use that term, because they shame us for revealing aspects of ourselves that most of us would prefer to keep hidden. But the 'uglies' also make us feel superior, by enabling us to demonstrate our compassion and sensitivity. Some of us pride ourselves in recognising their inner qualities, their perception or their intelligence, whilst in private we use them as a warning to our children about the 'cruel hand of fate' or 'the dangers of loose living' or 'the power of evil'. 'If the wind changes, you'll stay like that,' my grandmother used to say when I was pulling a face.

Psychologists tell us that different cultures arrive at their particular definition of beauty by determining an accepted norm of facial features; those who deviate the least from the accepted norm are considered the most 'beautiful'. It's a very persuasive idea, and it implies that our concept of beauty is based on a deep-seated conservatism where 'like' is attracted to and validates 'like'. Differences are undesirable and unacceptably ugly and – unless we stop and think about it – evil.

Coverings and Distortions

Like Punchinello, something interesting happens when you're clearly set apart from 'the norm'. If you deliberately distort your body with vast amounts of padding stuffed under your clothing, so that the best you can do is to hobble about, or be wheeled about on a cart; if you make yourself so ugly and misshapen that we feel uncomfortable looking at you, and then play a vicious parody of a 'normal' person doing absolutely anything, then the relationship between you and your target will change completely.

If B is parodied by a grotesque version of a human being – then it's no longer a case of one sentient individual viciously making fun of another. Now it's a case of an archetypal outcast – a leper, a beggar, a mad person, who's barely human at all – having the audacity to poke fun at 'normality'. Now we're in the same territory as the King being mocked by the Fool. Whether this is a natural fool or an allowed fool we don't know yet – all we know at the moment is that if you're going to dress up like that, then you're a fool, and you're a faintly disturbing fool, because your appearance is so much worse than life that it's a parody in itself.

If A looks fantastically grotesque, and then 'has a go' at B, who looks 'normal', we're unlikely to take offence in quite the same way. B will be less likely to feel insulted, because A will look like an outlandish joke of a person, far too ridiculous to be taken seriously. If you look 'worse than life' from the outset, you tend to feel less inhibited about making comments about somebody else, especially if they look socially more acceptable than you do. In being socially unacceptable yourself, you feel that you have licence to be more personal, and more confrontational with your comments, and you'll probably end up being more eloquent into the bargain. There'll be an air of the preposterous about you, and what you have to say will lose its bile. If your shape or your costume impedes your movement, attempts at an accurate physical parody will be so impaired that almost anything you do is likely to be funny; the whole interaction will be less personal and more theatrical. This is the grotesque parody of the buffoon, and to find it, you need to find your own personal version of Punchinello's hump, and his preposterous pot belly to set you apart from everyone else.

You start by stuffing your clothes with newspaper, cushions and bits of foam to make your body-mask. We might call it a 'mask' but unlike Wyan's little Bondress mask in Bali, this mask is less definable. You might be an androgynous series of blobs, hardly a recognisable human being at all. Wyan's 'mask' was called 'Man who thinks he's a dancer'.

But you won't have a clue as to who you are: you'll just be covered up. Like a child giggling under the duvet, you'll just feel safe and hidden and mischievous. These are the three most important words in playing buffoon. You feel safe because everything is hidden, and you delight in the mischief of it all. Your natural movement rhythms will be so distorted that we'll never know what you really feel about anything. So it's all a sham, an elaborate hoax – but is it? This is the enigmatic world of the buffoon: full of half-truth, distortion, ambiguity and basic unequivocal humanity.

The Playing Your Shape Game

Each body-mask will have a different distribution of weight. Decide how you're going to carry that weight. And ask yourself whether you're 'in the space above'. In other words, do you feel that you're taller than you really are, with your head in the clouds, or are you in 'the space beneath', and smaller than you really are, and closer to the earth? Most buffoons feel the latter, but this isn't always the case. Finally, determine where the extremities in your body-mask are. In other words, if you have a hump, or a big pointed head, or an enormous belly or huge buttocks, be aware of how this part of your body projects into the space, and see to what extent you can keep a fixed point with it. To what extent can you walk across the space without this protuberance going up and down as you walk? To keep this fixed point you have to find lightness and delicacy in your movement. There's a useful restriction here that ultimately will raise your awareness of how little you need to move in order to give your body-mask a clear physical presence in the space.

We're dealing with outlandish shapes here, and there's a lot for the audience to take in. We need stillness and simplicity in your movement or everything you do will look blurred and messy. You probably won't be able to do anything 'normally', so you're going to have to find the most comfortable way of walking, standing and moving about. Your job is to negotiate the restrictions imposed by your body-mask, and if you respect the discipline of the fixed point, you'll have to simplify your ideas, clarify the way you move and as a result you'll give yourself more space to play and more time to react. You'll be more mysterious to watch.

The grotesque fascinates us because it repels and intrigues us at the same time. Our first instinct is to look away in horror, but after that initial shock we become fascinated by the strangeness of your appearance. We can't imagine what sort of a body must be lurking under all that padding; we can't visualise your anatomy; you're too bizarre to arouse our pity, and too weird to be a person, yet you're discernibly a sentient human being. Anything beyond our understanding and beyond our imagining is mysterious.

A padded buffoon moving with a clear fixed point has an intriguing grace, and stillness that has the effect of emphasising the smallest and the most delicate of gestures. I've seen buffoons look hideous and beautiful at the same time. This is the paradox of the grotesque. We don't know what you are and we don't know what to make of you. In our confusion we'll latch on to anything we think we recognise, and when we find something, like a graceful movement, a childlike charm, or a clear intelligence at work, that quality is amplified by the fact that you look so incongruous.

It's no more than extreme dressing-up, to enable you to feel mischievous, and us to feel uncomfortable. The enduring lesson in padding yourself up like this is the feeling of mischief that you can get from being decidedly worse than life. Once you've experienced the full padding approach, you can get a similar feeling with an astonishing variety of other disguises. Grotesque parody like this cultivates a taste for dressing in the most unflattering way possible. Padding is optional. I like it because it's so extreme, and because it compels you to make bold choices, and enables you to cover up as much as you like. Padding also gives you a strong physical impulse to play with. But padding isn't essential; you can make an interesting group of buffoons from random clothes picked up from a charity shop. As long as you feel disguised and mischievous, most of the games in this section will work for you.

Lecoq and Gaulier have identified innumerable different types of buffoon based on the different designs that emerged in their various workshops. Gaulier discovered elegant little dwarfs, achieved by actors shuffling about on their knees; malevolent hunchbacks, that seemed to change in quality depending on whether the hump was on the left or the right; and insane leaders with wild eyes and no other deformity at all. When I worked with Lecoq, he was talking about luxurious buffoons, diabolical buffoons, and infant buffoons. In *The Moving Body*, he ends up dividing his buffoons into three categories: the mysterious, the grotesque and the fantastical. I doubt that there's much to be gained by looking for different types of buffoon. After all, we're not dealing with 'characters' here. The question isn't 'Who am I?' so much as 'What do I want to hide?' Like clown, buffoon is more about playing yourself than finding a character. It's far more important to determine how different buffoons fit together as a group; that's about as near as you're going to get to character.

The Dancing Game

To what extent can you maintain a clear fixed point with your body-mask, and dance to some light and delicate music?

This is an excellent way of discovering where you have the most mobility. The key here is to go with the padding, and try not to resist the restrictions the padding gives you. Dancing is a good way of discovering what it is that we like about the way you look and the way you move. No matter how grotesque you try to make yourself, we'll always find that little trace of humanity; it might only be a hand or a foot, a little smile, or a playful glint in the eye – whatever it is, we'll latch on to it.

Of course, from here on, you can dance in pairs, you can do buffoon formation dancing, or you can have dancing competitions if you like. But remember it's a game. What dance is to a buffoon isn't necessarily dance to anybody else – and I'm using the word 'dance' here in the widest possible sense.

In this context, any movement done with pleasure, for the audience, and with respect for your physical limitations is going to be interesting to watch. The more appropriate the dance – in other words, the more suitable it is for your shape and comfortable to perform – the more intriguingly parodic it will be.

The Centre of Good

Unlike pastiche, caricature and burlesque, a group of grotesque buffoons are not only commenting on us, 'the beautiful people', and targeting our hypocrisies, they're also implying Bakhtin's alternative values of equality and community: anti-hierarchical, anti-individualistic, anti-spiritual. This isn't a conscious political standpoint so much as a basic instinct. As obvious outsiders with no place in any conventional continuum of acceptable beauty, they stick together because there's an obvious safety in numbers. This is an essential part of the equation. Furthermore, unless we see something to admire about them, their comments will lack resonance. When confronted with an effective group of ridiculing buffoons, there's a tacit implication that they know something that we don't; that their way of life, for all its appalling limitations, is somehow better than we know. It's as if we get a tantalising glimpse of the way they live by the way they work as a group, and it's an ideal society. There's no conflict, no resentment. Everybody knows their place and likes it. If it's a buffoon's place to be sat on by everybody else – they love it; if it's their place to be beaten by the rest of the group – they're proud of their job. Buffoons operate best on the principle that there's safety in numbers. In small units, they always know their exact place in the group, and accept it without the slightest trace of resentment. Buffoons are devoid of ambition and appear to have no egos whatsoever.

This is the buffoonish 'centre of good'. The script analyst Robert McKee has a very persuasive theory about character. He maintains that all effective characterisation, no matter how 'evil' or contemptible that nasty creation might be, will be perfectly acceptable to us as a human being, as long as we've something to admire about him. Hannibal Lecter in *The Silence of the Lambs*, for example, could hardly be less sympathetic, but we admire his cleverness and his innate intelligence, and we respect his forethought. These qualities become his centre of good. Because we admire him in this way, we learn to respect him, and even begin to accept his appalling actions.

The centre of good in a group of buffoons lies in their complicity within the group. This is my starting point, and the Dancing Game – and all the games in Part One – will help to foster this complicity. With only your movement quality to imply that you live in an ideal society, the greater your complicity, the more concord, the more sensitivity, and the more awareness you can show us, the more you'll demonstrate that you've got something for us to aspire to. Buffoon is primarily a visual form. We respond, first and foremost, to what you look like, and this image is amplified by how you move.

The Buffoon Chorus

A chorus of buffoons seems to work best in small groups of five. This appears to be the optimum number that enables you to work with enough speed, spontaneity and mental agility before the group starts to find it difficult to function in a rapid improvisation. Strictly speaking, five isn't really a chorus: it's too small to imply that gravitas, sense of witness, and universality that gives a chorus its presence. Five is also too small a number to generate that sense of anarchy, passion and loss of control that's always the reverse side of chorus work. The bigger the group, the slower they tend to be in building their reactions, and hence the more gravitas they seem to command, or, if they turn into a mob, the harder they are to control. It's much more difficult to stop a group of twenty-one running about, with complicity, than it is to stop a group of five. A group of five is small enough to change rhythm very quickly, keep everybody fully engaged, and to maintain a high level of complicity. Notice that the best group sizes are all odd numbers. Odd numbers make better groupings because there's always an imbalance. Even numbers have a tendency to make more symmetrical groupings, and there's an implicit invitation to subdivide into smaller groups again, so that if you're not careful, groups can look as if they're taking sides.

The Grouping Game

A, a padded-up buffoon, runs to a position on stage followed by B, C, D, and E who group themselves around A in some way, looking at the audience. Then somebody else in the group runs to somewhere else on the stage, and again the rest of the group follow, and build another picture.

The game is to keep looking at the audience as much as you can, and to experiment with how your various shapes and sizes seem to fit together. If you get too close, and too tightly packed, you'll find an impro very difficult to sustain because you won't be able to move enough or to see each other enough. Sometimes it helps to play as a whole group reacting together, and on other occasions it helps for one of you to work alone, and the others to stay back in support.

All groups have a leader; somebody who appears to makes the decisions, and seems to have authority in the group. You don't need to look very hard for these people – they'll emerge by themselves, but all groups also have what Philippe Gaulier has called a 'chorafer'. This is the individual in the group who appears to be the most reactive; the one with the greatest spatial awareness, who seems to know instinctively when the group should stop, move, or exactly where the group should be on stage. You can't elect a chorafer, and the role might shift within a group as the work progresses, but the chorafer has a different function from the leader. The leader responds dramatically and is generally the spokesperson of the group; you can direct and relate to the leader. The chorafer's role is more instinctive: more to do with spatial awareness than direction; it's unlikely the provocateur will even know who the chorafer is. The chorafer initiates the movement of the group; the leader initiates the group's reaction to the provocateur. The chorafer might be 'runt of the litter', the most sensitive, wary, or even the most timid. The idea is to respect the chorafer, and if you don't know exactly who that person might be – so much the better. Awareness is everything. It doesn't help to cast the leader as the chorafer because they have a symbiotic relationship. For example, the leader might say that of course they'll all move to the other side of the stage but the chorafer might well start to move in the opposite direction. In an ideal society, these roles emerge naturally and without discussion, and you always agree with the outcome – whatever happens.

The Revealing Game

In how many different ways can a group reveal one person, as if they were going to do a solo?

There are several variations: the group might all step back to reveal someone standing in the middle, or they might all run forward together, and then all run back, leaving one person standing there alone. It's worth exploring other variations of this kind of reveal, such as the group travelling across the stage, all stopping, then all starting again, except for one person who's left standing there alone. There are many other variations. The game here is to see how many each group can find with the minimum discussion. The more able you become at making reveals, the more fluidly you'll be able to work as a chorus. It's visually satisfying to isolate a spokesperson from the group so that the chorus can amplify whatever they go on to do.

Playing the Audience

Behind the safety of your padding, and with your lovely new body to show off, meeting the audience is a delight to be savoured. Buffoons are proud of their appearance and want to show it off. I like to build up to the subject of playing the audience with themes such as models on a catwalk, strip shows, or lap dancing. All of these subjects are useful in encouraging you to find pleasure in being your new self, and teasing the audience, whilst at the same time playing with a relatively easy target for your parody. All the games detailed in Part One can be adapted for a buffoon chorus.

Games like the Demonstration Game, or the 'Don't Say the Obvious' Game can be adapted to games criticising members of the audience.

The Clapping Game is an excellent preparation for playing an audience, and it adapts well to being played by a small chorus; just remember to space the objects out a little more than you would do normally. The big challenge for a chorus in this game is to learn to think together as a group, and to follow the same associations, and to develop the same themes. To do this, you have to make sure that you're all looking in the same direction and at the same objects scattered on the floor. You can't rely on listening alone, so you have to take more space between you as a group so that you can move more easily, remain able to see each other, and maintain a single point of focus.

Debunking

Buffoons play the audience very much like clowns play the audience. Like clowns, they're constantly monitoring audience response, continually reacting to that response, and don't make any attempt to hide these reactions. Where clowns go to a fixed point, drop the theme, and go to a point of bafflement, buffoons also go to a fixed point and drop the theme, but instead go to a soft conspiratorial giggle behind their hands, or an ironic smile, or an expression of sincere apology. Any of these things are likely to happen whenever it becomes clear that they've gone too far, or whenever they're particularly pleased with themselves. Whether they're laughing at us or just laughing out of embarrassment, and whether their apology is really sincere, we'll never know. The giggle leaves whatever you've just said or done hanging in the air like a giant question mark. It's another version of 'only joking'. Like the point of bafflement, if you use it too much, it soon becomes irritating and self-defeating, but buffoons don't particularly mind irritating the audience. Our irritation is just another thing to play with.

The giggle, the smile or the apology are all potential debunking devices that keep everything in the 'here and now'. They stop the game, and add another dimension to the comedy. When you debunk the situation in clown, this is a daring and liberating thing to do, and if it's played effectively, can be disarming in its honesty. When you debunk the situation in buffoon, everything is brought back to a point of confrontation, and it's unsettling. Rather than drawing us closer to you, as it does in clown, it's alienating, and makes us think more closely about what's just happened. The more you debunk, the more you're likely to raise the stakes between you and the audience. Buffoons play with parody in the same way that clowns play with laughter. They use the provocateur in much the same way as a clown might. Where the clown uses the provocateur as a means of staying on stage, and getting more laughs, the buffoon uses the provocateur to stay on stage in order to see how far they can go before getting kicked off. Like clowns, it's imperative for buffoons to respect the provocateur – but only when the provocateur is looking at them. As soon as the provocateur looks away, they'll parody him mercilessly.

The Avoiding the Big Stick Game

The entire group find a hiding place in the room, and one at a time they cross the space, taking care not to catch the attention of the provocateur – who's reading a book, with a rolled-up newspaper nearby.

The object of the game is for each buffoon to cross the stage, past the reading provocateur. The buffoon's game is get as close to the provocateur as possible, and the provocateur's game is to tease the buffoon, and to be unpredictable.

Basically, this is a game of chicken for the buffoon: how close can you creep up to the provocateur, mocking everything that happens – your fear, the provocateur's concentration, how the provocateur is sitting – anything? Eventually, the buffoon gets hit with the newspaper, and instantly the rest of the group come out of hiding, conceal the victim in the group, and all try to talk their way out of the situation being as apologetic, and as polite as they can. If the provocateur doesn't believe them, someone else might get hit, and so the game continues.

The game only works if the provocateur really manages to intimidate the chorus. The group need to genuinely fear the provocateur or the stakes won't be high enough.

Because of the padding, the provocateur can really hit the buffoons as hard as he likes with the newspaper, which will probably make a loud noise on impact, sounding much worse than it really is. The buffoon accepts the beating with credible contrition, only to go to the soft conspiratorial giggle once the provocateur looks away, to debunk the situation.

The Mischief Game

Two groups of five buffoons are at opposite ends of the space. The provocateur goes up to one group, and they all flatter him or her, restricting their comments purely to what they see. The idea is for each member of the chorus to speak a short sentence, one at a time. They're always in agreement, and the ideal is to follow the logic. The 'And . . . And' Game is a good preparation for this. A typical speech might be as follows:

'We really like your hair today.'
'It really suits you like that.'
'It frames your face' (Conspiratorial giggle)
'No, we like your face.'
'You've got such a kind face.'
'Such a strong mouth.'
'Good teeth.'
' White teeth.'
'Brown eyes.'
'So understanding.' (Conspiratorial giggle)
'We feel we can talk to you.'
'We can say anything to you.'
'You understand us.'

Be specific, and accurate. Don't make anything up. Talk about what you see. Be very flattering, and be credibly sincere. The more genuine and flattering you try to be, the more sardonic you're likely to become.

When the provocateur turns away from you, to approach the other group, then the whole buffoon chorus parody anything you've been talking about. If the last thing you said was 'Nice hair', then play with that idea, and make gestures that imply that it's ridiculously long or greasy. If you finished with 'Strong mouth', then you copy each other in making whinging facial expressions. The gestures can be developed in the same way as the text – it's just a group version of the 'And . . . And' Game. The idea is to be playful and accumulative with your ideas, rather than vicious. It's far too easy to be vicious. Play your parody as a bit of fun, and keep it light and frivolous. If your movement is a natural development from what went before, then it's easier to sustain, and we'll appreciate the logical developments.

As soon as the provocateur turns round, the entire group giggle softly to themselves and huddle together. If the provocateur hears you giggling – you smile sweetly as if nothing has happened. It's sort of a version of Grandmother's Footsteps.

As the game progresses, if the provocateur sees their mockery, a victim is selected from the group who is ceremoniously beaten with the rolled-up newspaper.

The key is to keep your parody as small as you can. The smaller your parody, and the more ambiguous it is, the greater your respect for the provocateur will seem, and the stronger the tension will be between you.

The provocateur's job is to really intimidate the group with that rolled- up newspaper. The beatings are an essential element but the real tension is in the anticipation rather than the execution. One small beating should be enough to inspire an appropriate respect for the provocateur.

The Going Too Far Game

Most parodic games are based on a build-up game of one kind or another. The Numbers Game is an excellent example of what I mean. You can play this game with anything: praising somebody's face, or apologising to somebody, or even making a polite greeting to the audience.

A says, 'It's nice to see you.' (That's stating the theme, to the power of one.) B says, 'It's very nice to see you after all this time.' (That's developing the theme to the power of two.) C says, 'It's so nice to see you. It really has been a long time, and we've all missed you.' (That's developing the theme to the power of three.) D might say, 'It's awful when you miss somebody – you know – you can't stop thinking about them. We thought about you so much that we used to see you over there, and sometimes over there, and sometimes in . . . ' (That's developing the theme to the power of four.)

Notice that it's not just a question of each person speaking slightly longer than the person before on a chosen theme. The idea is to keep elaborating on the theme and allowing it to develop.

It's a game of making it worse – and you can only develop this game by listening to each other, and by going to the same level of physical intensity. If somebody lets the intensity drop, the action will lose its momentum. Any theme can be developed like this until it becomes completely abstract and absurd. There's a Monty Python sketch where four speakers rival each other for the worst childhood: 'Beds? We never had beds, just a mattress on the floor.' 'Floor? You were lucky . . . 'etc.

The above examples use text, but you can play exactly the same game with simple actions:

A smiles; B smiles and breathes heavily; C smiles, breathes heavily, and starts to sob; D smiles, breathes heavily, starts to sob, and goes down to their knees; E smiles, breathes, sobs, goes to their knees and beats the floor with their fists. A beats the floor and goes into a fit; B goes into a fit, twitches and dies; C goes into a fit, twitches, dies and becomes a ghost. And so the game continues.

You don't always have to go back to the beginning. The rule is to keep building on the previous idea, and you've got to keep an eye out for what the audience like. 'How far can you go?' is the controlling idea in parody. It's at its best when it's constantly evolving and constantly searching for a more fruitful theme.

The Group Association Game

This is a development from a simple word-association game, but it's played by five people at the same time, which is much more difficult to achieve. You've all got to watch each other, keep together, and find the developments from each other. It's an excellent complicity game.

Group A all say the same word at the same time and demonstrate to group B what they mean by it.

For example, group A might look at each other saying 'mmm', 'mu', 'muse', eventually arriving at the word 'music'. This rambling search for the word is one of the most interesting parts of the game.

Group B then take the word 'music', and see how far they can go with it by playing as many other words and action associations as they can. They must work in complicity and without a leader, trying to keep the attention of group A.

For example, they start with the word 'music', but eventually grope their way to: smile – cry – sob – razor – slit – wrist. They all say the words at the same time, and all do similar actions at the same time.

When group A have had enough, they put their hands up. Group B must then give their last word to group A, and so the game continues.

This game has all the advantages of the basic word-association game, whilst insisting the group follow each idea through, and learn to look to each other for developments.

The Excuse Game

This is a natural development of the Group Association Game.

In this version, the whole group have to speak together and at the same time, without a leader, whilst inventing an excuse.

The provocateur asks, 'Why are you late?' and the group have to grope their way to a logical reply.

A further development of this game is for the group to start their explanation with a movement that justifies the word.

For example, in reply to the question 'Why are you late?', the group might look at each other, somebody might touch a pocket and every-

body copies this gesture and the action develops into everybody tap-
ping their pockets and looking round, and they grope their way to the
sentence, 'We lost our rail ticket.'

All these association games build the complicity of the group. Once everyone has developed the skill and control to follow associations, they can play much easier and far more rewarding games that involve each member of the group speaking one phrase at a time, independently.

Confrontational Parody and Oblique Parody

All this work on buffoons and grotesque parody was originated by Lecoq, at his school in Paris in the sixties: 'I wanted to give [my students] a new freedom,' he told me, 'and to let them work from a part of themselves that gave them more spontaneity on stage.'

He didn't set out to invent a new theatre form but to investigate the grotesque as an agent of release. In doing so, he discovered a huge 'territory' on the margins of the sacred and the profane: a mysterious and liminal world, as much about tragedy and drama as it was about comedy and stupidity, where violence can be beautiful, and an endearing smile is the equivalent of a kick in the balls.

In *The Moving Body*, Lecoq writes about his work as follows:

> ❝ *So I went on to wonder where these [buffoons] came from. They could not derive from a realist space like the street or the metro. They must have their origins elsewhere: in mystery, the night, heaven, and earth. Their function was not to make fun of a particular individual, but more generally of everyone, of society as a whole. [Buffoons] enjoy themselves, for their whole life is spent having fun imitating aspects of human life. Their great delight is to make war, fight, and tear out each other's guts. However, their war games never follow the logical chronology of a story that unfolds. They bring a special style of composition: they so enjoy killing one another that with each killing they just want to start again. So they indulge in repeated massacres just for the fun of it.* ❞

Buffoons might not be realistic insofar that they're absurd exaggerations of real life, but there are undeniable elements of buffoon in all our cities. You've only got to watch the winos in the park, the homeless in their cardboard boxes, and the *Big Issue* sellers to see elements of buffoon round us all the time. Terry Gilliam's film *The Fisher King*

(1991) exploits this level of social degradation, and takes it to a point of pathos, but it does so by going beyond realism to a heightened level of the grotesque. This passage from Lecoq's book articulates his desire for the universal rather than the specific. He's trying to avoid the trap of the work becoming too small. He's chasing the bigger picture here, and going for an oblique parody that implies, hints and makes allusions, but never calls a spade a spade. In playing down social context, and refusing to engage directly with political issues, he's looking for a more poetic level of parody that might make a more profound statement about humanity whilst allowing us to find the appropriate political context for ourselves. He's advocating a style of parody where we have to do most of the work.

This passage underlines the difference in approach to buffoon between him and Philippe Gaulier. Gaulier was teaching at Lecoq's school in Paris when investigations into buffoon were in full swing, and when he eventually left to set up his own school, he took the work with him but approached it in a very different way.

For Gaulier, Lecoq's approach lacked specific references. He wanted more realism, more confrontation, and more targets. He wasn't content to be mystified and intrigued, he wanted to confront us with our innate hypocrisy – and ultimately with ourselves. He wanted a more savage parody to make us laugh without pulling the punches.

This is my paraphrase of his introduction to his work with buffoons at an exhibition class he gave in London in the early eighties:

> **❝** *In the bad lands, the swamps, the rubbish dumps that nobody wants, on the outer edges of the city, live God's little mistakes: all those people who don't belong with 'the beautiful people' because they're the wrong shape, or they don't think in the same way as everybody else. To the beautiful people, they're worth nothing. It's nothing to kill a buffoon. The beautiful people value their dogs more. They're so easy to kill that there isn't even any sport in it, but once a year, as a treat, the buffoons are let into the city to perform, and entertain the beautiful people. The buffoons can't resist the opportunity to have their moment of fun either. To please is to be rewarded; not to please is to risk the worst.* **❞**

He's setting the scene for confrontational parody here. He's opening the door and inviting buffoons into our space to have a go at us, 'the beautiful people', and play a game of brinkmanship, a game of 'How far can they go?' before they get kicked out again – and of course they will always eventually get kicked out. He's emphasising the 'here and now', fearing that the slightest trace of the 'there and then' will weaken this confrontation and ultimately be a cop-out.

This was my first encounter with grotesque parody, and Gaulier was inspirational. I recruited a buffoon chorus with a taste for the outrageous, and trained them into a sensitive playful unit. We spent much of our time exploring ways of provoking the audience to see how far we could go.

The Reading the Audience Game

An effective group of buffoons will be reading the audience all the time. It's a fundamental survival strategy because you can only stay on stage if the audience are sufficiently intrigued. If we grow to dislike you, and dislike what you're doing, to such an extent that the group can't rescue themselves with another game, then the complicity with the audience will be lost and the group must leave the stage. As always, when the buffoons find their complicity with the audience, they can start to play with our reactions and expectations.

The first stage of reading the audience is to acknowledge our mood, and try to reassure us as sincerely as you can. 'We can see that you're looking uncomfortable,' one member of the group might say. 'Don't be,' says another. 'Relax'. 'If you get nervous then we'll get even more nervous.' 'Then who knows what's going to happen?' Don't make anything up. Just react to what you see and work as a group.

If you still feel welcome, you can take the game a stage further by making comments about us. Once again, the restriction is to only talk about what you see, and not to make anything up.

'It's lovely to see that you've made an effort.' 'Yes, you look lovely.' 'You've washed your hair, haven't you?' 'It looks wonderful.'

We'll probably feel very ambivalent about everything at this stage. The more sincere you try to be, the more we're likely to mistrust you. Buffoons don't inspire trust.

The Provoking the Audience Game

A buffoon chorus look round the audience, and if they see two people sitting very close together, or holding hands, or dressed the same, or two people with the same haircut, they might as a group improvise something like:

'We can see you're very close. It's nice to be in love, isn't it? It's so warming. Don't be ashamed . . . We've all been there; well, most of us have. We've all been there. In fact, we're there now. Can't you tell? We've got so much in common, you and I – so much to talk about . . . Who's the dominant one between you two? You know, who wears the trousers – so to speak? Don't tell us. We know. It's obvious – once you know what to look for. Can you tell with us – can you?'

This is the most confrontational audience game I've ever developed. It could be effective if you have a drunk or a heckler, but most audience members freeze if they think they're likely to be picked on indiscriminately. It feels like a break in the conventional contract with the audience, but reciprocal confrontation – even if it means making a joke out of somebody who's fast asleep on the front row – is fair game. Some level of confrontation is essential to remind us all that theatre is a live event, and not merely television without the glass screen.

Inspired by Gaulier's teaching, my group decided to stage a grotesque version of *The Nativity*. The baby Jesus was played by a large malevolent hunchback, with a winning smile; the Angel Gabriel by an obese blob of a creature who couldn't stop giggling; and the Virgin Mary was a charming woman with elephantine buttocks. In the end, the Three Wise Men were represented by Colonel Gaddafi, who burst in and shot them all.

We opened to a small audience, who, for the most part, hated it. They loathed being put on the spot, and sat there in grim silence throughout. They hated our pointless gibes at religion. Our incendiaries targeting human hypocrisy just blew up in our faces. I had been so preoccupied with the quality of the chorus, and with staging the confrontation with the audience that I had failed to question the basic premise behind what I'd learnt with Gaulier: Do people necessarily enjoy being put on the spot, having their values and beliefs mocked and ridiculed by a padded actor making outrageous images and sardonic comments? I was too enamoured with the form to think about the content, or the experience itself, and I've never managed to offend so many people as quickly as I did then. To make matters worse, the Greater London Council decided to close the theatre because they said it was a fire risk. We were incensed; the group were convinced it was a conspiracy to stop the show, so we decided to put it on in the car park. We gave candles to the audience, and did the performance as planned. The word got round in the local pub that our show was so shocking that the GLC had banned it. That night we had a large rowdy crowd of young people, slightly the worse for drink, crowding round our little corner of the car park, holding their candles, and ready to be offended.

The chorus started with their customary apology:

" *'We're so sorry.'*

'We're so sorry to make you stand in the cold like this.'

'We're so sorry to make you stand in the cold, in a car park, with only a bit of hot wax for comfort.'

'We know it's not what you're used to. Please accept our apologies. We're so sorry.'

'No, you're not!' said a voice from the back of the crowd. The audience laughed in approval.

The chorus gathered themselves. 'Oh, the truth-sayer,' one of them said. The audience loved this. They were beginning to warm to their role.

'Yes, thank you,' said a voice from the chorus again.

'What would we do without you?' said another. The audience laughed again.

'We're so sorry; we didn't realise before. We didn't know. We're so sorry ... '

'Prove it,' another member of the audience said. Another roar of approval came from the crowd. The chorus fell to their knees. 'Oh! Oh!' they howled in unison. The atmosphere was electric. 'Please. Please,' they pleaded. 'We'll never do it again.' (Followed by a conspiratorial giggle.)

'Lick the gravel then,' demanded our 'Truth Sayer' in the audience — more laughter from the crowd — he was really enjoying himself now. 'Yes! Yes! Thank you. Thank you. Thank you,' said the chorus as they plunged their faces into the gravel. One of them did this with such force that she cut her lip. Blood was trickling down her chin.

'Look, I bleed for you. We sacrifice our life's blood for you. Yes. For you! For all of you.'

Now the entire group were banging themselves into the gravel, standing up, and throwing themselves to the ground, grinding their padded humps, and padded buttocks into the earth. The crowd loved it. They'd not seen anything like this before. The large malevolent hunchback playing baby Jesus slammed his hands into the gravel.

'Look!' he bellowed, holding his reddened palms at the audience. 'I've got the stigmata! I am the Son of God!'

(*Personal Journal 1984, Ivy House, London*) 🙰

That was the first line of the play. The group giggled, drew back, and without taking their eyes off the audience, they took their positions for the start of the play.

Confrontational parody is at its best when the audience are 'up for it'. On this occasion, our nativity play was like a stand-up gig. The audience had come to see something offensive. They'd come to be shocked. Some of them looked as if they were daring themselves to be there to affirm their 'street cred' rather than to have a good time. The drama came as much from the spontaneity of the chorus, and how they played the crowd, as it did from the material itself. Our ribald version of *The Nativity* was no more than a crude attempt to shock. There was no ambiguity, no empathy, no centre of good, no pathos, no mystery, and definitely no poetry. It was a clear case of form over content. Was all this work on the grotesque no more than a bad case of personal aesthetics outweighing theatrical effectiveness? I think it was. This was buffoon played at a vicious level, but the only people laughing were the converted. Here, all the buffoons were allowed fools. They were all sufficiently intelligent to know exactly what they were doing, to have an opinion and, what's more, they understood enough to bear a grudge. To go deeper into the grotesque, I felt the need to look at the natural fool, those buffoons who don't value anything, and laugh at everything because they barely know what's going on in the first place. I wanted to explore a more oblique parody, one that was more generalised, where the targets were broader, and where the subject matter was more universal. I wanted to make the theatrical equivalent of strong imagistic poetry rather than a vicious diatribe designed to shock.

Three things inspire parodic play: the Group Association Game, the Reading the Audience Game, and the prevailing question of 'How far can you go?' There are innumerable versions of these games, but they identify the skills you have to develop to find your way deeper into the ridiculous. The main difference between confrontational parody and oblique parody is that the targets in the former are always explicit. You always know what you're saying and who you're getting at, and no matter how much you try to respect the audience, the more deference you show us, the more vicious your mockery seems to be. Of course, it would be different if we could genuinely beat you for what you've just done, but we all know that you're immune to anything like that, and the only real danger is the threat that we might walk out on you. Oblique parody is essentially ambiguous, and often completely nonsensical.

The Beyond Meaning Game

This is a development of the Group Association Game; only, the idea here is to go beyond language and into a world of half-meanings and visual associations. Real words are forbidden, and the group can only communicate in sound and movement.

The provocateur asks a simple direct question: How does a paper clip work? Or how does a zip fastener work? Or what does a comb do?

Immediately, somebody in the group makes a sound and a move-ment, and without thought, everybody copies that sound and move-ment, and develops it through associations in the normal way. Of course you'll have some idea about what a comb does, or how a paper clip works, for example, but it's more interesting to be obtuse. Delegate the answer to the group, and let the associations develop from one to another – out of your control – so peripheral meaning and strange images start to proliferate.

Insist on complicity. If you stop and think, it will look as if you're planning something, and if you work too quickly, it will look as if you're trying to get something right. This work is most effective when it develops slowly, and you allow the ideas to come together in their own way. If you're baffled – it doesn't matter. Looking the way you do, why should we expect anything else? Providing you keep your complicity, nine times out of ten you'll come to some sort of logical answer to the question. The key is not to try to find an answer but simply to play the game. There should be no thought at the beginning. If you get too analytical about what you're trying to do, the game will become too literal. Literal interpretations are boring. Our main interest in burlesque parody is the outlandish and the absurd. Leave the connections to the audience; your job is to keep the game going.

There are two things at work in this game: the fact that the audience assume you're working on a clear and rational explanation, and the fact that the game imposes the restriction on you that everybody must delegate every decision to everybody else. Delegation is the driving force behind all oblique parody, deflecting us from conventional reason and logic, and propelling us into the never-never land of the ridiculous. Those constantly evolving sounds and movements generate a continual mosaic of possibilities and the result is a burlesque answer to the question that will either shed light on the subject or intrigue us with its outlandishness. The Beyond Meaning Game puts us in a similar frame of mind to people going to Bedlam in the eighteenth century to be entertained by the lunatics. To be honest, because it doesn't matter what you do in these circumstances, all your attempts at communication will probably be more entertaining in the end than what you have to say. We'll be following your every move with an astonished twinkle in our eyes. What to you is a rigorous game is pure invention to us.

The game's simple questions about mundane domestic objects can just as easily be replaced with more complex ones like: What is democracy? What is politics? What is religion? What is anarchy? What is death?

Interesting things happen to these freely developing actions and images once we attach a more abstract concept to them. If I ask you, 'What is democracy?' and you all start to slowly raise your hands in the air, and jump up and down, or alternately, if you all start to slowly descend to the floor sobbing, we'll instinctively read your actions as a rational answer to the question, and we'll read meanings into your actions that are purely fortuitous from your point of view. Whatever you do will look like a pertinent answer to the question, and every action will have meaning to us. You're just following the group – but we don't know that. Every pause you make to look round to see what each other is doing will look as if you're getting inspiration. It'll look profound and mysterious, particularly if you can follow a slow and seamless development to a finished action. We accept all your attempts at communication as being completely genuine and to an extent they are; only the game is structured to deliberately obfuscate what you're trying to say. You can be as absurd and incongruous as you like, yet providing you maintain your complicity and don't try to make anything up, then incongruity will be the last thing on our minds.

Once you're confident in balancing the free associations with the desire to communicate a specific idea, you can play a more sophisticated version of the Beyond Meaning Game with more language. In rehearsals for *Don't Laugh, It's My Life* (Told by an Idiot, 1996), the actor Steve Harper was playing an old lady in a grotesque half-mask. She was obsessed with religion, and we developed the game of her reading anything she happened to find lying about as if it was a direct communication from God. She found an old cigarette packet, and evolved a short monologue from it about her faith, and the fact that God was talking to her. The box became the idea of God:

66 *It's a box, and everybody thinks it's empty but, look — there's silver foil inside — which means that every cloud has a silver lining. That's heaven — He's reminding us — and what's this: 'Silk Cut'? 'Silk' — that means that His love is soft as silk. But 'Cut', that's more difficult — 'Cut' — God moves in mysterious ways — 'Cut'. If we feel His love, we must show it. We must make cuts. Deep cuts.* **99**

I'm paraphrasing here, but you get the idea. In the course of the play, she came to the conclusion that we have to get closer to the ground in order to get closer to God: so she cut the legs off all the furniture in the house and eventually she cut her own legs off, as her ultimate act of contrition.

Oblique parody like this is reminiscent of the ancient idea of the Holy Fool with the ear of God except that, in this instance, you're completely sane; you're just delegating how you want to answer the question to the apparently random gestures of the group. I once put this game in a show where a buffoon chorus told the audience that the chorus knew everything, and that the audience could ask them any question they liked and receive an answer. As it happened, one night a Monsignor — a high-ranking priest and friend of one of the cast — was in the audience looking very grand in his robes. The group had barely made the invitation when he asked, 'Who is Jesus Christ?' The group retreated at the question and looked very humbly at the impressive figure in the audience. Then they made vague gestures in the air, accompanied by gentle 'Ah' sounds, then they moved about the room, and found the game of gently banging into each other, then gradually they all pointed to the Monsignor, and to his feet, and words started to emerge, 'There – There – Shiny shoes – Shiny shoes – Jesus Christ – is a shiny pair of shoes.' There wasn't the least offence provoked by this game, and it was replete with meaning. This is a prime example of the buffoon mocking meaning in order to make meaning. The audience were intrigued; we had all followed the meandering logic, and we all enjoyed the irony.

I began this book with the idea that comedy is a great leveller. Now, at the end of it, I've changed my mind. It isn't comedy that's the great leveller – it's parody. It's parody that turns the world upside down and reduces Picasso to a common forger. Parody teaches us that there's something ridiculous in every one of us and that we're at our most vulnerable when we're being earnest. The strongest comedy comes from the greatest seriousness. Parody isn't a lesson in getting us to 'lighten up a bit'; it's a reminder that no subject is beyond its reach. There are no unsuitable targets, but this freedom comes with responsibility and our only constraints are the political climate we find ourselves in, and our personal taste at the time. That is all.

Parody teaches us to know ourselves better, and to accept ourselves more. It's the dark side of comedy where laughter has the whip hand – and it hurts. But it also makes us stop and think. At its best, parody tells the truth, uncompromisingly; at its worst, it's vicious and banal. Parody is the comedy of survival. We deal with authority, injustice, fear, pretension and stupidity through parody. At school we ridicule the teachers we don't like, at university we ridicule ideas, at work we mock the bosses, and we all ridicule the politicians to the day we die. You can test the health of a society by the amount of parody its leaders are prepared to tolerate. In campaigning against the law intended to outlaw religious hatred in the UK – which, critics feared, would also prohibit the right to ridicule religion – the comic actor Rowan Atkinson remarked:

66 *There should be no subjects about which you cannot make jokes. The right to offend is far more important than any right not to be offended.*   **99**

In theatre, this is the only absolute. When the ancient Greeks invented theatre they saw it as a place where it was possible to stage anything that was too dangerous or too contentious to be tolerated in the 'real-life' healthy society. Theatre grew out of a culture that valued the evolution and the dissemination of ideas more than the delicate sensibilities of small groups of easily offended individuals. It was a culture that could distinguish between fiction and reality, and that could respect the power of make-believe. The best parody gets under our skin because it's a blatant fiction, with that irritating grit of something deeply recognisable at the same time. It's the comedy of comment, and the distance between pastiche and buffoon indicates the range of exaggeration you have to play with and the size of comment you're making. But pastiche, caricature, burlesque and buffoon are not mutually exclusive categories. They're the notes in the ascending scale of exaggeration. Parody is a perpetual game of seeing how far you can go; the ever-present risk is that you'll offend us to the extent that we won't be able to watch you any more. We'll hate you if you go too far, but we'll hate you just the same if you don't go far enough.

Mobility is the big lesson to be learnt in playing parody. Like a mischievous child deliberately testing its parent's tolerance, when playing parody you do something or say something, then gauge our reaction to it. Then you try to push that comment a little further and then a little further again – so that you bring us to the edge of our tolerance. But you must do this without losing your charm and your sense of fun. It's impossible to keep the two plates – potential offence and likeability – spinning in the air without resorting to irony, ambiguity, sardonic inference, bizarre imagery or ludicrous juxtaposition.

If you make yourself look worse than life by assuming outrageous deformities, you can generally get away with making comments that are far more daring and extreme than somebody who looks distinctly 'normal'. If you look outrageous, we expect you to do outrageous things. If your buffoon plays something relatively mundane – doing housework, baby-sitting, being a waiter in a restaurant – it's difficult for us to take you seriously since whatever you do will clash with what you look like. Extreme appearances make normality look ridiculous. In

Gaulier's confrontational style of buffoon, you remain hidden behind your fixed distorted body-mask, have little scope for mobility, and you soon end up playing the illusion of a grotesque. I'm sure Bakhtin would have been fascinated by this radical interpretation of grotesque realism. Towards the end of his life, Lecoq was creating buffoons in brightly coloured carnivalesque costumes that softened the grotesque by introducing a ridiculous element. The effect implied a more ambiguous relationship with the audience but Lecoq was still working with a fixed persona and his investigations remained locked in a personal aesthetic which was difficult to apply. The preposterous disguise inspired by the Ad Hoc Game is transparent, and this gives you scope to drop your disguise and declare the game.

Ultimately, any fixed persona is limiting. The freer you are to play the audience, the more you can play a drop, declare the game, and the more mobility you'll have to move up and down the scale of exaggeration from pastiche to buffoon and back again. If you deny yourself the freedom of going up the scale, it will be much harder to captivate us with the prospects of doing something both entertaining and offensive at the same time.

Physical parody all boils down to the art of dressing up: the art of assuming a disguise, exploiting it and then dropping it occasionally. Buffoon takes every aspect of physical comedy as far as you can go, but if you cling on to Lecoq's idea of creating a mysterious and preposterously deformed creature in order to be able to do what you like on stage, you'll deny yourself the real benefits of exploring parody. Leave aside your padding and find that same freedom in playing with costume pieces and props. Buffoon is a form that allows you to be as confrontational as a political extremist and as bizarre and playful as a clown – all at the same time. The trouble is that there aren't many plays or theatrical events that can happily accommodate preposterously deformed people who perpetually play the audience and dissolve into sardonic giggles all the time. Buffoon is a means to an end – and the end is a taste for being worse than life, for poking fun, and mocking people. This mockery can be affectionate or vituperative – it's up to you. It can be immensely funny or deeply disturbing, but you can't play effective parody if you haven't got something to say. Your comments raise the stakes in trying to be funny because they put you in danger of offending us.

I've long fantasised over a particular ending to Bertolt Brecht's delightful parody of Hitler's rise to power, *The Resistable Rise of Arturo Ui*. I once described it to a colleague who assured me that no theatre in its right mind would ever stage it, so here it is:

At the end of the play, Arturo Ui is finally in power. Imagine a group of actors that we haven't seen before in the production, playing present-day Nazis, with blonde hair, black suits, and white Alsatian dogs, suddenly bursting into the theatre and interrupting the play. Imagine them marching through the auditorium and onto the stage, threatening the audience at gunpoint and beating up the actor playing Arturo, insisting that he takes off his uniform and making him strip down to his underwear. Then imagine them trashing the set, and making all the Jews, blacks and homosexuals in the audience stand up. Then they leave us, as abruptly as they came in. Finally, imagine the actor playing Arturo saying the concluding lines of the play, 'The bitch that bore him is in heat again.' There could hardly be a simpler or more confrontational parody. It could hardly be less funny, and cause more discomfort and more anger. But it's a great ending.

Life was a funny thing that occurred on the way to the grave.

Quentin Crisp

Acknowledgements

I would like to thank Alison Sinclair, who encouraged me to write in the first place and who supported me through the early stages of this project. I am most indebted to my wife, Mary, and my son and daughter, Toby and Lucy, whose patience, support and personal expertise fed my enthusiasm.

We all owe much to our teachers and my thanks goes to Pauline Stuart and Rosemary Linell, who encouraged me to make my own work at a time when devising wasn't remotely fashionable, and later to Yoshi Oida, Jacques Lecoq, Philippe Gaulier and Monica Pagneux. All these teachers, in their different ways, convinced me of my own ability and left me with more questions than answers.

But deep learning comes from application, and I'm particularly indebted to my immediate colleagues, to Paul Hunter and Hayley Carmichael, whose commitment, drive and consummate skill remain an inspiring provocation.

JOHN WRIGHT
London, 2006

John Wright offers open public workshops, specially commissioned workshops, and designated research and development projects for companies or individual artists all over the world.

The idea is to be as flexible as possible. A course can last for a month, a day or anything inbetween. 'School for Devisors' and 'School for Mask' have been John's biggest open workshops to date, but his shorter courses on comic timing, writing with objects, playing with rhythm, making parody or working the audience are immensely popular.

For further information, visit:

www.toldby.dircon.co.uk

www.thewrightschool.co.uk

Bibliography

Bergson, Henri, *Laughter: an Essay on the Meaning of the Comic*, Los Angeles: Green Integer, 1999 (First published as *Le rire* in 1900)

Heilpern, John, *Conference of the Birds: the Story of Peter Brook in Africa*, London: Penguin, 1979

Johnstone, Keith, *Impro: Improvisation and the Theatre*, London: Methuen, 1981

Koestler, Arthur, *The Act of Creation*, London: Hutchinson, 1964

Komparu, Kunio, *The Noh Theater: Principles and Perspective*, New York: Weatherhill/Tankosha, 1983

Lecoq, Jacques, *The Moving Body: Le Corps Poetique*, London: Methuen, 2002

Mamet, David, *True and False: Heresy and Common Sense for the Actor*, London: Faber and Faber, 1998

Wellsford, Enid, *The Fool, his Social and Literary History*, London: Faber and Faber, 1935

Woolf, Virginia, 'Modern Fiction' (1919) in *The Common Reader*, London: The Hogarth Press, 1925

Index of Games